Beginning Backbone.js

James Sugrue

ISBN-13 (pbk): 978-1-4302-6334-0

ISBN-13 (electronic): 978-1-4302-6335-7

President and Publisher: Paul Manning
Lead Editor: Louise Corrigan
Technical Reviewer: Chris Wiegman
Editorial Board: Steve Anglin, Ewan Buckingham, Gary Cornell, Louise Corrigan, James DeWolf,
    Jonathan Gennick, Jonathan Hassell, Robert Hutchinson, Michelle Lowman, James Markham,
    Matthew Moodie, Jeff Olson, Jeffrey Pepper, Douglas Pundick, Ben Renow-Clarke, Dominic Shakeshaft,
    Gwenan Spearing, Matt Wade, Steve Weiss, Tom Welsh
Coordinating Editor: Kevin Shea
Copy Editor: Kim Wimpsett
Compositor: SPi Global
Indexer: SPi Global
Artist: SPi Global
Cover Designer: Anna Ishchenko

Distributed to the book trade worldwide by Springer Science+Business Media New York, 233 Spring Street, 6th Floor, New York, NY 10013. Phone 1-800-SPRINGER, fax (201) 348-4505, e-mail orders-ny@springer-sbm.com, or visit www.springeronline.com.

For information on translations, please e-mail rights@apress.com, or visit www.apress.com.

Apress and friends of ED books may be purchased in bulk for academic, corporate, or promotional use. eBook versions and licenses are also available for most titles. For more information, reference our Special Bulk Sales–eBook Licensing web page at www.apress.com/bulk-sales.

Any source code or other supplementary materials referenced by the author in this text is available to readers at www.apress.com. For detailed information about how to locate your book's source code, go to www.apress.com/source-code.

Contents at a Glance

Contents

About the Author

James Sugrue has worked in the software development industry for more than 13 years. He is currently based in Cork, Ireland, working as the principal front-end architect for Carma, a real-time transportation start-up. James began his career with a German safety automation company, working his way from graduate to architect, while helping shape the company's technology road map.

Always on the lookout for new and exciting technologies, James lives to code and spends much of his spare time building mobile and web application for fun. He has also been a regular editor at JavaLobby and EclipseZone for more than five years. This is his first book.

www.jamessugrue.ie

About the Technical Reviewer

Chris Weigman is a WordPress plug-in developer for iThemes.com where he works on the Better WP Security plug-in and other projects. He has a master's degree in computer science from Southern Illinois University and also teaches as an adjunct in the computer science department at St. Edward's University. When not behind the keyboard, Chris can often be found in the cockpit because he has certified flight instructor and commercial pilot licenses and does his best to make the most of them. Chris resides in Austin, Texas, with his wife and their four-legged children.

Acknowledgments

One of the reasons for the continued success of Backbone, in this fast-moving industry, is the community behind it. There are a number of authors of Backbone extensions and articles who have helped me achieve a higher level of understanding of the nuances of the library. They include Addy Osmani, Derick Baily, Phillip Whisenhunt, Ian Storm Taylor, Rico Sta Cruz, and Oz Katz. Thank you for sharing your knowledge.

Thanks to Jeremy Ashkenas, the father of Backbone, for creating such an addictive framework, with an excellent level of detail in its documentation.

The outstanding team at Apress helped ensure the book was the best possible quality. Chris Weigman was a fantastic technical reviewer and helped me see the book from a different perspective. Both Kevin Shea and Louise Corrigan provided excellent editorial guidance and support throughout the process.

Last but not least, thank you to my wife, Sarah, and my family for their patience, support, and encouragement while I was writing this book.

—James Sugrue

Introduction

Creating web applications in JavaScript in a well-structured manner can be difficult, but libraries such as Backbone have introduced much needed clarity. Since its release in 2010, Backbone.js has been considered one of the best options for dealing with large application code bases.

When I first used Backbone, I was impressed with its unopinionated nature and the clarity of the code. With the extensive level of community support and extensions available, there seemed to be very little Backbone could not accomplish.

Clearly, many other developers and organizations have been equally impressed with Backbone. You'll find it at the center of many applications and web sites that you regularly use, from the New York Times to Airbnb to SoundCloud.

If you are considering giving Backbone a starring role in your technology stack, this book will help you find its place and gauge its suitability. If you're new to Backbone, the first half of the book will get you started quickly. Those who have already started to use Backbone will find the second half of the book to be most useful, with discussions about best practices, Test-Driven Development, and modular architectures.

Who This Book Is For

This book is for anyone who is creating web applications with JavaScript. No matter what level of expertise you possess, there is a topic in the book for you.

Whether you are assessing the suitability of Backbone for your next project or have already adopted Backbone for your application development, you will find the book to have all you need to further your knowledge.

Readers are introduced to the basic concepts of object-oriented JavaScript at the beginning of the book and can continue the journey with deep dives into Backbone, along with explanations of the Model View * architecture.

Experienced Backbone developers and web application architects will find the more advanced chapters that deal with Backbone best practices, Test-Driven Development, and the creation of modular applications with RequireJS useful in ensuring high architectural quality for any web app they are building with Backbone.

How This Book Is Structured

The book has been split up into 12 chapters, each of which deals with a particular aspect of JavaScript, Backbone, or web application development processes.

Chapter 1, "Object-Oriented JavaScript," discusses the core object-oriented concepts surrounding JavaScript. While many readers will be able to skip this chapter, if you are new to JavaScript or have used only small parts of the language, this will assist greatly in your understanding of Backbone.

Chapter 2, "An Introduction to Backbone," introduces the library to the reader, giving a history of the library along with a description of some other Model-View-* frameworks that exist on the JavaScript landscape.

Chapter 3, "Backbone Models and Collections," discusses the parts of Backbone that deal with the data layer. Because most Backbone applications deal with RESTful APIs, this chapter helps you create your own Node.js server to communicate with the client-side application.

Chapter 4, "Backbone Views and Templating Libraries," is a guide to creating views with a combination of Backbone view class, HTML, and various tempting libraries. After reading this chapter, you will understand how to integrate libraries such as Underscore, Handlebars, and Mustache into your Backbone views.

Chapter 5, "Routers and Events," deals with the final Backbone classes that assist in creating decoupled applications, using routers to control the navigation across different views, and using events to communicate between different parts of the application.

Chapter 6, "From Start to Finish," takes everything that has been introduced in the earlier part of the book to create a fully functional Backbone application.

Chapter 7, "The Backbone Ecosystem," looks at the wide variety of extensions that have been developed by the online Backbone community to make development tasks easier and keep Backbone relevant when compared with newer JavaScript MV* libraries.

Chapter 8, "Testing Your Backbone Application," brings you through the Test-Driven Development practice, using two of the leading JavaScript testing frameworks: QUnit and Jasmine.

Chapter 9, "Using Grunt for Your Build Process," looks at how you can use the leading JavaScript task runner to introduce continuous integration in your project and reduce the need for repetitive tasks.

Chapter 10, "Extending Backbone with Marionette and Thorax," shows how you can greatly simplify your Backbone application code by leveraging either Marionette or Thorax.

Chapter 11, "Best Practices with Backbone," is a guide to some of the best practices that professional Backbone developers use to ensure they are getting the most from Backbone, without any unintended side effects.

Chapter 12, "Creating a Manageable JavaScript Code Base," ends the book with an introduction to RequireJS and how it can be used in conjunction with Backbone to make your code even more modular. This chapter also introduces some useful design patterns to use in your applications.

Downloading the Code

The code for the examples shown in this book is available on the Apress web site (`www.apress.com`). A link can be found on the book's information page on the Source Code/Downloads tab. This tab is located underneath the Related Titles section of the page. You can also access the code from GitHub, `https://github.com/jamessugrue/beginning-backbone`.

Contacting the Author

Should you have any questions or comments—or even spot a mistake you think I should know about—you can contact the author at `james@jamessugrue.ie` or @sugrue on Twitter.

CHAPTER 1

■ ■ ■

An Introduction to Backbone.js

Backbone.js helps provide a structure to your otherwise unwieldy JavaScript code base and might just be the perfect choice for your project. This chapter will introduce you to the world of Backbone.js, giving you a high-level view of what the framework is all about and an appreciation of why it exists.

We'll delve into detail on the Model View Controller pattern and discuss why it is useful for web applications. While going through the benefits of Model View * frameworks, of which Backbone is just one choice, we'll also compare Backbone to some of the other leading Model View * frameworks available for JavaScript today.

You'll see some examples of where you can find Backbone in use right now by big-name companies, and we'll give you honest reasons where Backbone might be the answer to your project, as well as where it won't work.

And just before we get deep into the coding, we'll tell you all you need to get Backbone downloaded and set up for your project.

What Is Backbone.js?

Since its release in late 2010, Backbone has been considered one of the leading libraries available that enables the creation of single-page web applications. Backbone is praised for being one of the more lightweight options and has found significant adoption with a large number of commercially successful web applications. Later in this chapter, we will examine what separates Backbone from competing solutions.

Backbone was created by Jeremy Ashkenas, who also wrote CoffeeScript. The library began its life as part of the DocumentCloud code base, an open source project that provides journalists with the ability to upload and annotate documents collaboratively. As a JavaScript-heavy application, what we now know as Backbone was responsible for structuring the application into a coherent code base. Underscore.js, Backbone's only dependency, was also part of the DocumentCloud application.

Mission Statement

To put it really simply, Backbone helps developers manage a data model in their client-side web app with as much discipline and structure as you would get in traditional server-side application logic.

To appreciate how important this is for JavaScript developers, we need to look at the history of how web sites and applications have traditionally been developed and how Backbone fits into this evolution.

Server-Side Logic

Up until 2005, web sites were pretty static, with all the real business logic implemented in the server side, using languages such as PHP, Java, and .NET. While these sites were far from the dynamic experiences we are accustomed to today, this approach allowed front-end developers to have very clean code bases, with HTML for structure, CSS for presentation, and perhaps a little JavaScript for things such as form field validation and pop-up windows. While not very exciting, it was a very controlled environment.

Ajax

During 2005, Ajax (Asynchronous JavaScript and XML) gained popularity and changed how web sites would be used forever. With the ability to call server-side logic without reloading the entire page, a new breed of dynamic web site was now possible. While this was a big step at the time, it seems relatively conservative now. Usually, Ajax would be used to update a small section of the page.

For example, when filling in a registration form, you could implement an Ajax call in your JavaScript that would check whether a particular username existed and highlight this information in an error section of the page.

To create these more engaging user interfaces, front-end developers had to use a lot more JavaScript, and this led to more complex code. This was one of the points at which the language began to be taken more seriously because Ajax enabled a more natural way of communicating between the client and the server.

Representational State Transfer (REST) provides an architecture for client-server communication over HTTP. All Ajax requests are made using RESTful services, and when creating Backbone applications, you will invariably be consuming such services in your data model. Later in this book, when dealing with models, we will see more about the importance of REST for your JavaScript apps.

jQuery

Another key milestone in JavaScript's maturity was the release of John Resig's jQuery in 2006, a framework that acknowledged the need for a more controlled approach to writing JavaScript for web applications. The framework provides the ability to search and manipulate the Document Object Model (DOM), deal with events, create animations, and create Ajax applications with a straightforward syntax. jQuery also abstracted away many of the cross-browser incompatibilities that plagued front-end engineers.

With its modular architecture, developers could write their own plug-ins that would run on top of JQuery. Suddenly, JavaScript developers were taken seriously, and more elegant user interfaces were possible.

Single-Page Web Applications

A single-page web application is one that requires just one page load and where all required elements can be loaded dynamically onto the page without needing to leave. This more immersive user experience is what desktop applications have always benefited from. Now that Ajax had proved itself and the JavaScript ecosystem was providing more robust libraries and frameworks, single-page applications were easier to implement.

These applications are not without their challenges. For a single page to deal with different stages in the application life cycle, page state is required. In addition, there is a need to enable the user to bookmark the application at a particular stage—this one of the places where Backbone really helps alleviate the complexity of implementing such solutions.

The wide array of smartphones and tablets, all with their own platforms and idiosyncrasies, have led a significant majority of developers to work on HTML5-based web apps that behave in a similar fashion to native apps. Single-page applications enable such applications to be built and made available directly from web sites, rather than requiring users to acquire the app through the app store on their device.

The Continuing Need for Structure

As browser-based applications continue to dominate, the architecture behind single-page applications becomes much more significant. With so much logic now residing in the client side, it's clear that the practices and patterns that have applied to traditional desktop applications are now relevant in JavaScript.

The core part of this is to have a data model at the center of your application. As your products grow in complexity, it is necessary to be able to track the state of many different components.

Gmail is a classic example of this (see Figure 1-1). You need to track whether a message has been read or not, as well as the date, subject, sender, and message content. The number of unread messages is also highlighted in the left menu. The more you look at the Gmail web application, the more you appreciate the complexity of the data model behind it.

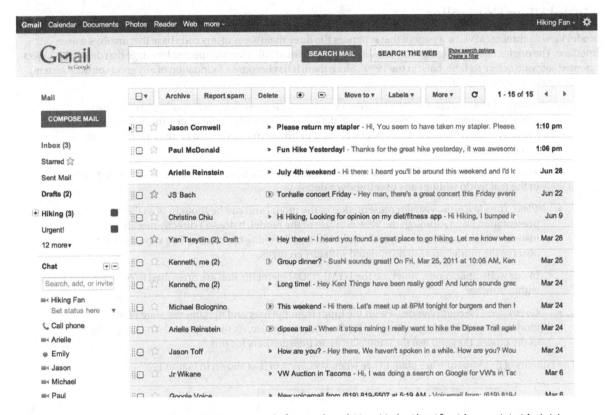

Figure 1-1. *Gmail, a classic web application example (Image from* http://cdn.theatlantic.com/static/mt/ assets/science/threadlist-large.png*)*

Trying to implement such a data model without some supporting framework would be pretty chaotic. Unless you are a team of one developer (and even then it's debatable), there is a measure of consistency required so that everyone understands how the data model is defined and represented.

This is exactly where Backbone comes in, making development more comfortable for developers to deal with data models, build module views, and send events across the application.

Design Patterns for Web Applications

Design patterns are credited with bringing maturity to software development. Ever since the seminal Gang of Four book *Design Patterns:Elements of Reusable Object-Oriented Software*, which introduced a series of reusable solutions and approaches for building applications, programmers have been using patterns to tame their code base. Following design patterns results in the improved readability of source code for any architect or developer and allows you to follow proven techniques and structures in application creation.

It was just a matter of time before this much-needed discipline was introduced to the JavaScript world where the most widely used and applicable patterns is among the oldest: Model View Controller. The emergence of real object-oriented JavaScript has allowed many frameworks to adopt variations of this pattern.

Model View Controller

Model View Controller (MVC) is a pattern that separates the three main areas of any code base that involves a user interface. The origins of this pattern go way back to the days of SmallTalk, a well-respected language that dealt with object-oriented software before its time, back in the 1970s. Since then, it has become a foundation of any good software system.

The pattern uses three key terms.

- *Model*: The *model* consists of all the data you want to represent in your application. You can think of it as pure data representations of data that is shown or manipulated through the user interface. When changed, the model will use a notification mechanism to alert observers, who can then decide whether to take action.

   Typical examples of model objects would be a User or Todo item: data representations of items in the real world without any user interface detail.

- *View*: The *view* is the visual representation of the model and can be thought of as the presentation layer. Although the view is aware of the model, it doesn't directly modify it, instead using the controller layer to deal with model-editing operations. The view will usually observe the model, so as to be updated with any changes.

   In our web applications, views are the HTML/DOM elements that are presented to the user within browser.

- *Controller*: The *controller* deals with the input from the user and updates the state of the model, essentially acting as the glue for the entire structure. As the user needs to change data in the model, they will use the controller as an intermediary for this.

The benefits of this structure are plain to see when you think of it as shown in Figure 1-2.

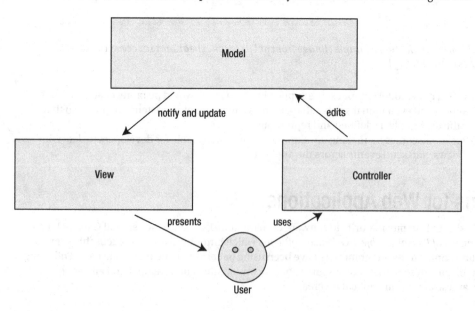

Figure 1-2. *An overview of the interactions of an MVC-based application*

To look at this really simply, the model is your data, the view is what you see in your browser, and the controller deals with the interactions between both of these layers.

To take this understanding one step further, let's illustrate how the MVC pattern would apply to a typical web application that includes a registration form.

The view in this case is the HTML form, which presents the user with the ability to input, or edit, data about themselves. The controller is the code that gets invoked when the user clicks Save. The controller will also apply some validation to the data provided in the form. Finally, the model is our data representation of the user. Figure 1-3 represents this in a sequence diagram.

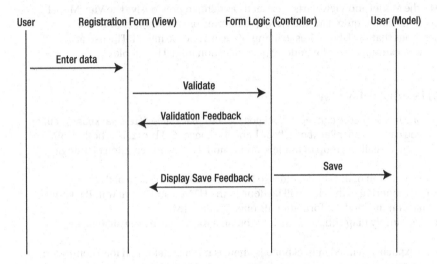

Figure 1-3. *MVC interaction sequence for a registration form*

This design pattern provides two key benefits: a separation of concerns and code reuse.

The model will always be isolated from the view and will contain only the domain object data. Therefore, the application that you develop for desktop browsers in this fashion could use the same model in a mobile version with no code changes.

Later in the book you will see how separating code like this results in code that is easier to test and is more maintainable, with the separation of concerns providing a more natural balance of work across a team of developers.

Model View *

As UI frameworks have evolved, variations of the MVC pattern have arisen, which all follow the spirit of the original pattern with slightly different flavors. These are known collectively as *Model View* * frameworks because the concept of a dedicated controller is usually abandoned.

There are two main variations on MVC that make up the MV* family. While these differences may seem almost academic (and they are), it is important to be somewhat familiar with them before delving into the JavaScript frameworks that enable these patterns.

Model View Presenter

As you can see from the name its name, the Model View Presenter (MVP) pattern differs only in the replacement of the controller with a presenter. The presenter is responsible for the interaction between the view and the model and contains all the business logic for the view.

The important distinction is that a higher level of decoupling is introduced, where the presenter communicates with the view through an interface. The addition of this interface means that it is easier to test the business logic independently of the real view, and the logic for your application can be written before any UI code has been written.

Also, there is typically no direct link between the view and the model, with the presenter passing on the data and acting as a true intermediary between both.

Model View ViewModel

In Model View ViewModel (MVVM), the Model and View parts are exactly as defined previously. The ViewModel is a single entity that is responsible for the data required for the view, as a filtering or combination from the "lower-level" model and all the operations that the UI requires to manipulate or view the model. The use of a ViewModel can sometimes feel like duplication, unless the underlying application model is complex.

How Backbone Supports Model View *

As you'll see later in the book, Backbone has four core concepts: Backbone.Model, Backbone.View, Backbone.Router, and Backbone.Collection. For now you can consider Backbone.Model and Backbone.Collection as both dealing with the model side of things. A collection is really a group of models, and a model is a representation of a single object, or a row of data.

Backbone.View represents the presentation of data but could also be seen as taking on some of the responsibilities of a controller. The real rendering of the view will be done in the HTML, and the view in Backbone really just provides the capability to pass on the model information through to the HTML.

Typically the Backbone.Router will simply map URLs to functions, but in a way it can also participate in controller duties.

So, while the model and view are explicitly defined in Backbone.js, there is no such definition for a controller; instead, some of the tasks that the controller would undertake are shared between the view and router.

Let's take a variation of our original MVC diagram and apply it to Backbone to see how interactions would look (see Figure 1-4).

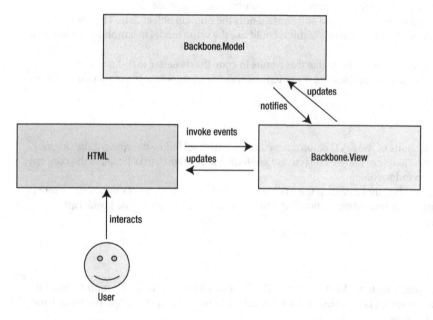

Figure 1-4. An illustration of the structure of Backbone's MV implementation*

All of the data that needs to be represented in the HTML view is stored in JavaScript objects rather than the DOM. The model is one of Backbone's big strengths as it provides functions to save and retrieve data from a server using RESTful services.

Other JavaScript Model View * Frameworks

There's a wide array of MV* frameworks available for JavaScript development. Backbone tends to be the most discussed, thanks to the number of tutorials and the strength of documentation provided by the team.

Now that we have a rough idea of how Backbone applications are structured, let's take a look at how some of these other frameworks compare.

Knockout.js

Knockout.js was first released in July 2010, and it follows the MVVM pattern. Unlike Backbone, Knockout provides bindings between sections of the user interface and the underlying data model, resulting in the UI updating dynamically when the model changes. In Backbone, this updating needs to be written by the developer. It can be downloaded from Knockoutjs.com, as illustrated in Figure 1-5.

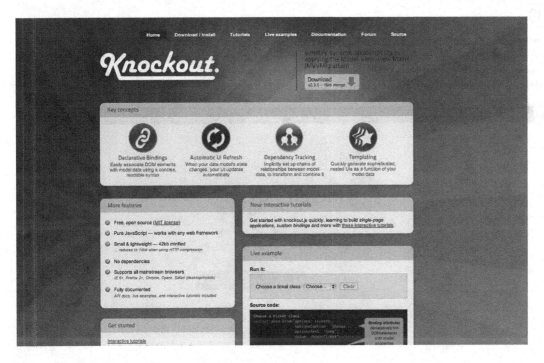

Figure 1-5. *Knockout.js web site*

In Knockout, the data bindings are included in the HTML. In this example, `firstName` is the attribute from the model we want to display.

```
<p>First name: <input data-bind="value: firstName" /></p>
```

The ViewModel is where the model is bound to the UI. When the ko.observable() function is used to define the attribute, the view will be automatically updated.

```
var myViewModel = {
        firstName : ko.observable('James');
};
```

When the model is defined, it is then bound to the UI using the applyBindings function.

```
ko.applyBindings(myViewModel);
```

As you can see, it's really easy to get started with Knockout, and it requires less JavaScript code compared to same type of app created in Backbone.js. It's not without its drawbacks—more complex UI interactions can be difficult to get right.

Although both frameworks provide structure to your JavaScript application, Backbone is mostly concerned with providing an MVC solution and tries to stay out of the user interface. Meanwhile, Knockout utilized the MVVM pattern for automatic user interface updates. Where Backbone excels is in how it deals with models, retrieving and persisting data using RESTful services. Accomplishing this in Knockout requires a lot of extra code. A project with a simple user interface and basic data models could benefit from using Knockout, but for more elaborate efforts, Backbone is a solid choice.

AngularJS

AngularJS was released in 2009 by Google. It takes an approach similar to Knockout, in that the data bindings are added directly to the HTML page. One of the main design goals of the framework is to remove DOM manipulation from the application logic. This leads to controllers and models being written in plain JavaScript rather than extending framework-defined versions. AngularJS can be downloaded from http://angularjs.org, as illustrated in Figure 1-6.

Figure 1-6. AngularJS web site

Angular provides a number of ng-* attributes to use within your HTML to accomplish the data binding between the UI and the model. Where Backbone uses Underscore or other alternative templating libraries, Angular allows model data to be injected directly into the HTML source.

The following snippet of HTML shows how a controller is a user for an HTML page, and the list of people in this controller are iterated through and displayed:

```
<body ng-controller="AddressBookController">
 <ul>
 <li ng-repeat="person in people">
{{person.name}}
</li>
</ul>
```

Written as a simple JavaScript object, the controller merely needs to allow the data to be retrieved for the view.

```
function AddressBookController($scope) {
  $scope.people = [
   {"name": "James"},
   {"name": "Sarah"},
  ];
}
```

Some developers might find that Angular is too opinionated, forcing you to write your application in a particular fashion.

Ember

Ember.js was released in 2011 as a rebranding of SproutCore 2.0. SproutCore is a slightly older framework, which included its own widget set. In an effort to expose the MVC framework that ran underneath SproutCore, without the need to use these widgets, Ember.js was born. Ember can be downloaded from http://emberjs.com/ as illustrated in Figure 1-7.

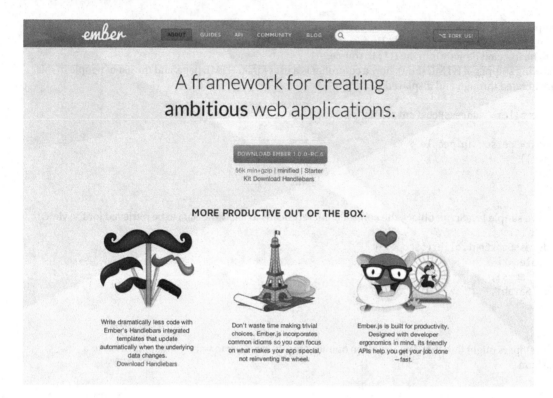

Figure 1-7. *EmberJS web site*

Ember is another framework that uses a data binding approach, allowing the view to automatically update when the model changes. This data binding works between models too so that if the data in a related object changes, both are kept in sync.

Like Backbone, Ember uses a templating library, Handlebars in Embers' case, to inject model data into the HTML. Ember also introduces a dedicated controller to complete the full MVC stack, but the model layer is represented with simple JavaScript objects.

The following is an example of a Handlebars template:

```
<script type="text/x-handlebars" id="index">
  <h1>Address Book</h1>

  <ul>
  {{#each person}}
    <li>Hello, <b>{{name}}</b>!</li>
  {{/each}}
  </ul>
</script>
```

Meanwhile, the model and application are created in JavaScript.

```
App = Ember.Application.create();

App.Person = Ember.Object.extend({
  name: null,
});

App.IndexRoute = Ember.Route.extend({
  model: function() {
    var people = [
      App.Person.create({
        name: "James"
      }),
      App.Person.create({
        firstName: "Sarah"
      })
    ];
    return people;
  }
});
```

The amount of JavaScript code required in Ember is similar to that in Backbone. But again, Backbone's strength is in the dedicated model object.

Summary

What you will have noticed here is that most other frameworks provide some built-in functionality to update the view when the model changes. Backbone is often considered a lower-level framework because all of this work has to be accomplished by the programmer using additional code. Some may see this as a negative, but it results in a more transparent view into how your application is actually working behind the scenes. Because you write the UI update code yourself, it is easier to debug when there are issues. This level of control is one of the most widely quoted reasons for developers using Backbone.

Also, as one of the more mature frameworks available, Backbone has a richer set of documentation, tutorials, and examples across the Internet.

Backbone Adoption in the Real World

While debating whether Backbone is right for your project, it can be useful to see which other industry leaders have adopted the technology in real-world applications used every day. This section of the book lists some high-profile examples and gives five good reasons to use Backbone, along with another list that describes where it might not be suitable.

Companies Using Backbone

Some of the brightest companies in the world use Backbone to power their latest applications. Let's take a look at three of these companies and find out why they have chosen Backbone. You'll find many more case studies listed at the official Backbone web site.

Airbnb

Airbnb is one of Y Combinator's greatest success stories, providing a collaborative sharing service for people to rent living space across 192 countries. Airbnb has used Backbone in a number of its products, from its mobile web application to web site features including wish lists and matching and in its own internal applications. An example of how Backbone is used in the mobile website can be seen in Figure 1-8.

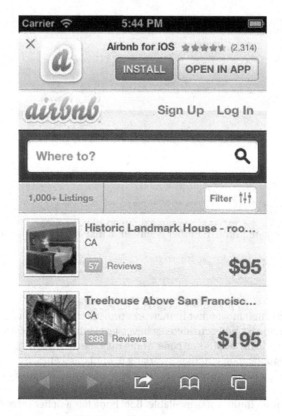

Figure 1-8. *Backbone features extensively in Airbnb's technology stack*

While initially Airbnb used Rails in the back end with Backbone on the client side, it has evolved the mobile application to now use Node.js on the server, which also includes Backbone. This results in the ability to share application logic that is relevant on both sides, without the need to rewrite in different languages.

You can find out more about Airbnb's use of Backbone at its developer blog at
`http://nerds.airbnb.com/weve-launched-our-first-nodejs-app-to-product/`.

SoundCloud

SoundCloud is a German-based music distribution platform with the ability to upload or listen to user-created content. The team initially used Backbone as the underpinning of its mobile web application but has since utilized it for the front end of its desktop web site too, an example of which can be seen in Figure 1-9.

Figure 1-9. SoundCloud desktop web site with player controls

One of the reasons that the engineering team chose Backbone was that "it doesn't prescribe too much about how it should be used." Similar to Airbnb, SoundCloud decided to use Handlebars as the templating engine because of the ability to add custom helpers and the precompilation of the templates.

To read more on SoundClouds architecture, check out its blog at `http://backstage.soundcloud.com/2012/08/evolution-of-soundclouds-architecture/`.

Foursquare

Foursquare is a location-based social networking app that allows users to check in to venues across the world and share status with the friends. Foursquare uses Backbone to create the model classes for all the real-world objects in its problem domain: users, venues, and check-ins. Backbone was used because it provides "a simple and lightweight mechanism to capture object data and state, complete with the semantics of classical inheritance." However, in place of Backbone.sync, the team provides its own service URI to abstract the Ajax calls to the API. You can see an example of the website, using Backbone, in Figure 1-10.

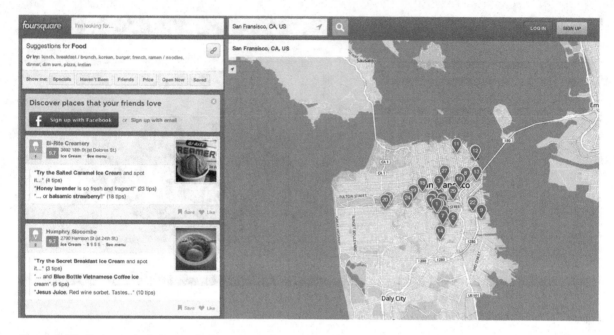

Figure 1-10. *Foursquare desktop web site*

Find out more at the Foursquare engineering blog, found at
`http://engineering.foursquare.com/2011/12/08/web-sites-are-clients-too/`.

Five Reasons to Use Backbone in Your Project

In case you're still not convinced that Backbone is the right choice for your project, here are the five top reasons to consider using it.

- *Backbone is a library, not a framework*: There's a subtle difference between libraries and frameworks. Frameworks are very prescriptive about how they are used in your project and usually impose a certain style of coding that might not suit. As you saw in the section comparing different MV* options, Backbone is the option that leaves you with the most freedom, and it can be refactored into any existing JavaScript application without having to overhaul the app in order to utilize the library. Backbone can be extended if you require additional functionality. You can use any templating library alongside Backbone, so if Underscore doesn't meet your needs or you are familiar with something like Handlebars, you can use that instead. Because there is no two-way data binding in Backbone by default, you won't hit any surprise performance issues. The library's simplicity insulates you from such problems.

- *JavaScript applications need structure*: If you want to create commercial-quality JavaScript applications, you need to impose some type of structure. Backbone's MV* approach suits almost every type of application, helping separate code that deals with the data model and the view. Most client-side applications will deal with a RESTful API, and this is one of the areas that Backbone excels at, providing synchronization functions in your model that will implement all create, update, and delete REST calls for that data object. Using a framework like Backbone brings a common, well-defined approach to JavaScript development that the entire project team can easily follow. The best practices that Backbone encourages are easy to maintain.

- *Rich documentation and a large user community*: Using any new technology can be daunting, but a mature documentation set and a large community base can help take the sting out of this. With Backbone you get this in abundance. The documentation available at `http://backbonejs.org` is simple to follow, with annotated source code and examples that help you understand every aspect of the library. Pair this with the numerous blogs and tutorials that you will find across the Internet and you know that you're not alone. There are a huge number of plug-ins and extensions available for Backbone that have been created by the user community. It's likely that if you encounter an issue, someone has already found a way to resolve it. We'll take a closer look at Backbone plug-ins and extensions later in this book.

- *It scales well, and credible companies are using it*: In the previous section we saw just a few big-name companies that use Backbone. But if you go to `http://backbonejs.org`, you will see that there are a huge list of companies that have adopted Backbone. The library is not just being used for experimental projects; in the case of Airbnb, Backbone proved to be such a good solution that it is now using it on the server side. This proves that it's a library that scales well and that it can integrate well with any other JavaScript library, even Node.js. The maturity of the library counts for a lot, and because Backbone has been around for almost three years and has reached version 1.0.0, it has the edge on a lot of other MV* solutions.

- *Your code base is a jQuery mess*: Backbone isn't just for fresh projects. It's likely that you have some legacy applications that could use some cleanup. You may have been using jQuery extensively, manipulating the DOM manually and making `$.ajax` calls. If this is the case, Backbone can be the perfect replacement, with the `Backbone.Model` object enabling you to use simpler code to achieve the same results. Don't forget that you don't need to use absolutely everything that Backbone provides. You can pick and choose what suits your application at the time.

Three Reasons Backbone Might Not Be Right for You

In some cases using Backbone might not make sense for your application. Using the wrong library for any project can have devastating consequences. This list shows when Backbone is not such a good idea:

- *Proof-of-concept applications*: Sometimes you just want to get a quick experiment together to prove what a particular user interface could look like. If you're creating something really simple, it's likely that Backbone would be too much and that you might get something together faster by using something like AngularJS. If you're not already up to speed with how Backbone works, some other solutions bring you from zero to app in less time. However, if the proof of concept turns into a real application, it is worth considering Backbone for the real implementation.

- *You're not comfortable with lower-level JavaScript*: As one of the less opinionated MV* solutions, Backbone leaves a lot of work for the developer to do. The two-way data binding between model and view is one of these tasks. While a lot of the development community is happy to write the code for this binding, some may find it a daunting. More opinionated frameworks that give more guidance into the implementation details of the entire application can be useful, but beware of potential performance issues.

- *You are creating a small web page*: Backbone is suitable for developers who are creating web applications, not just trivial web pages. There is no doubt that Backbone would be overkill for something that simple.

For some it might be difficult to see where this line is, so I would say that Backbone is overkill unless any of the following is true:

- You need to make Ajax calls to save and retrieve data from the server

- You have a number of complex view sections on your page

- You are already using a lot of jQuery to manipulate the DOM

It's difficult to find reasons not to use a library as powerful as Backbone. If you're comfortable with JavaScript, using Backbone isn't going to be a huge leap and will improve your coding skills as you follow the best practices and patterns that are encouraged within the library's code base.

Getting Backbone Set Up

Now that you've decided that Backbone is right for you, it's time to get your development environment set up.

Downloading Backbone

The official site for Backbone.js is at `http://backbonejs.org`. At the time of writing, the library had reached version 1.0.0.

As you can see, in Figure 1-11, you'll have three options for download: development, production, and edge. Usually, you will want to use the development version when working on your own machine. Development versions include the code in a nonminified format, so it is easy to debug and read through and includes all comments.

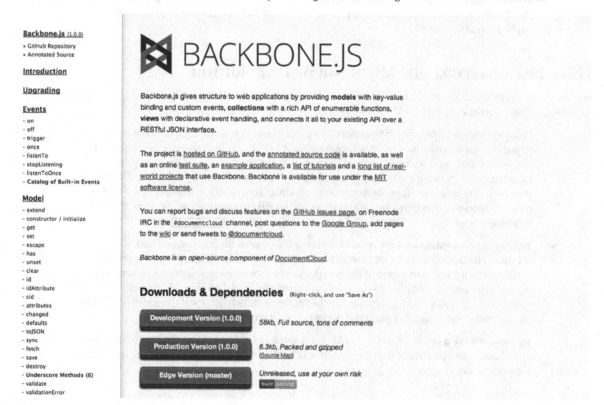

Figure 1-11. *Backbonejs.org*

When you are deploying your app onto a production server, you should use the production version. As you can see from Figure 1-11, this is a much smaller file, and as such it will download faster to the web browser, improving site performance.

The edge version is the code that is being worked on by the committers at the moment. Most of the time you will want to avoid this, unless you want to explore any new features that the team is developing.

For now, download the development version and save the backbone.js file in your development folder.

Backbone is always dependent on Underscore.js, which you will find linked from the Backbone web site. This can be downloaded from http://underscorejs.org, as in Figure 1-12. Again, you should download the development version of the library.

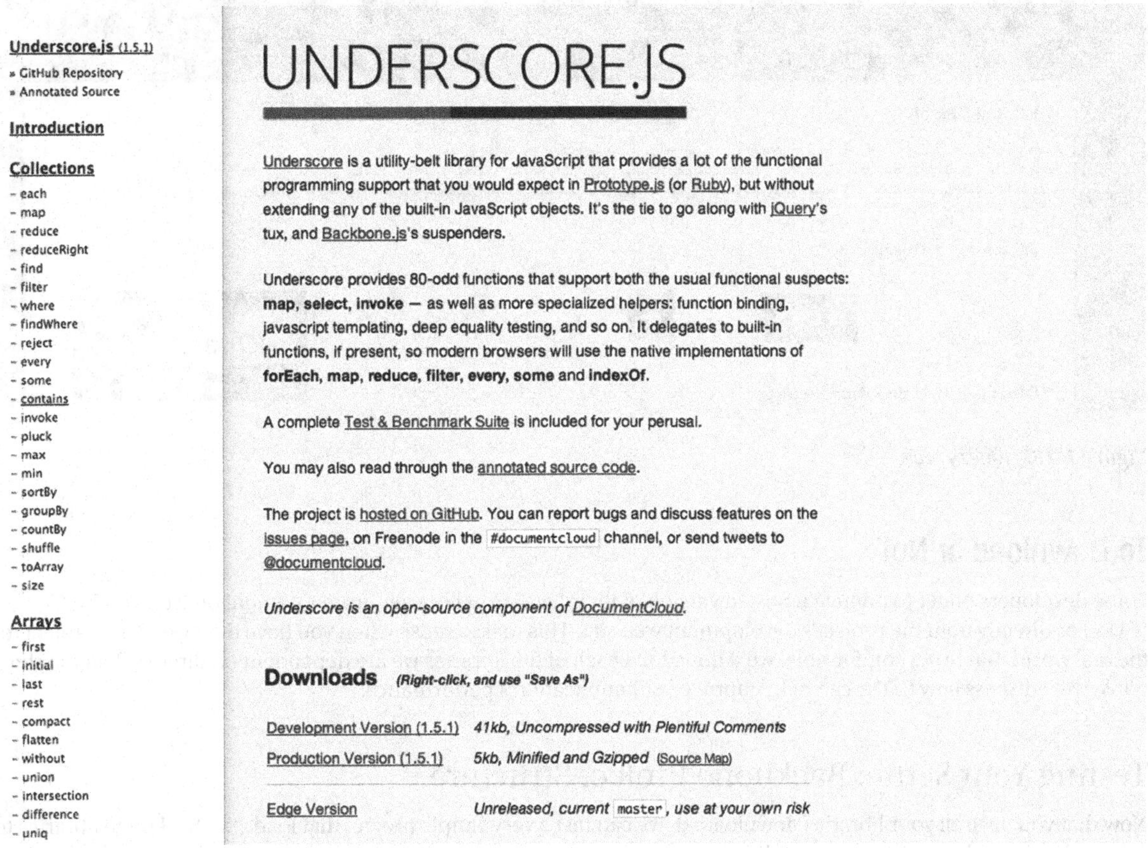

Underscore.js (1.5.1)
» GitHub Repository
» Annotated Source

Introduction

Collections
- each
- map
- reduce
- reduceRight
- find
- filter
- where
- findWhere
- reject
- every
- some
- contains
- invoke
- pluck
- max
- min
- sortBy
- groupBy
- countBy
- shuffle
- toArray
- size

Arrays
- first
- initial
- last
- rest
- compact
- flatten
- without
- union
- intersection
- difference
- uniq

UNDERSCORE.JS

Underscore is a utility-belt library for JavaScript that provides a lot of the functional programming support that you would expect in Prototype.js (or Ruby), but without extending any of the built-in JavaScript objects. It's the tie to go along with jQuery's tux, and Backbone.js's suspenders.

Underscore provides 80-odd functions that support both the usual functional suspects: **map, select, invoke** — as well as more specialized helpers: function binding, javascript templating, deep equality testing, and so on. It delegates to built-in functions, if present, so modern browsers will use the native implementations of **forEach, map, reduce, filter, every, some** and **indexOf**.

A complete Test & Benchmark Suite is included for your perusal.

You may also read through the annotated source code.

The project is hosted on GitHub. You can report bugs and discuss features on the issues page, on Freenode in the `#documentcloud` channel, or send tweets to @documentcloud.

Underscore is an open-source component of DocumentCloud.

Downloads (Right-click, and use "Save As")

Development Version (1.5.1)   41kb, Uncompressed with Plentiful Comments

Production Version (1.5.1)   5kb, Minified and Gzipped (Source Map)

Edge Version   Unreleased, current `master`, use at your own risk

Figure 1-12. Underscorejs.org

If you are using Backbone.View, and we will be, you need to depend on a DOM manipulation library, with a choice of jQuery or Zepto. Because jQuery is considered an industry standard and because of the wealth of information and plug-ins available for it, we will also depend on this.

You can download jQuery from www.jquery.com, as illustrated in Figure 1-13. At the time of writing, there is a choice of v1.10.12 or v2.0.3. If you have the luxury of supporting only more modern browsers, then the v2.*x* stream is the one to choose. But if you have to support Internet Explorer 6, 7, or 8 (and most of us still do), then you should download from the v1.*x* stream.

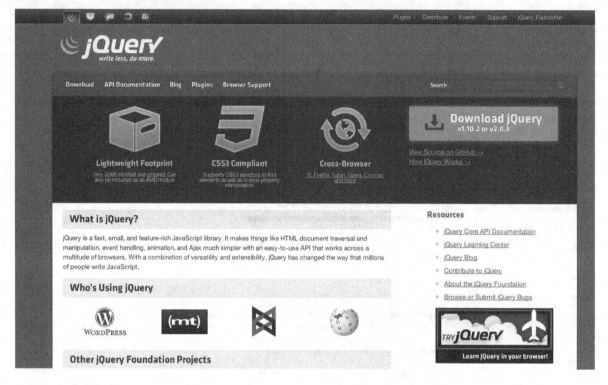

Figure 1-13. jQuery.com

To Download or Not

Some developers prefer to point at a hosted version of their JavaScript libraries, from a content delivery network (CDN) or directly from the project's development web site. This makes sense when you have deployed your project to the real world. But to get comfortable, we'll download each of the libraries we are dependent on directly. Later in the book, we'll discuss how CDNs can help improve your application's performance.

Testing Your Setup: Backbone Project Structure

Now that you have all your libraries downloaded, we can test a very simple project that loads the Backbone libraries to ensure that everything is set up correctly.

All of these libraries should be downloaded to a `js/external` folder. This is just a convention used to separate the JavaScript that you write from the libraries that you are depending on.

You will need to create an `index.html` file so that the app can be run from a browser. This should be added to the root directory, resulting in the folder structure outlined in Figure 1-14.

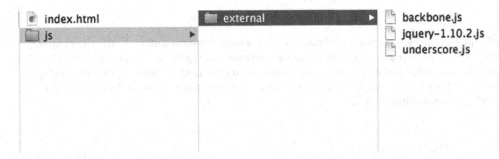

Figure 1-14. *Folder structure for simple Backbone app*

In index.html we will just create a simple HTML page and include the dependent libraries at the bottom of the page. Libraries should be loaded in the order of dependency; because Backbone depends on Underscore and jQuery, both of these libraries should be loaded first.

```
<!DOCTYPE HTML>
<html>
<head>
    <meta charset="UTF-8">
    <title>My App</title>
</head>
<body>

<script src="js/external/jquery-1.10.2.js"></script>
<script src="js/external/underscore.js"></script>
<script src="js/external/backbone.js"></script>

<script>
  // Your Backbone code goes here
</script>
</body>
</html>
```

There's no custom Backbone code in this application so far; that will come later in the book when we start to explore Backbone in depth. For now this file just includes a placeholder comment to show where you would add your code. Note that all the scripts are loaded at the end of the page, rather than in the header. This is a standard practice used by JavaScript developers so that page rendering happens sooner, without scripts to block it.

Now, simply open index.html in a browser—if there are no errors loading the libraries, then you are ready to start some serious Backbone apps over the next few chapters.

Some Tips for Your Development Environment

Setting up your machine for JavaScript development is a personal thing; different people like different tools. Here is a selection of the tools that I use for my own JavaScript development.

Apache

You're definitely going to need some version of Apache to host your web app locally. Although for the type of apps we'll create in this book, PHP and MySQL aren't going to be required, so it's hard to beat XAMPP (www.apachefriends.org/en/xampp.html) for ease of installation across Mac or Windows platforms.

Google Chrome

When developing JavaScript, Chrome is my browser of choice, purely because of the strength of the developer tools included. The Chrome Developer Tools (Figure 1-15) are among the best web debugging tools available. From the Sources tab you can open any JavaScript and add breakpoints, allowing you to inspect the values of variables and go step by step through the execution of your program. Figure 1-15 illustrates a breakpoint within backbone.js as the script is loaded in the code previously illustrated.

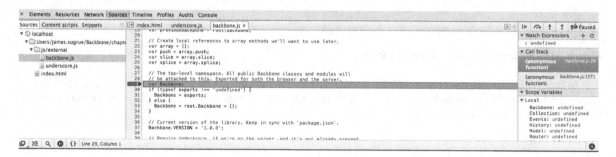

Figure 1-15. *Chrome Developer Tools*

The Console tab is another indispensable tool for JavaScript developers. You can type your code directly into the console and have it evaluated. When the debugger is paused, you can access all variables currently in scope from the console. Similarly, you can make changes to your JavaScript directly in the Sources view.

Later we'll see some other useful features that Chrome Developer Tools provides. It's worth noting that Firebug contains similar tool, if that is your browser of choice.

Sublime Text 2

Finally, you'll need a good text editor for writing your JavaScript. Thankfully, there's no need for any heavyweight IDEs when writing client-side web apps. The editor of choice for the Java community today seems to be Sublime Text 2 (see www.sublimetext.com). Apart from the obvious syntax highlighting, the editor has a wide range of plug-ins available to help you run jslint through your source code and much more. There's even a plug-in that allows you to hook into Chrome Developer Tools and debug your JavaScript from within Sublime.

Summary

In this chapter we introduced Backbone, along with a number of other JavaScript libraries and frameworks that attempt to introduce structure into web applications using variations of the Model View Controller pattern. I hope the difference between these leading projects are clear now and you can see where Backbone differs in the level of control it affords the developer.

We also looked at why Backbone might be a good choice for your project and saw a few brief case studies of how some big companies are using Backbone for their own projects. Finally, this chapter listed everything you need to get started, from the JavaScript libraries you need to download to the developer toolbox that makes working with JavaScript a frictionless experience.

CHAPTER 2

■ ■ ■

Getting Object-Oriented

Before we discuss Backbone.js in detail, we'll discuss some JavaScript basics, with a focus on supporting object-oriented concepts from JavaScript. If you're already familiar with JavaScript, feel free to skip this chapter. However, if you're new to creating JavaScript applications, this is will be an important step in getting the most from this book. If you're coming from another programming language, you'll be amazed by the things JavaScript is capable of doing. No longer a language for simple web form processing or hobbyists, JavaScript has become one of the most popular languages in the software development ecosystem.

The Rise of JavaScript

Having first appeared under the guise of LiveScript in 1995, JavaScript has been a major part of the development of the Web as we know it today. By allowing client-side scripting, JavaScript enables more dynamic web sites and applications.

JavaScript is an interpreted language, meaning it doesn't need to go through a compilation process before execution, like Java and C# do. Instead, JavaScript code is run one statement at a time by the browser. Because JavaScript is an interpreted language, most people expect there to be little in the way of structure to create real objects in JavaScript. Despite its origins focusing on creating client-side scripts on the browser for web sites, it is more commonly being used for the creation of large-scale applications. This has brought about a wealth of frameworks that help create "single-page web applications"—applications that can communicate with back-end services asynchronously without the need to reload the entire page for each action.

Backbone is one of the leading frameworks in this category. Before we look at how Backbone applications work, let's look behind the scenes at the roots of the language.

JavaScript Versions

In an effort to standardize JavaScript across browsers, ECMAScript was released in 1997. Since then it has gone through a number of releases, the most recent of which is ECMAScript 5.1, released in June 2011. Support for the features in the latest version of the specification varies widely across browsers; to find out which features your target browsers support, check one of the many compatibility tables available online such as Juriy Zaytsev's overview at `http://kangax.github.io/es5-compat-table/`.

The features that have been introduced in this version include improved object creation, object property definition, native JSON support, and useful array interrogation methods. These improvements have played a huge part in the continuing dominance of the language on the Web.

Future versions of ECMAScript, termed ES.next, will include module definitions, observables to detect changes in an object state, and the addition of real Map and Set implementations.

Looking at the road map for the language, there is no doubt that JavaScript will be alive for a long time. Every iteration of ECMAScript continues to strengthen the language, adding features that have been proven to be useful without causing the language to become overcomplicated.

Executing JavaScript Snippets

Throughout this chapter you will encounter a number of code snippets that you may want to try for yourself. The simplest way to execute these little bits of code is to use Chrome Developer Tools, included in your standard Chrome distribution. The console provided allows you to enter JavaScript and see it execute immediately. We'll be taking a closer look at Chrome Developer Tools in the next chapter. For now, you can access the tools using the Tools/Developer Tools menu option from Chrome.

To write something out to the console, simply use the `console.log` statement, which will accept any type of output. The Chrome console even gives you code completion for your JavaScript. If Firefox is your browser of choice, the Firebug add-on gives you similar capabilities.

You will also find a number of services online that allow you to execute JavaScript and share snippets you create, such as jsfiddle.net and codepen.io.

What Is an Object Anyway?

An object is a representation of something in your problem domain that contains a number of attributes. The classic example of an object is a person. In your code, you'll want to refer to different attributes of person, such as their name, age, and gender.

Along with these attributes, an object also contains methods so that you can make changes to the state of any of the attributes. Sticking with our person example, you might have a `setAge` method that allows you to change the age of your person.

Putting it all together, an object is a combination of state (attributes) and behavior (methods). The benefits to using objects in your code include the following:

- *Modularity*: Each object is independent of any other, so you can make changes to your object without affecting any others.

- *Encapsulation*: The attributes stored within each object can be hidden from other objects, so you just expose the basic information and hide internal state.

- *Reuse*: If an object already exists to represent your data or accomplish a particular task, you can simply reuse it or, better yet, extend its functionality.

We'll see how each of the practices listed here can be applied to your JavaScript code later in this chapter. But first, we'll go back to basics in a short primer of the JavaScript building blocks.

JavaScript: The Basics

JavaScript isn't a bloated language, and it provides you with just enough to get going. But don't mistake that for a language that is lacking power and features. Let's take some time to go through the various data types and objects that JavaScript provides, along with a refresher on the basic syntax.

Primitive Data Types

JavaScript contains five primitive data types: String, Number, Boolean, Undefined, and Null. In the case of the first three types, these are actually objects that wrap real primitive types, and as such they provide additional methods to deal with the data they represent.

As JavaScript is a dynamic language, a variable can change type during its lifetime. The left side of the equal sign doesn't specify the type of the variable, like in statically typed languages, but instead takes the following form:

```
var <variablename> = <value>
```

Let's now take a look at each of the data types in turn.

String

A String is simply a sequence of characters. You can use either single quotes or double quotes to create your String, provided you end with the same quotation mark you started with. The following are two valid String declarations:

```
var doubleQuoteString = "A String in double quotes";
```

If you want to include a quotation mark in your String, you can escape it using \, like so:

```
var escapedQuote = 'He said \'hello\'';
```

As mentioned earlier, String is an object wrapper around a simple type, so there are a number of properties and methods available for String operations (see Table 2-1).

Table 2-1. *Listing of String functions*

Method/Property	Purpose
.length	Returns the number of characters in the String.
charAt(index)	Returns the character at the specified index.
charCodeAt(index)	Returns the Unicode of the character at the specified index.
concat(String1, ..., StringN)	Joins Strings and returns a copy of the result.
fromCharCode()	Converts Unicode to characters.
indexOf(value)	Returns the position of the first occurrence of the value in the String. Returns -1 if it does not exist.
lastIndexOf(value)	Returns the position of the last occurrence of the value in the String. Returns -1 if it does not exist.
match(regExp)	Finds a match for the regular expression within the String, returning the matches as an array.
replace(*regExp*, *value*)	Finds a match for the regular expression within the String and replaces the resulting subString with a new value.
search(regExp)	Finds a match for the regular expression within the String and returns the position of the match.
slice(startPos, endPos)	Extracts the part of the String between the specified start and end positions.
split(token)	Splits the String into an array of subStrings, using the specified token as the delimiter.
substr(startPos, numChars)	Extracts a subString from the String, beginning at the start position through the specified number of characters.
subString(startPos, endPos)	Extracts a subString from the String, between the specified start position and end position.
toLowerCase()	Returns the String in all lowercase characters.
toUpperCase()	Returns the String in all uppercase characters.
trim()	Returns the String without any of the whitespace at either end.
valueOf()	Returns the primitive value of the String.

The String object is immutable, which means that all of these methods do not alter the original String but instead return a new String.

Number

Unlike most other programming languages, JavaScript uses a floating-point representation for numbers, and that's it! Depending on how you want to represent the number, you can create integers, doubles, and add scientific notation for larger numbers.

```
var count     = 10;    //number with no decimal places
var cost      = 2.99;  //number with two decimal places
var pi        = 123e5; //12300000
```

When no decimal place is defined, the range of a Number is from -2^{53} to 2^{53}. For floating-point numbers, the range goes from -2e31 to 2e31.

There are two special values for numbers: Infinity, when a math overflow exception occurs, and -Infinity, when a number is smaller than the minimum supported value.

Boolean

Booleans are simple values used for testing in conditional statements and can be one of two values, true or false. It's worth noting that true is treated as a String and not a Boolean.

```
var lightsOn = true;
```

Undefined and Null

Many people get confused with the difference between undefined and null, mainly because of their experiences in other programming languages. In truth, it's quite simple to see how it works. Undefined is the default value assigned to any variable. So, if I created a variable as follows and printed its value, it would be undefined.

```
var initialVariable;
console.log(initialVariable);
```

Null has to be assigned by the programmer to empty a variable and is not a default value.

```
var initialVariable = 'hello';
initialVariable = null;
```

Both of these types are considered primitive data types in the JavaScript world.

Core Objects in JavaScript

There are a few more useful objects provided to you by the JavaScript language to help deal with dates, simple mathematical operations, regular expressions, and arrays.

Date

While many libraries exist to help you deal with date and time, the JavaScript Date object is pretty powerful on its own. Date objects can be constructed using any of four constructors, the most useful being the form that take no parameters, giving you the current date and time. You can also build a Date obect at a particular time by providing a millisecond value.

```
var now = new Date();
```

You can extract the various parts of a date using a complete list of getX() methods, such as getMinute(), getDay(), and getMonth().

Of course, more eloquent approaches are available to retrieve date representation, with utility methods to return readable dates such as the following:

```
var calendarString  = now.toDateString();
var time            = now.toTimeString();
```

Math

JavaScript has a built-in Math object that allows you to perform simple mathematical operations. This object contains a number of useful constants such as Math.PI, Math.E, and Math.LOG2E.

Although it is an object, you never create an new instance of Math to use it. Think of it more as a utility object with a number of convenience methods.

For example, to round a number up to the nearest whole number, use this:

```
var doubleValue = 2.1;
var intValue = Math.ceil(doubleValue); //intValue would now be 3
```

Table 2-2 enumerates some of the available methods that you may find useful.

Table 2-2. *Listing of Math functions*

Method	Purpose
abs(x)	Returns the absolute value of x.
ceil(x)	Returns x rounded up to the nearest integer. ceil(2.1) would result in 3.
floor(x)	Returns x rounded down to the nearest integer. floor(2.1) would result in 2.
log(x)	Returns the natural logarithm of x.
pow(x,y)	Returns the result of x to the power of y.
random()	Returns a random number between 0 and 1.
round(x)	Rounds x to the nearest integer. round(2.1) would return 2.
sqrt(x)	Returns the square root of x.

Note that the previous table is not a complete list. The Math object also allows you to perform sine, cosine, and tangent calculations on numbers.

RegExp

Regular expressions are useful when you need to perform pattern matching operations on Strings. When creating a new expression, you pass through the pattern as a parameter, along with a number of flags. There are two forms that your RegExp creation can take.

```
var pattern = new RegExp('javascript','i');
```

Or

```
var pattern = /javascript/i;
```

Both of these would perform a search for the word *javascript* while ignoring case because of the i modifier. You'll remember that the String object has a match method that accepts a regular expression as a parameter, so let's put both together in a short code example.

```
var myString = 'I love Javascript';
var pattern = new RegExp('javascript', 'i');
var match = myString.match(pattern);
```

The result of match in the previous case would be an array containing one String: 'Javascript'.

■ **Note**   There's a lot more to regular expressions; you can find a complete explanation of this object on the Mozilla Developer Network at https://developer.mozilla.org/en-US/docs/Web/JavaScript/Reference/Global_Objects/RegExp.

Basic Syntax

You need to know a few basic things about every language. JavaScript is pretty simple, with few rules, so this won't take long.

Declaring Variables

As you've already seen, variables can be declared simply using the var keyword.

```
var greeting = 'Hello';
```

If you are using an object rather than a primitive, you may need to use the new keyword to construct the object.

```
var now = new Date();
```

The *scope*, or availability, of a variable depends on where it has been declared. A variable declaration made outside of any function will be global, while a declaration made within a function block will be visible only within that block.

Loops and Conditionals

It's impossible to create a JavaScript program without needing to use a conditional at some stage. In this section, we will look at the if/else conditional, as well as for and while loops.

if conditions in JavaScript take the following form:

```
if (<condition>){
   <action>
}
else{
  <alternate action>
}
```

While on the topic of conditions, it's important to note the difference between == and ===. The double equals just checks for equality, but the === provides more precision, ensuring that both the value and type are equal. For the most part, you'll want to use this precision equality operation.

```
if (userInput === 'run'){
   console.log('running application');
}
```

You see a shorter form of the previous example used in some programs where the condition and both outcomes are expressed in a single line.

```
var outputString = (price < 10 ) ? 'Reasonable ' : 'Too Expensive';
```

You may also need to iterate through arrays or perform repeated actions using for or while loops. Again, the syntax is simple. A for loop is similar to Java.

```
for(var i = 99; i >= 0; i--){
        console.log(i + 'bottles of beer on the wall.' + i + ' bottles of beer');
}
```

while loops just include a conditional test, leaving the variable initialization and the changing of variable state outside of the construct.

```
while(<condition>){
        <actions>
}
```

There is also a variant of the while loop available, where a piece of code can be executed before testing the condition.

```
do{
<actions>
}
while(<condition>)
```

Arrays

Arrays are a fundamental part of any programming language, giving the ability to create lists and collections. JavaScript provides everything you'll need to deal with arrays effectively.

There are two ways to create a new array; the second of which is more favorable, as shown here:

```
var myArray = [];
```

```
var myArray = new Array();
```

Items can then be added to specific indexes of the array. Arrays have a zero-based index, which means that the position 0 is the first element in the array.

```
myArray[0] = 'first item';
```

Items can also be pushed onto the array, taking the next available position.

```
myArray.push('first item');
```

If you already know what items you need in the array, you can use a more condensed syntax for creation.

```
var myArray = new Array('first item', 'second item', 'third item');
```

Table 2-3 enumerates all the operations that are possible in an array.

Table 2-3. *Listing of JavaScript Array functions*

Method/Property	Purpose
.length	Returns the number of items in the array and can also be used to set the size of the array.
indexOf()	Finds an element in the array and returns its position. Returns -1 if an element cannot be found.
join()	Joins all elements of the array to create a String.
lastIndexOf()	Finds the last occurrence of an element within the array and returns its position, -1 if the element cannot be found.
pop()	Removes the last element in the array and returns the element.
push()	Adds the element to the end of the array and returns the new length of the array.
reverse()	Reverses the order of the elements in the array.
shift()	Removes the first element from the array and returns that element.
slice()	Selects part of the array and returns this as a new array.
sort()	Sorts the elements of the array. A sort function can be provided as a parameter to enforce a particular sorting strategy.
splice()	Adds or removes elements from the array. The method accepts two lists of elements: the elements to remove and the ones to be added.
toString()	Returns a String representation of the array.
unshift()	Adds elements to the beginning of the array and returns the new length.
valueOf()	Returns the primitive value of the array.

■ **Note**   An array can contain a mixture of object types. You can also create *n*-dimensional arrays by placing arrays within arrays.

Closures

Closures can be a slightly confusing topic for some, but more than likely you will find yourself using them in the course of your JavaScript coding without realizing. jQuery makes heavy use of closures.

A *closure* is an inner function that can access the outer functions' variables. Just as we mentioned earlier in this chapter, a variable has a global scope or a function scope. The closure, being within a function, can access both of these scopes, as well as its own inner scope. Furthermore, the closure can access the outer functions' parameters.

Let's investigate this with a simple code example where two closures provide functionality to calculate the area of a circle or a rectangle.

```
function calculateArea(height, width, shape){
      var pi  = Math.PI;
      //first closure
      function getCircleArea(){
        var circleArea = pi * (height*height);
        return circleArea;
      }

      //second closure
      function getRectangleArea(){
        var area = width * height;
      return area;
      }

      if(shape === 'Circle'){
            return getCircleArea();
      }
      else{
            return getRectangleArea();
      }
}
```

So, you're creating a closure any time you define a function within another function. This could be thought of as an object with just one method and that method is private because it can't be executed from outside of that function.

Making JavaScript Object-Oriented

If you have programmed in a traditional object-oriented programming language, you will be familiar with terms such as *constructors*, *attributes*, and *methods*, as well as the additional concepts of encapsulation, inheritance, and polymorphism. The following section will introduce how each of these concepts can be applied in JavaScript.

Creating a Simple Object in JavaScript

Creating an object in JavaScript can be quite straightforward. You simply create a new instance of Object and add properties as required.

```
var myObject = new Object();
myObject.id = 100;
```

Another common approach to creating an object is to follow the object literal pattern on creation, where all the properties are listed as parameters within the constructor.

```
var myObject ={id: 100};
```

Both of the previous examples result in the same object, where you can access the id attribute using this:

```
var objectId = myObject.id
```

Defining Constructors

The previous section just scratches the surface of how to create objects. More often than not, you will want to use a constructor to create your object. A constructor allows you to pass through some initial variables and set up the initial state.

In other languages, this is achieved using classes, but JavaScript doesn't have classes; it has functions. This is where you really get to see the language flex its muscles.

Imagine you want to create an object that will represent a message. You'll need to define the subject, recipient, and message content. Using either of the previous approaches would be verbose and error prone. To create our representation, we create a new function for Message, with the parameters listed, as shown here:

```
function Message  (subject, recipient, content){
this.subject = subject;
        this.recipient = recipient;
        this.content = content;
}
```

Now if we want to create a new instance of this Message object, we can call our constructor function along with the new keyword. Using new is essential when calling functions that are meant to act as constructors.

```
var myEmail = new Message('Javascript is cool', 'you@gmail.com', 'Creating objects is simple');
```

This brings us a little further down the line: we are able to access our attributes as before, but we have a definition for our object and its attributes.

Creating Methods

We can elaborate on the previous example to add methods to our object. Methods allow us to provide access to variables within the object, change the state of the object, or perform operations on the object. Adding a method is achieved by creating a function within our "constructor" function.

```
function Message  (subject, recipient, content){
        this.subject = subject;
        this.recipient = recipient;
        this.content = content;
```

```
//expose the method
this.showMessage = showMessage;
function showMessage(){
        console.log('To:' + recipient + 'Subject: ' + subject + 'Message:' + content);
}
```

```
}
```

Now we can easily invoke this method, which simply prints the message structure to the console.

```
var myEmail = new Message('Javascript is cool', 'you@gmail.com', 'Creating objects is simple');
myEmail.showMessage();
```

Note that before we added the function, we have a line that exposes the showMessage method as part of this object. Without this line, the execution of the previous code would have led to the following error:

```
TypeError: Object #<Message> has no method 'showMessage'
```

However, you may want to do this to keep method *private*, internal to the object but not to callers of the object.

JavaScript Prototype

You'll often hear that JavaScript is prototype-based, rather than class-based. This simply means that while classes aren't present, you can still achieve code reuse and inheritance by cloning objects that exist as prototypes.

Every JavaScript function has a prototype project, which has nothing assigned to it by default. When properties and methods are attached to this, they will be available to instances of that function. Let's see how we could use this for our Message object created earlier by adding the show method via the prototype property.

```
function Message  (subject, recipient, content){
        this.subject = subject;
        this.recipient = recipient;
        this.content = content;
}
```

```
Message.prototype.show = function(){
        console.log('To:' + this.recipient + 'Subject: ' + this.subject + 'Message:' + this.content);
};
```

```
var myEmail = new Message('Javascript is cool', 'you@gmail.com', 'Prototype is useful');
```

```
myEmail.show();
```

Any number of functions and attributes can be added using the prototype property. If you were to examine the contents of Message.prototype, you would see that Message has a constructor, a show method, and the __proto__ property, which you can ignore for now.

```
> Message.prototype
Message {show: function}
constructor: function Message(subject, recipient, content){
show: function (){
__proto__: Object
```

It is worth noting the difference between the `prototype` property, which we have just discussed, and the `prototype` attribute. The attribute applies to the instance of the object that has been created, and the value of that attribute will specify the object's parent, or type.

In our previous example, the value of the `prototype` attribute for `myEmail` would be `Message.prototype`. Any object created from a constructor function will inherit from that constructor. But when an object is created using the object literal pattern, you will notice that the prototype will be `Object.prototype`.

Encapsulation

As you build up an object model, there will be common functionality that you want to expose to every instance of a particular object that is created. For example, you would expect to be able to send and show any message. So, let's build on our original `Message` example to illustrate how this can be achieved using the Combination Constructor/Prototype Pattern.

For convenience, here is the `Message` object constructor:

```
function Message  (subject, recipient, content){
        this.subject = subject;
        this.recipient = recipient;
        this.content = content;
}
```

Now, instead of defining each part of the prototype in isolation, we can use the following shorthand to assign the constructor and a number of methods to the `Message` object:

```
Message.prototype = {
        constructor: Message,

        sendMessage: function(){
                        console.log('Sending message to ' + this.recipient);
                   },

        show : function(){
                        console.log('To:' + this.recipient + 'Subject: ' + this.subject + 'Message:'
                        + this.content);
        }
};
```

The complete definition of the `Message` object is now in one place, and the same methods are available to all instances of `Message` we create. Each message created can have its own instance properties that are passed through to the constructor.

```
var workMessage = new Message('Work complete'', 'boss@mycorp.com', 'My work is done here');
var socialMessage = new Message('Time to go out', 'friend@gmail.com', 'Finished work now.');
workMessage.send();
socialMessage.send();
```

Inheritance Using Prototype

Inheritance is one of the big wins from any object-oriented code base, allowing you to provide basic behavior in one object that can be used and extended by any other object. The prototype property allows JavaScript to provide an inheritance mechanism.

For a simple illustration of how this inheritance works, let's look at how we would create a base definition of an Animal, which has a talk method:

```
function Animal(name){
        this.name = name;
}

Animal.prototype.talk = function(){
        console.log(this.phrase);
}
```

Now we create Dog object that can take a phrase attribute.

```
function Dog(phrase){
        this.phrase = phrase;
}
```

And we define the Dog's prototype to be Animal. It now inherits everything that the Animal object provided.

```
Dog.prototype = new Animal();
```

Creating a new instance of the Dog object and invoking the talk method, which was provided by the Animal object, will result in bark being output to the console.

```
var myDog = new Dog('bark');
myDog.talk();
```

We could achieve the same effect as earlier by using the following additional statement to ensure that instances of Dog use the correct constructor:

```
Dog.prototype.constructor = Dog;
```

With inheritance, you will also want to be able to call the parent constructor. This can be achieved using the constructor property, which will always point to the superclass. This allows us to ensure the name property is set correctly.

```
function Dog(phrase){
        this.phrase = phrase;this.constructor('Dog');

}
```

Overriding Methods

You will also want to apply a similar pattern to methods that the child object overrides. This occurs when you need to provide some additional functionality to that which you inherit. This is pretty straightforward in JavaScript thanks to the .call method of any Function object. Let's illustrate this by extending the functionality of the talk method.

```
Dog.prototype.talk = function(){
        console.log('The dog says');
        Animal.prototype.talk.call(this);
}
```

When calling the parent class method, you can pass though a different object as context for it, which in our case is our Dog object. You could also pass through any parameters for that method right after the this declaration.

When calling the parent object method earlier, we needed to know that the parent was Animal.prototype. We can make the code more elegant by keeping a record of what the parent object is.

```
Dog.prototype = new Animal();
Dog.prototype.constructor = Dog;
//define the parent property
Dog.prototype.parent = Animal.prototype;
Dog.prototype.talk = function(){
        console.log('The dog says');   //use the parent property to invoke the method
        this.parent.talk.call(this);
}
```

The Prototype Chain

When a "subclass" such as this invokes any method or attribute, the prototype chain is interrogated in order to find the value. If the current object doesn't define a method, the parent is checked and so on until the root of all objects is reached: Object.

Running the following code will result in the execution of the Object.toString() method because no other definition exists in the prototype chain, but a definition does exist in Object.

```
myDog.toString();
```

Parasitic Combination Inheritance Pattern

The approach to inheritance we have taken so far is quite straightforward. However, we can create an inheritPrototype function in our JavaScript code base that will provide a more elegant approach to inheritance. Before we discuss that, we first need an understanding of the Object.create() method that JavaScript already provides.

Object.create

Object.create was originally written by Douglas Crockford but has since become part of the JavaScript language. This method allows you to create a new object using a prototype that is provided as a parameter, along with optional property descriptors.

Creating a simple Object that inherits everything we have defined for our Animal object is as simple as this:

```
var dog = Object.create(Animal.prototype);
```

Adding additional properties to the dog object can be done from this point. Or you can use the additional property descriptor's parameter. A property descriptor takes the name of the property along with a definition of its value and whether the property can be altered.

```
var dog = Object.create(Animal.prototype, {
              'legs':{value: 4, writable: true},
              'barks': {value: true, writeable: false}
});
```

In summary, what you're really doing with Object.create is passing in the object you want to inherit from. Note that Object.create was introduced in ECMAScript 5.0/JavaScript 1.8.5.

inheritPrototype

The idea behind the inheritPrototype function is that you can pass in the parent and child objects, and the function will then make the child object inherit everything from the parent object.

```
function inheritPrototype(childObject, parentObject){
        var parentCopy = Object.create(parentObject.prototype);
        parentCopy.constructor = childObject;
        childObject.prototype = parentCopy;
}
```

The previous code might look complex, but it's fairly digestible if you take it line by line.

First, a copy of the parent object is created that will have everything that parentObject contains. This is used as a temporary object for our copy process; in the end, this parentCopy will actually be used as the child object.

The second line simply says that the constructor of this temporary object will be the child's constructor. And finally, the prototype of the childObject will be parentCopy. At this point, childObject will have inherited everything from parentObject.

Now, we can create a Dog, first defining its constructor and then using our inheritPrototype function.

```
//define Dog constructor
function Dog(phrase){
this.phrase = phrase;
}
```

```
//set up the Dog object to inherit from Animal
inheritPrototype(Dog, Animal);
```

From this point, new properties and methods can be added to the Dog object. Had we defined these before using the inheritPrototype function, the additional definitions would have been overwritten because of the copying that takes place.

Controlling Access to Methods and Properties

When using prototype, all properties and methods that are added are accessible to any callers. However, sometimes you want to keep some properties hidden and use only particular methods within the object, not externally.

Private members can be created by not including them on the prototype or exposing them using this.

Let's take the Message object as an example. Perhaps we want to send secure messages and have a private key that is used for sending the message.

```
function Message  (subject, recipient, content){
        //private property
        var privateKey = '11111';
        //private method
        function encryptMessage(content){
        return content || privateKey;
        }

        this.subject = subject;
        this.recipient = recipient;
        this.content = content;

        //expose the method
        this.showMessage = showMessage;
        function showMessage(){
                console.log('To:' + recipient + 'Subject: ' + subject + 'Message:' + content);
        }

          this.sendMessage = sendMessage;
          //public method using a private method
          function sendMessage(){
             console.log(encryptMessage(this.content));
          }
}
```

While this example gets the point across, remember that JavaScript is an interpreted language, and anyone could look at your source and see this secret key. In real-world applications, compiled server-side code would deal with confidental data like this.

Providing a Namespace

When creating any nontrivial code base, a namespace is important to help avoid any collisions in object names and to make navigating the code a little easier.

The Message object is an example of where an object collision could easily happen. Message isn't clearly related to e-mail, SMS, or Twitter. So, someone joining a project with poor documentation might create their own Message definition for a different purpose.

To see this in action, let's create a namespace for our Message, which will take the form com.apress.chapterone. Each of the namespace parts must be defined in sequence.

```
var com = com || {};
com.apress = com.apress || {};
com.apress.chapterone = com.apress.chapterone || {};
```

The definition of Message changes to utilize the namespace parts.

```
com.apress.chapterone.Message = function Message(
```

The usage of a Message object will now need to respect the namespace as follows:

```
var myMessage = new com.apress.chapterone.Message(
```

This is probably the simplest approach to namespace management that exists for JavaScript, but it is the most effective and easiest to understand.

Object-Oriented Frameworks for JavaScript

While the previous gives you an appreciation of the intricacies of object-oriented JavaScript, there are a number of libraries, Backbone included, that provide utilities and patterns that make implementing object-oriented concepts in JavaScript easier for the programmer. While we look at the main contenders here, it is likely that Backbone will be sufficient in most cases.

PrototypeJS

Currently in version 1.7.1, Prototype.js (http://prototypejs.org/) provides more natural approaches to defining classes and dealing with inheritance. Not to be confused with the prototype language feature, the library provides many other useful features such as programming shortcuts and abstractions of Ajax to ensure cross-browser compatibility.

To use PrototypeJS in your code, simply download the library and include it in script tags ahead of your own source.

Creating a class is simple, with properties passed through to a Class.create method.

```
var Animal = Class.create({
    talk: function(phrase){
        console.log(phrase);
    },
    move : function(){
            console.log('Animal moving');
    }
});
```

The real power in PrototypeJS is in how subclassing is achieved. The create method allows you to specify the class you want to inherit from as a first parameter. Also, each function can be refined by using the $super parameter, which points to the parent class implementation of the function.

```
var Dog = Class.create(Animal,{
    talk: function($super, message{
            console.log('Dog says');
            $super();
    }
});
```

These small additions alone provide a less cumbersome approach to inheritance in your JavaScript.

MooTools

MooTools (www.mootools.net) is another compact JavaScript framework that provides some object-oriented mechanisms, along with other DOM and Ajax-related functionality, similar to Prototype.js. Some developers may find MooTools more familiar as it introduces Extends and Implements concepts, similar to the Java programming language.

Creating a class is also more closely aligned to Java, as MooTools uses the new keyword for creation.

```
var Animal = new Class({
        initialize: function(name){
                this.name =name;
        },
        talk : function(phrase){
                console.log(phrase);
        }
});
```

initialize is a special function that acts as a constructor for the class, so creating a new Animal would be achieved using this:

```
var animal = new Animal('Cow');
```

Extending a base class and calling the super constructor are pretty simple too.

```
var Dog = new Class({
        //define extends relationship
        Extends: Animal,
        initialize: function(name, phrase){
                //call super constructor
                this.parent(name);
        }
});
```

Defining an implements relationship follows a similar pattern, where the initialize function can be omitted.

Backbone.js

Luckily for you, Backbone.js has provided enough object-oriented concepts to eliminate the need for you to utilize any additional libraries such as Prototype.js or MooTools.

We'll see later in this book how you can easily extend any object and how you can take advantage of the initialize function to act as a constructor when creating new object instances.

Summary

This chapter provided an overview of JavaScript basics with an emphasis on how object-oriented programming concepts can be applied. You should now have a clear understanding of the prototype language feature and an appreciation of the intricacies of supporting features such as inheritance. At the very least, you will appreciate how much Backbone helps to remove all the boilerplate code related to object-oriented programming.

With this knowledge, understanding how Backbone works will be much easier. You will see how much Backbone helps in supporting OO concepts and creating a manageable code base in the following chapters.

CHAPTER 3

■ ■ ■

Backbone Models and Collections

There are two main parts to the model layer of any Backbone.js application: the representation of the data (Backbone.Model) and the grouping of your data into sets (Backbone.Collections). An understanding of how each of these parts works and interacts will give you the ability to create a well-structured data layer for your Backbone applications.

■ **Note**   Throughout this chapter, as you are using the code samples, you can simply load index.html from Chapter 1 and use the Chrome Developer Console to try these snippets. Because you have loaded Backbone, Underscore, and jQuery, all the snippets will execute correctly.

System Setup

Before we go further, you will need to do a few things to ensure your system is working properly. First, all your code should be executed from an Apache web server, rather than simply from the file system. In my examples, I have a folder named backbone in the htdocs of an XAMPP installation. When serving index.html from this server, the URL to visit is http://localhost/backbone/index.html.

The structure of index.html should follow that from the previous chapter. Ensure that you have included the Backbone, Underscore, and jQuery libraries, and put any JavaScript code shown in this chapter between with the script element at the end of the file.

You will also notice that for any back-end API calls I used Node.js. This can be downloaded from http://nodejs.org, and you should ensure that your local installation is working properly before setting up the server.js file that we will create in the "Exchanging Data with the Server" section.

Finally, don't forget to use the Chrome Developer Tools when you run into problems; it always provides the best chance at narrowing down bugs in your JavaScript code.

Backbone Models

Every application begins with the definition of a model. It's the data that you need to manipulate and represent in the app. As we described in previous chapters, the model is a layer in which the data resides and will likely contain many objects. As a rule of thumb, you should break your problem domain into individual elements and describe each of these as a model object.

To create a model object in Backbone, you will need to use the `Backbone.Model`. As you'll see for all Backbone objects that you create, you'll use an `.extend` method to create your own version of the class, as in the following code:

```
MyModel = Backbone.Model.extend({
    //object properties would go here
});
```

All objects in the library have this Backbone namespace, so it's always really clear when you're using Backbone objects.

In real applications, it is likely that you will never create a model in this way but instead will pass through properties to construct your object correctly. In the previous code snippet, the empty brackets ({}) represent an object literal. This is where all the properties and functions that you want to be available in the model will reside.

■ **Note** An object literal contains a list of comma-separated definitions in the form of key : value, where value can be a function or another object.

Constructors

When creating new model objects, you may want some behavior to be executed on construction, such as setting up different handlers or setting some initial state in your mode. To achieve this in Backbone, just define an `initialize` function when creating your model object.

To see this `initialize` function in action, let's create a simple Book object where a line is written to the console on object creation.

```
Book = Backbone.Model.extend({
    initialize: function(){
        console.log('a new book');
    }
});
```

This `initialize` function gets called as soon as we create a new instance of the `Model` object. In this case, on creation of a new Book object, we'll see the line "a new book" on the console.

```
var myBook = new Book();
```

Another common requirement for models is to have some default attributes available. You may want to do this so that optional parameters, not passed through on object creation, have some definition. In Backbone, this is done using the `defaults` object literal.

```
Book = Backbone.Model.extend({
    initialize: function(){
        console.log('a new book');
    },

    defaults: {
            name: 'Book Title',
            author: 'No One'
    }
});
```

Now when the object is created, these default values are provided for each instance.

Model Attributes

With data being the main reason that you have a model, let's first focus on attributes. This section covers all the attribute-related operations that are available to you when using `Backbone.Model`.

Getting Attribute Values

The attributes in any model object can be easily retrieved by using the `.get` function and passing through the name of the attribute that you want to access. Because we're using the simple default values, the following line would print out "Book Title" after you have initialized the Book object.

```
console.log(myBook.get('name'));
```

During object creation, it is possible to pass through the values of the attributes in the model so that each instance can be unique.

```
var thisBook = new Book({name : 'Beginning Backbone',
                         author: 'James Sugrue'});
```

Now when you retrieve the values of either attribute, the value passed through on creation will be used in place of the default.

```
console.log(thisBook.get('name') + ' by ' +        thisBook.get('author'));
```

Now when you retrieve the values of either attribute, the value passed through on creation will be used in place of the default.

You can also use the `.attributes` property to get a JSON object that represents all of the model data.

```
console.log(thisBook.attributes); // a JSON representation of all attributes
```

Changing Attribute Values

Changing attribute values outside of the constructor is done in a similar way, using the structure of a function call in the format `.set('<variable name>', <value>)`. For example, to change the book name, use this:

```
thisBook.set('name', 'Beginning Backbone.js');
```

You can add new attributes to your object in the same manner as shown previously.

```
thisBook.set('year', 2013);//creates a new attribute called year
```

Deleting Attributes

You may find that you need to delete attributes you have no use for from your model. In the following example, a new attribute is added and subsequently deleted. The second `console.log` statement results in undefined being returned as the attribute value.

```
thisBook.set('year', 2013);
console.log('Book year ' + thisBook.get('year'));
thisBook.unset('year');
console.log('Book year ' + thisBook.get('year'));
```

Backbone provides a neater way to check for the presence of an attribute in a model, using the .has function, which returns a Boolean.

```
//check for the existence of an attribute
var hasYear = thisBook.has('year'); //results in false
var hasName = thisBook.has('name'); //results in true
console.log('Has an attribute called year  : ' + hasYear);
console.log('Has an attribute called name  : ' + hasName);
```

You can also delete all attributes from your model using the clear function.

```
//create a new object
var newBook = new Book({name: 'Another Book', author: 'You'});
newBook.clear();//remove all attributes
console.log('Has an attribute called name  : ' + newBook.has('name'));//results in false
```

Both the unset and clear functions take an additional options object, in which you can add a Boolean indicating that no change event should be triggered from the model when the operation is complete. The "Model Events" section later in this chapter explains how these events operate.

```
thisBook.unset('year', {silent: true});
```

Cloning Models

It's common that you might want to make a complete copy of your Backbone model, keeping all the same attributes. Rather than needing to worry about the details of how to create a deep copy, you can simply use the .clone() method to create a cloned model instance.

```
var clonedBook = thisBook.clone();
```

Attribute Function Reference

Table 3-1 describes the most useful operations relating to attributes that you can carry out on a Backbone model.

Table 3-1. *Attribute Functions for Backbone Models*

Operation	Description
.get(<attribute name>)	Returns the value of the attribute with the given name. If no such attribute exists, undefined is returned.
.set(<attribute name>, attribute value>	Sets the value of the given attribute to the value provided in the second parameter. If the attribute doesn't already exist, a new attribute is created with this value.

(*continued*)

Table 3-1. (*continued*)

Operation	Description
.has(<attribute name>)	Checks for the existence of the given attribute in the model object.
unset(<attribute name>)	Removes an attribute from the model, if it exists.
clear()	Removes all attributes from the model object.
.attributes	Returns a JSON representation of all attributes in the model.
.clone()	Creates a new instance of the model with all the same attributes.

Adding Functions to Your Model

So far our model has been all about the attributes, but you can also add your own functions to deal with repetitive tasks. The following example illustrates how to include a printDetails function in place of all the console.log statements used so far:

```
Book = Backbone.Model.extend({
    initialize: function(){
        console.log('a new book');
    },

    defaults: {
        name: 'Book Title',
        author: 'No One'
    },

    printDetails: function(){
        console.log(this.get('name') + ' by ' + this.get('author'));
    }
});
```

This function is now available to all instances of the Book object.

```
    //use the printDetails function
thisBook.printDetails();
```

Model Events

Although we'll be dealing with events later in the book, one specific type of event that is critical for models is the change event, where the values of an attribute, or set of attributes, are altered.

Listening for Changes

With Backbone change handlers, the easiest type of change handler listens for changes across the entire model. Event handlers are added to Backbone objects using the .on() function, which accepts the type of handler as a string and accepts a reference to a function that will be run when the change happens.

The best time to create this listener is in the model `initialize` function. By altering the code you have so far, you will see that any time a set is called, this function is invoked.

```
Book = Backbone.Model.extend({
    initialize: function(){
                this.on("change", function(){
                            console.log('Model Changed');
                });
    },

    defaults: {
        name: 'Book Title',
        author: 'No One'
    },

    printDetails: function(){
        console.log(this.get('name') + ' by ' + this.get('author'));
    }
});
```

You can listen for changes in specific attributes by using the format change:`<attribute name>` rather than change. The following addition creates another handler that deals only with changes to the name attribute:

```
initialize: function(){
            this.on("change", function(){
            console.log('Model Changed');
            });
            this.on("change:name", function(){
            console.log('The name attribute has changed');
            });
    },
```

We noted earlier that the `.set` function allowed an optional parameter for silent updates. If this is used, then the change handler won't be invoked.

```
//set the variable (expect change handler)
thisBook.set('name', 'Different Book'); //change handler invoked
thisBook.set(,'name', 'Different Book', {silent:true});//no change handler invoked
```

Figuring Out What Has Changed

Backbone includes a number of properties that keep track of what is changed in your model. If you are using a global change handler, this can be a really useful way to see what's going on.

You can check whether an individual attribute has been altered using hasChanged(`'<attribute name>'`).

```
this.on("change", function(){
   console.log('Model Changes Detected:');
   if(this.hasChanged('name')){
            console.log('The name has changed');
   }
```

```
    if(this.hasChanged('year')){
        console.log('The year has changed')
    }

});
```

You can get a set of all the attributes that have changed using the `.changed` property.

```
Book = Backbone.Model.extend({
    initialize: function(){
        this.on("change", function(){
        console.log('Changed attributes: ' + JSON.stringify(this.changed));
        });
    },
```

You can also get a set of the previous state of all attributes using the `.previousAttributes()` function. The following line could also be added to the change handler:

```
console.log('Previous attributes: ' + JSON.stringify(this.previousAttributes()));
```

Finally, you can retrieve the previous value of a specific attribute using `.previous('<attribute name'>)`.

```
if(this.hasChanged('name')){
    console.log('The name has changed from '  + this.previous('name') + ' to ' + this.get('name'));
}
```

Attribute Changes Reference

Table 3-2 describes the most useful operations related to attributes changes in your model.

Table 3-2. *Functions Related to Attribute Changes in Backbone Models*

Operation	Description
`.on('change', <function>)`	Provides a global change handler that responds to any attribute changing in the model
`.on('change:<attribute name>', <function>)`	Listens for changes on a particular attribute
`.hasChanged(<attribute name>`	Returns true if the attribute has changed since the last change event
`.previous(<attribute name>)`	Returns the previous value of a particular attribute
`.changed`	Returns a complete set of all the changed attributes in the model

Model Validation

Backbone provides a validation mechanism for model data, meaning that you can have all the logic that determines whether the state of the model is correct or not within the model, rather than in some external JavaScript or form-processing code.

If you provide a validation method, it will be run every time the .save function is invoked and during every set/unset operation when {validate:true} is provided as an optional parameter.

Let's imagine our Book model insists that a name exists and that the year is after 2000. A validation method for these rules would look as follows:

```
Book = Backbone.Model.extend({
        initialize: function(){
        },

  defaults: {
  },

  printDetails: function(){
  },

  validate: function(attrs){
        if(attrs.year < 2000){
                return 'Year must be after 2000';
        }
        if(!attrs.name){
                return 'A name must be provided';
        }
  }
});
```

If you break any of these rules when manipulating the model, the operations will fail to change the attribute values.

```
//try setting the year to pre 2000
thisBook.set('year', 1999, {validate: true});
console.log('Check year change: ' + thisBook.get('year'));
//try removing the name from the model
thisBook.unset('name', {validate: true});
console.log('Check if name was removed ' + thisBook.get('name'));
```

When a validation error has been detected, an event is fired. By adding an "invalid" event handler, you can provide feedback on the validation error. As with all event handlers, this should be added to your initialize function.

```
Book = Backbone.Model.extend({
initialize: function(){
        this.on("invalid", function(model, error){
                console.log("**Validation Error : " + error + "**");
        });
```

Without the validation flag, the validation function will not be executed on set. However, you can check whether the model is in a valid state at any time with the isValid() function.

```
//check if model is valid
console.log('Is model valid: ' + thisBook.isValid());
```

```
//break the validation rules by not using the validate flag
thisBook.set('year', 1998);
//check if the model is valid
console.log('Is model valid: ' + thisBook.isValid());
```

Exchanging Data with the Server

The final set of functionality available for Backbone models relates to how the data can be stored from, and sent to, a server that provides a REST API. Before we get to the Backbone mechanisms around this, we'll first set up a simple back end to provide responses to our API calls.

■ **Note**   Keep in mind that `Backbone.Collection` looks after a lot of the RESTful operations, rather than needing to make calls for every model object. To illustrate the underlying mechanisms, we'll look at the model operations first.

Node.js Server Back End

As we're working with JavaScript anyway, I will outline a simple server that uses Node.js, but feel free to replace it with a REST server implementation of your own choice. We won't be using this extensively, as the focus of this book is on the client side. However, it will be useful to respond to Backbone application requests for illustration purposes.

First you'll need to install Node.js from `http://nodejs.org`. Once it's installed, use the NPM package manager to install the express node package, a minimal web application framework for Node.js that makes it really easy to get a simple server with a REST API running.

```
npm install express
```

Finally, just copy the following code into `server.js`. As you can see from the code, it provides some simple endpoints served from `http://localhost:8080/books`.

```
/**
 * A simple API hosted under localhost:8080/books
 */
var express = require('express');
var app = express();
var bookId = 100;

function findBook(id){
    for(var i =0; i < books.length; i++){
        if(books[i].id === id){
            return books[i];
        }
    }
    return null;

}
```

```
function removeBook(id){
    var bookIndex = 0;
    for(var i=0; i < books.length; i++){
        if(books[i].id === id){
            bookIndex = i;
        }
    }
    books.splice(bookIndex, 1);
}

app.configure(function () {
    //Parses the JSON object given in the body request
    app.use(express.bodyParser());
});

var books = [
{id: 98, author: 'Stephen King', title: 'The Shining', year: 1977},
{id: 99, author: 'George Orwell', title: 1949}];
/**
* HTTP GET /books
* Should return a list of books
*/
app.get('/books', function (request, response) {

    response.header('Access-Control-Allow-Origin', '*');
    console.log('In GET function ');
    response.json(books);

});
/**
* HTTP GET /books/:id
* id is the unique identifier of the book you want to retrieve
* Should return the task with the specified id, or else 404
*/
app.get('/books/:id', function (request, response) {
    response.header('Access-Control-Allow-Origin', '*');
    console.log('Getting a  book with id ' + request.params.id);
    var book = findBook(parseInt(request.params.id,10));
    if(book === null){
        response.send(404);
    }
    else{
        response.json(book);
    }

});
/**
* HTTP POST /books/
* The body of this request contains the book you are creating.
* Returns 200 on success
*/
```

```
app.post('/books/', function (request, response) {
    response.header('Access-Control-Allow-Origin', '*');

    var book = request.body;
    console.log('Saving book with the following structure ' + JSON.stringify(book));
    book.id = bookId++;
    books.push(book);
    response.send(book);

});
/**
* HTTP PUT /books/
* The id is the unique identifier of the book you wish to update.
* Returns 404 if the book with this id doesn't exist.
*/
app.put('/books/:id', function (request, response) {
    response.header('Access-Control-Allow-Origin', '*');
    var book = request.body;
    console.log('Updating  Book ' + JSON.stringify(book));
    var currentBook = findBook(parseInt(request.params.id,10));
    if(currentBook === null){
        response.send(404);
    }
    else{
        //save the book locally
        currentBook.title = book.title;
        currentBook.year = book.year;
        currentBook.author = book.author;

        response.send(book);
    }
});
/**
* HTTP DELETE /books/
* The id is the unique identifier of the book you wish to delete.
* Returns 404 if the book with this id doesn't exist.
*/
app.delete('/books/:id', function (request, response) {
  console.log('calling delete');
  response.header('Access-Control-Allow-Origin', '*');
  var book = findBook(parseInt(request.params.id,10));
  if(book === null){
      console.log('Could not find book');
    response.send(404);
  }
  else
  {
    console.log('Deleting ' + request.params.id);
    removeBook(parseInt(request.params.id, 10));
    response.send(200);
  }
```

```
  response.send(200);

});

//additional setup to allow CORS requests
var allowCrossDomain = function(req, response, next) {
    response.header('Access-Control-Allow-Origin', "http://localhost");
    response.header('Access-Control-Allow-Methods', 'OPTIONS, GET,PUT,POST,DELETE');
    response.header('Access-Control-Allow-Headers', 'Content-Type');

    if ('OPTIONS' == req.method) {
      response.send(200);
    }
    else {
      next();
    }
};

app.configure(function() {
    app.use(allowCrossDomain);
});

//start up the app on port 8080
app.listen(8080);
```

To kick off the server, use node server.js on the command line. This server is very simple but will do enough to get the Backbone persistence calls to execute correctly.

Identifiers

Backbone models have three attributes that deal with uniquely identifying them during data exchange with the server: id, cid, and idattribute.

The id attribute is a unique string or integer value, just like a primary key in a relational database. This id attribute is useful when retrieving the model from a collection, and it is also used to form part of the URL for the model.

The cid attribute is generated automatically by Backbone when the model is first created; it can be used to serve as a unique identifier when the model has not yet been saved to the server and does not have its real ID available.

Sometimes the model you are retrieving from the back end will use a different unique key. For example, the server might use an ISBN as the unique identifier for a book, or a user ID field might be the identifier used for a User model when saved. The idAttribute attribute allows you to provide a mapping between that key to the ID in your model, meaning that the server will use that attribute to populate the ID.

Saving Models

The save function invokes the operation to save the model to the server, invoking the Backbone.sync function. We'll see later how the sync function can be replaced to provide alternative means of persisting models, but for now we'll follow the default behavior that's already built into Backbone.

Now that we have a back-end service to hook into, we can set the urlRoot attribute of the Model object.

```
Book = Backbone.Model.extend({
        urlRoot: 'http://localhost:8080/books/',
```

This URL tells Backbone where to point when performing any operations that require responses from a back-end service. As our node.js server is running on port 8080 and we've set up endpoints to respond from /books/, our URL is constructed as in the previous code listing.

In cases where the id attribute has not been set and save is called, the model will invoke a create operation (HTTP POST) on the back-end REST service, while an update (HTTP PUT) operation will be used when the ID has been specified. This is a simple way of ensuring that a single save function can be used regardless of whether your model has been newly created or has been edited since last retrieved from the server.

The save function can be called with no parameters or can take the set of attributes you want to persist to the server, along with an options hash that contains handlers for both success and error cases.

```
thisBook.save(thisBook.attributes,
{
        success: function(model, response, options){
                console.log('Model saved');
                console.log('Id: '  +thisBook.get('id'));
        },
        error: function(model, xhr, options){
                console.log('Failed to save model');
        }
});
```

Success and error handlers are important when making calls to remote API endpoints, and you cannot be certain that a call to save a model will always be successful. Once the call is complete and has returned, the appropriate callback will be invoked, either success or error. Don't forget that calls are made asynchronously, so any lines of code after the save method won't wait for the save to be completed first.

The save method will have invoked the following piece of code served up by the Node.js server:

```
app.post('/books/', function (request, response) {
    response.header('Access-Control-Allow-Origin', '*');

    var book = request.body;
    console.log('Saving book with the following structure ' + JSON.stringify(book));
    book.id = bookId++;
    response.send(book);

});
```

The most important part of this function is that it provided a new ID for the book and returned the new structure of the book object in JSON format. Now that this book object has an ID assigned to it, any subsequent save methods will invoke the update operation on the back end.

Remember that, if specified, the validation function will be called during the execution of save(). If the validation fails, the model will not be sent to the server.

Retrieving Models

If you want to reset the state of your model object to the same as it is on the server side, you can invoke the fetch() function. Again, this function accepts an options hash that includes success and error callbacks.

```
thisBook.fetch({
success: function(model, response, options){
        console.log('Fetch success');
},
```

```
error: function(model, response, options){
        console.log('Fetch error');
}
});
```

If the execution of the fetch function detects that there is a difference in the models between the server and client sides, a change event will be triggered. This can be useful when you want to ensure that the application is in sync with the back-end service or when you need to populate your model objects on application start-up.

Deleting Models

The final server operation that you may want to carry out is a delete operation to remove the model from the back end.

```
thisBook.destroy({
        success: function(model, response, options){
                console.log('Destroy success');
        },
        error: function(model, response, options){
                console.log('Destroy error');
        },
        wait: true
});
```

If the model is new and doesn't yet exist on the server, the destroy operation will fail. Adding a wait:true option will ensure that the model is successfully removed from the server before it is removed from any Backbone.Collection that contains it on the client side.

Parsing Server Responses

When invoking the save() or fetch() function, you may want to parse the model to enrich your data model by adding additional attributes or removing unnecessary attributes. You can do this by adding a parse() function to your model definition. The following example shows how to add a new attribute to your data model after a save or fetch operation:

```
Book = Backbone.Model.extend({
        parse: function(response, xhr) {
                response.bookType = 'ebook';
                return response;
        }
});
```

Note that as well as adding new attributes, you could make other changes to make the data returned from the API work for your front-end application, such as changing the currency of an attribute.

Extending Your Own Models

As in any object-oriented language, you will sometimes want to create a hierarchy within your model layer. One of the great things about Backbone models is the extend mechanism, which you can use to extend your own models.

As you'll recall, when creating new models, you need to use `Backbone.Model.extend` in the creation.

```
Book = Backbone.Model.extend({
```

You can use the same format to extend this further. In the following example, let's create an EBook model, extending the original Book model with an additional method:

```
EBook = Book.extend({
        getWebLink: function(){
        return 'http://www.apress.com/'+this.get('name');
        }
});
```

```
var ebook = new EBook({name: "Beginning Backbone", author: "James Sugrue"});
console.log(ebook.getWebLink());
```

To call a function in the parent class, you need to call it explicitly using the prototype and passing through this so that the current model is used as the context.

```
EBook = Book.extend({
        printDetails: function(){
                console.log('An ebook');
                Book.prototype.printDetails.call(this);
        }
});
```

The previous code results in the `printDetails` function from the Book model being executed after an additional print statement defined in the EBook model is displayed. If there were any parameters involved in this function, they would be passed along after the **this** reference.

We'll see later that there are some Backbone plug-ins available that make this call a little simpler.

Backbone Collections

In the previous section we focused on the single models, but usually Backbone applications use `Backbone.Collection` to provide ordered sets of models. This has some useful side effects, such as being able to fetch an entire collection from a back-end server and listening for events across any of the models in a collection.

When defining a collection, you will always pass through the model that is being contained. To follow on with the book example used in the `Backbone.Model` section, we will define our collection of books as a library.

```
//Define a collection based on book
var Library = Backbone.Collection.extend({model: Book});
```

Just as with `Model`, an `initialize` method can be provided in your definition of the collection, which can be invoked on construction of a new instance of the collection. This can be useful to set up event listeners for the collection.

```
var Library = Backbone.Collection.extend({model: Book,
        initialize: function(){
                console.log('Creating a new library collection');
        }
});
```

When a new `Library` object is created, you'll see the `console.log` statement from the `initialize` function print out to the console.

```
var myLibrary = new Library();
```

Constructors

When creating an instance of the collection, you can pass through an array of model objects to populate it with some initial content.

```
var bookOne = new Book({name: 'Beginning Backbone', author: 'James Sugrue'});
var bookTwo = new Book({name: 'Pro Javascript Design Patterns', author:'Dustin Diaz, Ross Harmes'});

var myLibrary = new Library([bookOne, bookTwo]);
console.log('Library contains ' + myLibrary.length + ' books');
```

The `.length` property allows you to get the number of models currently contained within the collection. Note that the `.size()` function returns the same number.

Manipulating Collections

As the collection is used throughout the life cycle of an app, the contents are bound to change, so you will need to manipulate your collection after construction. While it is possible to use the `.models` property to get a raw array of the models contained, there are more useful utility methods available to manipulate the collection.

Adding Models

Adding a new model to your collection can be easily done using the `.add` method.

```
var bookThree = new Book({name: 'Pro Node.js for Developers', author: 'Colin J. Ihrig'});
myLibrary.add(bookThree);
console.log('Library contains ' + myLibrary.length + ' books');
```

The `.add` method will also accept an array of books.

```
var bookFour = new Book({name: 'Pro jQuery', author: 'Adam Freeman'});
var bookFive = new Book({name : 'Pro Javascript Performance', author: 'Tom        Barker'});

myLibrary.add([bookFour, bookFive]);
console.log('Library has ' + myLibrary.length + ' books');
```

If a model is already present in the collection when passed through to `.add`, it will be ignored. However, if {merge: true} is included in the call, the attributes will be merged into the duplicate model.

```
myLibrary.add(bookOne, {merge:true});console.log('Library has ' + myLibrary.length + ' books');
```

Note that an add event is fired when models are added to the collection.

You can also use the .push() function to add a model to the end of the collection, providing either an array or a single model, as in the .add function.

```
myLibrary.push(bookFive);console.log('Library has ' + myLibrary.length + ' books');
```

To do the opposite of .push() and add the model to the beginning of the collection, use the .unshift function.

```
myLibrary.unshift(bookFive);
console.log('Library has ' + myLibrary.length + ' books');
```

Removing Models

As you'd expect, a .remove function is available for removing a single model or array of models.

```
myLibrary.remove(bookFive);
console.log('Library contains ' + myLibrary.length + ' books');
myLibrary.remove([bookThree, bookFour]);
console.log('Library contains ' + myLibrary.length + ' books');
```

A remove event is fired when models are removed. An options object used in the listener can access the index of the element that has been removed.

```
var Library = Backbone.Collection.extend({model: Book,
        initialize: function(){
                this.on("remove", function(removedModel, models, options){
                        console.log('element removed  at ' + options.index);
                });

        }
});
```

The .pop() function removes and returns the last model in the collection.

```
var lastModel = myLibrary.pop();
```

To remove the first model in the collection, use the .shift() function rather than .pop(). This will also return the model you are removing.

```
var firstModel = myLibrary.shift();
```

Resetting Collections

The reset function exists to provide the ability to replace the set of models in a collection in a single call.

```
myLibrary.reset([bookOne]);
console.log('Library contains ' + myLibrary.length + ' books');
```

You can empty the collection in one go by calling the reset method with no parameters.

```
myLibrary.reset();
console.log('Library contains ' + myLibrary.length + ' books');
```

Using reset fires a single reset event rather than a sequence of remove and add events. This is useful for performance reasons because your application needs to react just once to a reset operation.

Smart Updating of Collections

The set function is described by the official Backbone documentation as a way to perform smart updates on a collection. By passing through an array of models, set abides by the following rules:

- If a model doesn't yet exist in the collection, it will be added. The rule will be ignored if {add: false} is provided.

- If a model is already in the collection, the attributes will be merged. The rule will be ignored if {merge: false} is provided.

- If there is a model in the collection that isn't in the array, it will be removed. The rule will be ignore if {remove: false} is provided.

The following code snippet shows how the remove rule can be ignored:

```
myLibrary = new Library([bookOne, bookTwo]);
console.log('Library contains ' + myLibrary.length + ' books');
myLibrary.set([bookTwo], {remove: false});
console.log('Library contains ' + myLibrary.length + ' books');
```

Without {remove:false}, the result of the second evaluation of myLibrary.length would have been 1.

Traversing Collections

A number of functions are available to run on your collections in order to retrieve individual models and iterate over the entire collection. The following section goes through these in detail.

Retrieving Models

Provided that you know the id of your models, you can retrieve a model from a collection using the .get function. Recall that until a model has been synchronized with a back-end service, the cid attribute is used instead.

```
var aBook = myLibrary.get('c5');      console.log('Retrieved book named ' + aBook.get('name'):
```

If no model matches the id or cid that is used as a parameter, this function returns undefined.

If you don't want to use IDs, you can also use the .at function, which accepts the index at which the model is present in the collection. If the collection is not sorted, the index parameter will refer to the insertion order.

```
var anotherBook = myLibrary.at(1);
console.log('Retrieved book named ' + anotherBook.get('name'):
```

Iterating Through Collections

Although you can use a simple for loop to iterate through your collection as follows:

```
//a simple loop
for(var i = 0; i < myLibrary.length; i++){
        var model = myLibrary.at(i);
        console.log('Book ' + i + ' is called ' + model.get('name'));
}
```

There is a more elegant utility function provided by Underscore that helps iterate through collections, namely, the forEach function.

```
//using forEach
myLibrary.forEach(function(model){
        console.log('Book is called ' + model.get('name'));
});
```

Other Utility Methods

Making the most of Backbone's dependency on Underscore, Backbone.Collection has a number of utility methods available. Some of these have already been listed in previous sections. Let's explore the remaining functions.

Sorting Collections

Using the sortBy function, you can choose an attribute to use as a basis to sort your collection.

```
//sort collection
var sortedByName = myLibrary.sortBy(function (book) {
   return book.get("name");
});
console.log("Sorted Version:");

sortedByName.forEach(function(model){
        console.log('Book is called ' + model.get('name'));
});
```

Note that sortBy returns a sorted array representation of the models in the collection and doesn't actually change the order of the models within the collection.

By utilizing comparators, you can impose a sorted order that will always be used for your collection. It's probably most useful to define your comparator function during collection definition. The following example illustrates how to create a comparator to order books by name:

```
var Library = Backbone.Collection.extend({model: Book,
initialize: function(){
                //initialize function content..
        },
        comparator:  function(a, b) {
                return a.get('name') < b.get('name') ? -1 : 1;
        }
});
```

The collection will now always be sorted by name. However, if you change an attribute value in one model, the collection will not rearrange the ordering. Instead, the order can be applied by invoking the sort function for the collection.

```
myLibrary.at(0).set('name', 'Z');
myLibrary.forEach(function(model){
        console.log('Book is called ' + model.get('name'));
});
//force sort
myLibrary.sort();
myLibrary.forEach(function(model){
        console.log('Book is called ' + model.get('name'));
});
```

Note that the sorting order will be reapplied when a new model is added to the collection, unless the {sort: false} option is passed through when adding.

Shuffle

If you need to get a randomized version of the models in your collection, the shuffle() function will return an array of the models that have had a shuffling algorithm applied.

```
var shuffled = myLibrary.shuffle();
```

Iterating through the collection now will present the books in a different order than before.

```
myLibrary.forEach(function(model){
        console.log('Book is called ' + model.get('name'));
});
```

Getting a List of Attributes

Sometimes you may want to get a list of all the instances of a particular attribute in your collection. This can be done easily using the .pluck() function.

```
console.log('List of authors in collection:');
var authors = myLibrary.pluck('author');
authors.forEach(function(authorName){
        console.log(authorName)
});
```

Searching

A number of useful search mechanisms are available, based on passing through a set of key-value pairs to search functions.

For example, to get an array of model objects that match a certain criteria, use the `.where` function.

```
var results = myLibrary.where({author:'James Sugrue'});
console.log('Found: ' + results.length + ' matches');
```

The `findWhere` function can be used to find the first model that matches the query, rather than returning an array of matches.

```
var result = myLibrary.findWhere({author:'James Sugrue'});
console.log('Result: ' + result.get('author'));
```

You can also group model objects by common attribute values. For example, if each of the books had a Boolean indicating whether they were published, we could group them as follows:

```
var byPublished = myLibrary.groupBy('published');
myLibrary.forEach(function(model){
        console.log('Book is called ' + model.get('name'));
});
```

There are a lot more utility methods available to `Collections`, which you can read about at `http://backbonejs.org`. However, those listed here should be enough to get you started.

Exchanging Data with the Server

To wrap up our overview of `Collections`, we will take a look at how collections interact with the server. In the first half of the book, when looking at `Backbone.Model`, we saw how individual models could be retrieved, saved, updated, and retrieved using a REST API running on another server.

Collections can help organize this in a more efficient way, by managing all models and providing utilities to make saving models to the server a little easier.

Setup

The first thing you need to do is tell the collection where it needs to point to for its data persistence, using the `url` attribute. We'll be pointing to our Node.js server, running a `/books/` API endpoint on port 8080.

```
var Library = Backbone.Collection.extend({model: Book,
        url: 'http://localhost:8080/books/',

        initialize: function(){
        ....
```

Retrieving Data from the Server

Just as with `Backbone.Model`, collections have a `.fetch` method that is used to retrieve the collection data from the server.

```
var myOnlineLibrary = new Library();

myOnlineLibrary.fetch({
                success: function(e){
                        console.log('Got data');
                },
```

```
        error: function(e){
                console.log('Something went wrong');
        }
});
```

As with all functions that deal with online operations, you can provide success and error callbacks to detect whether the operation completed correctly.

Similar to Backbone.Model, a parse method can be defined at the collection level, which allows you to customize the data returned from the server. The response parameter contains an array of all model objects that are retrieved after the execution of .fetch.

```
var Library = Backbone.Collection.extend({model: Book,
        //        ......
        parse: function(response, xhr) {
                //customisations here
                return response;
        },
});
```

Saving Data to the Server

While retrieving data is done in a batch, saving models to the server is still done on an individual basis, as in the Backbone.Model sections of this chapter.

```
//add a model to the collection and save to server
myOnlineLibrary.add(bookOne);
bookOne.save({
                success: function(e){
                        console.log('Book saved to server');
                },
                error: function(e){
                        console.log('Error saving book);
                }
});
```

However, if you use the Backbone.Collection.create function rather than .add, the model is both added to the collection and persisted to the server.

```
//add to the collection and save all at once
myOnlineLibrary.create(bookTwo);
```

Deleting Data from the Server

Removing models from the server is done at the individual model level using the .destroy method, as described in the previous section.

```
bookOne.destroy({
        success: function(e){
                console.log('Book deleted')
        },
        error: function(e){
                console.log('Error deleting book');
        }
});
```

Collection Quick Reference

This section provides an overview of the functions, properties, and events that are related to `Backbone.Collection`.

Collection Method Reference

As you can see, there are a number of useful functions available for dealing with collections in Backbone. Table 3-3 describes them for quick reference.

Table 3-3. *Methods Available for Collections*

Function/Property	Description
`.length` `.size()`	Returns the number of model objects contained within the collection
`.models`	Returns a raw array of all the model objects
`.add([models])`	Adds a single model, or an array of models, to the collection
`.push([models])`	Adds a single model, or an array of models, to the end of the collection
`.unshift([models])`	Adds a single model, or an array of models, to the start of the collection
`.remove([models])`	Removes a single model, or an array of models, from the collection
`.pop()`	Removes and returns the model at the end of the collection
`.shift()`	Removes and returns the model at the beginning of the collection
`.reset()`	Replaces the models contained in a collection or empties the collection by calling with no parameters
`.get(id)`	Retrieves a model from the collection using the id or cid as the parameter
`.at(index)`	Retrieves a model at a particular index from the collection
`.foreach(function)`	Iterates through each model in a collection
`sortBy()`	Returns an array of models from the collection, sorted by a particular attribute
`.sort()`	Reapplies the sorting order on a collection
`.where({key:value})`	Finds all models within the collection that have the specified key-value
`.findWhere({key:value})`	Finds the first instance of a model that has the specified key-value
`.url`	Finds the location at which to point to for the REST API endpoint
`.fetch()`	Retrieves the entire collection from the server
`.create(<model>)`	Adds a new model to the collection and saves to the server

Collection Event Reference

Just like models, collections have a number of events that get fired when the contents change. Table 3-4 lists them for quick reference.

Table 3-4. *Events Related to Backbone Collections*

Function/Property	Description
add	Detects when a model has been added to the collection
remove	Detects when a model has been removed from a collection
reset	Detects that the collection has been reset
sort	Detects that the collection is being sorted
change	Detects that a model within the collection is being changed.
change:<attribute name>	Detects that <attribute name>, a model within the collection, is being changed

Summary

This chapter focused on the data layer of a Backbone application, with the first section describing the functionality available to Model objects and the second half dealing with collections. We saw how collections neatly encompass Model objects; most importantly, we learned about the interactions between a server that exposes a REST API running on a Node.js server and a Backbone client application.

CHAPTER 4

■ ■ ■

Backbone View and Templating Libraries

The previous chapter focused on the classes and functionality that Backbone provides to power the model layer of your web application. Now the focus shifts to the view layer, with Backbone.View being the main class behind it all. We'll also look at how templating libraries work to make updating your HTML pages a whole lot easier. As well as looking at Underscore, we'll spend some time looking at Handlebars and Mustache, two leading template libraries for JavaScript applications.

Code Setup

To execute the code in the examples, we will continue to use index.html from the previous chapter. Because we will be using the models and collections previously defined, any JavaScript code snippets for the view should be placed after their definition and instantiation, as follows:

```html
<!DOCTYPE HTML>
<html>
<head>
    <meta charset="UTF-8">
    <title>My App</title>
</head>
<body>
<script src="js/external/jquery-1.10.2.js"></script>
<script src="js/external/underscore.js"></script>
<script src="js/external/backbone.js"></script>

<script>
        Book = Backbone.Model.extend({
          //all the Book model definition source from Chapter 3.
        });

        /**
         * Define a collection based on book
         **/
        var Library = Backbone.Collection.extend({model: Book,
          //all the Library collection definition from Chapter 3.
        });
```

```
        //instantiate books
        var bookOne = new Book({name: 'Beginning Backbone', author: 'James Sugrue', year: 2013});
         var bookTwo = new Book({name: 'Pro Javascript Design Patterns', author:'Dustin Diaz,
Ross Harmes', year: 2012});

        //create library
        var myLibrary = new Library([bookOne, bookTwo]);

        //Here is where all your Backbone view code will appear
</script>
</body>
</html>
```

Backbone Views

When speaking of Backbone.View, we are referring to the JavaScript objects that are created in a Backbone application to organize the code into logical views. This means that although a view can update the HTML that is present in a view, usually with a templating library, the view will listen for changes in the model and render the changes on a designated section of your HTML page.

Creating a Backbone View

Creating your own view definition is done through the Backbone.View.extend() function. Just as with Backbone.Model and Backbone.Collection, you can pass an initialize function that will get invoked on construction of a new instance.

```
//Define the Library View
LibraryView = Backbone.View.extend({

        initialize: function(){
                console.log('View created');
        },

});
```

To create a new instance of your view, simply use the new operator.

```
//Create an instance of the view
var myView = new LibraryView();
```

You can pass additional options when creating the view, such as the model that the view is being attached to and the element that the view should be attached to. In the following code snippet, an instance of a Book model is passed through to the LibaryView, which can be accessed in the initialize function of the view:

```
var thisBook = new Book({name : 'Beginning Backbone',
                         author: 'James Sugrue'});
//Create an instance of the view
var myView = new LibraryView({model: thisBook});
```

We'll see how other attributes such as collection, el, id, className, tagName, and attributes can be passed through on construction of the view later in this chapter.

Binding to the Physical View

To bind your View class to an HTML page, you will need to utilize the el attribute, which is at the center of any view. el is the reference to the DOM element on your HTML page that is associated with the view.

The DOM element is available at all times, whether the view has been rendered or not. Because of this, the entire view can be created before it is rendered, at which point the element is inserted into the DOM at once, with as few repaints as possible.

There are two ways to use el: by referencing an existing DOM element or by creating a new one.

By passing an el attribute to the constructor, you are telling the view which DOM element it should attach to. For example, if the HTML page had a div created to contain the library view contents, you would want to pass a reference to that element when constructing the view.

```
<body>
<div id="myLibraryViewSection"></div>
```

The reference is made using standard CSS selectors that use #<element_id> or .<element_class>.

```
//Create an instance of the view with a model and an element
var myView = new LibraryView({
model: thisBook,
el: '#myLibraryViewSection'
});
```

You can also create the el for the view dynamically by passing a number of properties to the view when constructing it.

- tagName: The name of the HTML element to use for the view. If none is specified, the value of tagName will default to div.

- className: The CSS class that will be used to render this element. This property is optional. You can specify a number of classes for the element, passing them through as space-separated values.

- id: The ID to assign to the element. This property is optional.

- attributes: Additional attributes to assign to the element, such as data- attributes in name-value pairs.

```
//Create a view that will build its own DOM element
var myNewView = new LibraryView({model: thisBook,
 tagName: 'ul',
 className: 'libraryview',
 id: 'library',
 attributes: {'data-date': new Date()}
});
console.log(myNewView.el);
```

The result of myNewView.el will now be as follows:

```
<ul id='library' class='libraryview' data-date='Mon Aug 05 2013 13:54:20 GMT+0100 (IST)'/>
```

If none of these properties is passed through, the el is created as an empty div element.

All of the properties are accessible through the view's object, regardless of whether the el was newly created or passed through as a reference.

■ **Note** When constructing the el for the view, it will not be appended to the DOM automatically.

Rendering Content

To get your view content onto a page, you will need to override the render function. Left unimplemented, the content of the view will never be rendered.

To have the view render automatically on construction, you could call the render function from the view's initialize function.

```
//Define the Library View
LibraryView = Backbone.View.extend({

        initialize: function(){
                this.render();
        },
        render: function(){
                this.$el.html('Hello Library');
                                return this;
        }

});
```

Of course, a more useful render function would make use of the model or collection that is present in the view.

```
render: function(){
                this.$el.html('Book Name: ' + this.model.get('name'));
                return this;
        }
```

Note how the render function has a return this statement at the end. This is a convention that is encouraged by Backbone to allow chained calls. With the function returning a reference to the view, you can do further operations that require that reference. This can be particularly useful when you are dealing with nested views, providing access to the el property of the subview. The following code shows how you could append all of the subviews onto the parent view, thanks to the easy access to the el property:

```
render: function(){
        for (var i = 0; i < this.subviews.length; i++){
                this.$el.append(this.subviews[i].render().el);
        }
        return this;
}
```

As you can see from the previous snippets, because you have access to the $el property, HTML can be set directly on the element. However, this approach is prone to error and leads to a lot of messy HTML code within your JavaScript source. It is preferable to use one of the many templating libraries to provide a cleaner, more efficient rendering implementation. We'll look at the templating options available later in this chapter.

Note that rather than using a single model in our rendering, we could also pass a collection to the view when creating a new instance.

```
var myLibraryView = new LibraryView({
        collection: myLibrary,
        el: '#myLibraryViewSection'
});
```

The render method could now deal with the entire collection of models.

```
render: function(){

        for(var i =0; i < this.collection.size(); i++){
                        this.$el.append('<li>Book Name: ' + this.collection.at(i).get('name') + '</li>');
        }
        return this;
}
```

It can be a good idea to give each element that you render a unique ID so that it can be easily found at a later stage, should you want to manipulate or hide it. In this case, we could consider the name as the unique identifier and tag each <li> as follows:

```
render: function(){

    for(var i =0; i < this.collection.size(); i++){
      var bookname = this.collection.at(i).get('name');
      this.$el.append('<li id=\'' + bookname + '\'>Book Name: ' + bookname) + '</li>');
    }
    return this;
}
```

Whether you need to use a model or a collection will vary depending on your view requirements.

Finally, it is possible to remove the view entirely from the DOM. This will also result in all event listeners being disposed of.

```
myLibraryView.remove();
```

Finding Elements Within the View

It is common to need to find nested elements within your view and run other jQuery functions within the view's scope. Backbone provides an additional $el property that functions as a shorthand for $(view.el).

For example, to find a subelement within your view, you can use the following code. This will find the element with the ID Beginning Backbone if it exists within the view. Recall that in the previous sections we assigned unique identifiers to each of the <li> tags in the view.

```
$el.find('#Beginning Backbone');
```

Similarly, Backbone provides a $(<selector>) function as shorthand for $(view.el).find(<selector>), making any code that deals with subelements more elegant and readable.

```
$('#Beginning Backbone');
```

Both snippets of the previous code achieve the same result: finding an element with the ID of myelement within the scope of the current view.

Changing DOM Element

There may be situations in which you want to switch the DOM element that the view is applied to during the application life cycle. This can be achieved with the .setElement() function, which takes a reference to the new element to be used. The following code assumes you have a div created in your HTML with an ID of anotherViewSection:

```
myView.setElement('#anotherViewSection');
```

This function will also create a new version of the $el reference and ensure that any events that were registered under the old element get transferred to the new one.

View Events

Now that the view is rendering, you will probably want to add some events to make it interactive. Once again, this is made simple in Backbone with the ability to specify a hash of events in the view definition.

The events listed in the hash will use jQuery's on function to provide callbacks for DOM events with the view. The format {'event selector': 'callback'} is used to define the events that will be handled. The following example shows how to add a click listener to elements with the ID of book:

```
//Define the Library View
LibraryView = Backbone.View.extend({
        events: {
            'click #book' : 'alertBook'
        },
        render: function(){

            for(var i =0; i < this.collection.size(); i++){
                this.$el.append('<li id="book">Book Name: ' + this.collection.at(i).get('name') + '</li>');
                        }

                    return this;
            },

            alertBook: function(e){
                    alert('Book clicked');
            }
});
```

If no selector is defined, the event will be bound to this.el, the root element of the view.

For example, to add a click handler to the entire view, you could simply use this:

```
events: {
    'click : 'alertBook'
},
```

If you need to define events individually for each instance of the view or if a view has different modes of operation, you can use delegateEvents(). This function is called from the View constructor automatically, so you don't need to call it when your events hash has been defined. Calling delegateEvents will remove any existing callbacks and use the events hash provided to create a new set of event handlers.

The following would change the listener for the alert from a click to a mouseover:

```
myLibraryView.delegateEvents( {
    'mouseover #book ' : 'alertBook'
});
```

You can remove all events by passing an empty events hash to delegateEvents or by calling the undelegateEvents function. By adding a line such as the following to your view, you can remove all the events handled in myLibaryView. Type the following line into your Chrome Developer Tools console, and notice how the view no longer responds to any events you have created handlers for.

```
myLibraryView.undelegateEvents();
```

Dealing with self and this

A lot of the code that you will see in Backbone applications will have functions where a reference to the original this object is saved as self.

```
var self = this;
```

This is done to maintain a reference to the original this, even when the context changes. You'll see this happen a lot in closures in your code, especially in any event handlers you create.

Using this approach, the render function would change to use the self reference in place of this.

```
render: function(){
    var self = this;
    for(var i =0; i < this.collection.size(); i++){
        self.$el.append('<li id="book">Book Name: ' + self.collection.at(i).get('name') + '</li>');
    }

                return self;
},
```

Backbone View Quick Reference

Table 4-1 describes the properties and functions available in Backbone.View.

Table 4-1. *The Most Important Properties and Functions in Backbone.View*

Function/Property	Description
el	This specifies a reference to the DOM element to be used to contain this view.
$el	This specifies a cached jQuery object for the view's element.
$(<selector>)	When jQuery is included, the $ function will run queries scoped within the view's element.
model	This specifies the model that this view should render.
collection	This specifies the collection that the view should render.
id	This specifies the ID assigned to the view's root element.
className	This specifies the CSS classes for the view's root elements.
tagName	This specifies the HTML tag for this view's root element.
attributes	This specifies additional attributes to use for the element. This property can also be used to access the available attributes.
setElement(<selector>)	This changes the root element of this view.
remove()	This removes the view from the DOM completely.
render()	This is the function that deals with all the rendering of the view.
events	This is a hash of events and their handler functions to be used in this view.
delegateEvents(<events>)	This sets a new set of events and handlers for the view, removing the previous events.
undelegateEvents(<events>)	This removes all the view's events.

Templating in Backbone

Templating libraries make the separation of logic and presentation even more pronounced. By having templates defined outside of your JavaScript source, you can avoid having a mess of HTML strings in the render methods of your views.

The idea of a templating library is to take JSON objects from your JavaScript application and insert them into an HTML template, which includes conditionals and other logical expressions as well as placeholders for the object values.

Backbone doesn't force you to use any particular templating library, and as you can see from the previous section, you can just use plain HTML. We'll look at three templating libraries in this chapter. First we'll deal with Underscore, which your Backbone application will already depend on. Then we'll look at Handlebars and Mustache, two of the most popular templating libraries.

Templating with Underscore

As well as providing a number of useful functions for your Backbone application, Underscore contains functionality to deal with templating.

Templates are placed in your HTML page as a script, with a type of text/template so that the templates we create are ignored by the browser as it is rendering the HTML page. The template should also have an ID so that it can be found by your JavaScript.

```
<script type="text/template" id="library-template">
</script>
```

Underscore allows you to use JavaScript expressions within the template to loop through data and perform other conditional operations. Consider first what the data looks like in the render method from the previous section. We have a library that contains a number of books. Because we want to render a collection, rather than a single model, a loop will be required in the template.

```
<script type="text/template" id="library-template">
<ul>
    <% for (var i = 0; i < library.length; i++) { %>
      <% var book = library[i]; %>
      <li>
        <b><%= book.name %></b> by <%= book.author %>
      </li>
    <% } %>
 </ul>
</script>
```

This template expects that the JSON structure passed through for rendering is named library and that it is a collection of one or more items with the attributes as listed earlier (name and author).

Notice how any JavaScript code can be placed within the <% ... %> section, such as the for loop, and how all HTML code appears outside of these sections. Data can then be displayed using <%= variable %> sections.

With the template defined in the HTML, the view needs to be aware of this in the render method. The key to this is the template() function provided by Underscore.

This function compiles the JavaScript template into a function that can be evaluated for rendering. The parameters for the template are the string that represents the template and the data to be rendered, along with an optional parameter for the template settings.

Populating the value of the template string is done by finding the element in the page with the appropriate ID and evaluating the HTML of the result.

```
$("#library-template").html()
```

As the template expects the data in a particular structure, with the name 'library', the JSON representation of the collection is passed as the second parameter, with the expected identifier.

```
{'library': self.collection.toJSON()}
```

Finally, the template can be rendered by appending to the view's $el attribute.

```
self.$el.append(output);
```

The full code listing for our Underscore-enabled template function is as follows:

```
render: function(){
      var self = this;

      var output = _.template($("#library-template").html(), {'library': self.collection.toJSON()});

      self.$el.append(output);

                  return self;
   }
```

Note that the Underscore library is referred to using the _ namespace throughout the code. The render function defined earlier is straightforward, but it has a flaw: every time render is invoked, the template is compiled. It is neater to store the compiled template as an attribute for your view.

```
LibraryView = Backbone.View.extend({
        //other view related code
        template: _.template($("#library-template").html()),
        //....
});
```

Now when the view is created, the template is compiled and is ready for use. This leads to a cleaner render function.

```
render: function(){
        var self = this;
        var output = self.template({'library': self.collection.toJSON()});
        self.$el.append(output);
        return self;
},
```

The templateSettings parameter can be used to change the delimiter styles, by using a different regular expression in the interpolate parameter. For example, to use {{ }} rather than <% %>, you could use the following settings:

```
var templateSettings = {
    interpolate : /\{\{(.+?)\}\}/g
};
```

These settings can be made global for all Underscore templates by defining them at the _. level.

```
_.templateSettings = {
    interpolate : /\{\{(.+?)\}\}/g
};
```

This line would be applied to your entire application, so it would need to be declared before any view has been created in your JavaScript source code.

As you can see, using templates with Underscore is quite simple. With pure JavaScript used inside the template for logic and conditions, the code is really easy to follow. But there are other, more compelling options, which we will cover in the following sections.

Templating with Handlebars

Handlebars (www.handlebarsjs.org) is one of the most popular templating libraries in the JavaScript community. The library follows the Mustache.js style, where the philosophy encourages logic-less templates. Note that this is a different approach than Underscore. As a result of this, Handlebars templates will not accept arbitrary JavaScript within the templates, forcing you to use built-in constructs. However, there is the ability to add your own helpers, which we will look at later.

Like all templating libraries, Handlebars accepts the template structure and compiles it to a JavaScript function that accepts JSON data for presentation. One of the advantages of Handlebars is that, in following the same style as Mustache templates, the libraries are interchangeable, while you can keep the same templates. Also, with its template precompilation options, Handlebars is considered one of the most advanced libraries available.

Using Handlebars with Backbone

Including Handlebars in your Backbone project is surprisingly easy. For starters, you'll need to download the latest version of the library from www.handlebarsjs.org. To match the structure of the code used so far in the book, you can download this to the js/external folder and include it in index.html as follows:

```
<script src="js/external/handlebars.js"></script>
```

Now let's replace the template we created for Underscore with a Handlebars-compatible version. As before, the template is contained within a <script> tag with an ID, but the type of the template is now text/x-handlebars-template.

```
<script type="text/x-handlebars-template" id="library-template">
```

The approach to the loop is where the differences between Handlebars and Underscore are clearest to see, with Handlebars incorporating expressions in the form of {{#<expression name>}}.

```
<script type="text/x-handlebars-template" id="library-template">
<ul>
      {{#each library}}
    <li>
      <em>{{name}}</em> by {{author}}
  </li>
      {{/each}}
 </ul>
</script>
```

As you can see from the previous code, Handlebars templates look a lot more elegant than the Underscore equivalent. Rather than using a for statement, the #each expression is used to iterate through the collection, which was passed with the identifier library.

While {{#each}} is used to initiate the loop, it is then terminated using {{/each}}. All blocks in Handlebars follow this pattern. The variables are presented by simply placing the variable name within the curly braces.

If the library object contained another object underneath, its primitive values could be accessed using dot notation. For example, imagine that each book had the following structure, with an object contained in the book to represent the publishing date:

```
var bookOne = new Book({name: 'Beginning Backbone', author: 'James Sugrue',
                  publishDate :{year: 2013, month: 'December'} });
```

The publish year could then be accessed within the loop using {{publishDate.year}}.

```
<script type="text/x-handlebars-template" id="library-template">
<ul>
      {{#each library}}
    <li>
      <em>{{name}}</em> by {{author}} published in {{publishDate.year}}
  </li>
      {{/each}}
 </ul>
</script>
```

Including the Handlebars template is as simple as changing the `template` attribute of the view to compile using Handlebars instead of Underscore.

```
LibraryView = Backbone.View.extend({
        //....
      template: Handlebars.compile($("#library-template").html()),
        ...
});
```

Note how the only change was to replace `_.template` with `Handlebars.compile`.

In fact, the `render` method is the same as before, because the only code that was tied to the template library was the declaration of the template variable.

```
render: function(){
        var self = this;
        var output = self.template({'library':self.collection.toJSON()});
        self.$el.append(output);
        return self;
},
```

As you can see, Handlebars provides a neat way of creating templates. The expression language is straightforward but quite powerful. The following section will give you more insight into what is possible with Handlebars.

A Quick Guide to Handlebars

Since the syntax of Handlebars templates requires more than plain JavaScript, this section will go through some of the basic expressions to help get you started.

Displaying Variables

Variable values can be output to the template using the form `{{name}}`. This will print out the value `name` in the current context, which can be altered by block expressions that loop through collections.

```
<h1>{{name}}</h1>
```

If you are dealing with nested variables, you can use dot-separated paths to determine the value. For example, if the template was dealing with a `person` object, you could display the details as follows:

```
<h1>{{person.name}}</h1>
<p>Birthday: {{person.birthday}}</p>
```

Comments

Comments can be inserted into templates using either `{{! comment }}` or `{{!-- comment --}}`.

```
{{! Name of the person }}
<h1>{{person.name}}</h1>
```

The {{!-- }} style is used when you need to comment out Handlebars expressions.

```
{{!-- unused expression for now {{name}} --}}
```

Block Expressions

Blocks in Handlebars are represented with a {{#expression}} statement and a {{/expression}} statement to complete the block.

each

As we've already seen in the library example, the each helper allows a list to be iterated over.

```
{{#each library}}
     <li>
       <em>{{name}}</em> by {{author}} published in {{publishDate.year}}
     </li>
{{/each}}
```

Note that you can use {{this}} within the block to reference the current element that is being iterated through. You can also access objects and properties outside of the current context by using paths. An example of this would be to use {{../<property name>}} to look at the property that is at the same level as the list you are currently iterating through.

Conditionals

There are a number of conditional statements available for use in your template definition. The following section lists some of these.

if else

In the event that there are conditional sections of a template to be rendered, Handlebars includes an if else structure. A parameter is passed through to the {{#if }} expression to be evaluated.

```
{{#if book.published}}
     <p>Book now available</p>
{{else}}
     <p>Book coming soon : {{book.pubishDate}}</p>
{{/if}}
```

unless

The unless helper works as the inverse of the if statement shown earlier. It takes a parameter and ensures that it evaluates to false before entering the template section.

```
{{unless book.published}}
<p>This book is not yet published</p>
{{/unless}}
```

Built-in Helpers

Handlebars comes with a few built-in helpers to make it easier to use.

with

The with helper allows the context to be changed within a template so that a particular object is used. Rather than using {{object.property}}, this helper allows you to specify that you are dealing with a particular object within the block in the following form:

```
{{#with object}}
        {{property}}
{{/with}}
```

To see this in action, let's consider the following Person object:

```
{{#with person}}
        <h1>{{name}}</h1>
        <p>Birthday: {{birthday}}</p>
{{/with}}
```

log

The log helper allows simple logging within the template, which can useful for debugging.
The helper delegates to Handlebars.logger.log, which can be overridden if custom logging is required.

```
{{#with person}}
        <h1>{{log name}}</h1>
{{/with}}
```

Providing Helpers

The real power in Handlebars is the ability to write your own helpers in order to deal with cases where the built-in expressions and helpers are not enough. You can create your own helpers in JavaScript code that will then be used during the compilation of any of your templates.

Let's create a simple helper that adds two numbers. You need to use the Handlebars registerHelper function and provide the helper name, followed by the operation that will be carried out.

```
Handlebars.registerHelper('add', function(param1, param2){
        return param1 + param2
});
```

You can now use this in your templates as follows:

```
<p>In 20 years time {{name}} will be {{add person.age 20}} years old </p>
```

Don't forget that there's a huge community of Handlebars users who share their own helpers.

Precompiling Templates

Handlebars provides a powerful precompilation ability that results in time savings for client-side execution and allows you to use the Handlebars runtime library, `handlebars.runtime.js`, which doesn't include the runtime compilation capability. At the time of this writing, the unminimized runtime library was 11KB, while the full Handlebars library was 73KB. When targeting mobile devices, such savings can be significant.

You will need Node.js installed on your development or build machine to run precompilation. In Chapter 3, we created a Node.js server to act as a back end to our application. If you haven't already installed node.js, you can download it from `http://nodejs.org`. Once you have node.js installed, you can use the node package manager (NPM) to download the `handlebars` package.

```
npm install handlebars -g
```

All templates will need to be stored in an external file, which is passed to the precompiler on the command line.

```
handlebars <inputfile> -f <outputfile>
```

This will result in a JavaScript file being created that contains the compiled template, which can then be included within your application.

Templating with Mustache

Mustache.js is another logic-less templating library, available from `http://mustache.github.io`. Mustache is popular across a broad spectrum of languages, including Ruby, Java, Objective-C, and many more.

The template format is much the same as that used in Handlebars, although without the helpers.

Using Mustache with Backbone

You will first need to download the latest version of Mustache.js from `http://mustache.github.io`. Again, to match the conventions used throughout this book, this should be saved in the `js/external` folder and included in `index.html` as follows:

```
<script src="js/external/mustache.js"></script>
```

The template will look similar to the Handlebars version.

```
<script type="text/x-mustache-template" id="library-template">
<ul>
	{{#library}}
	<li>
	<em>{{name}}</em> by {{author}}
    </li>
	{{/library}}
  </ul>
</script>
```

Note that iteration through the list is achieved using {{#<listname>}} rather than using the {{#each}} block helper that exists in Handlebars. The loop is terminated using {{/<listname>}}. However, everything else is much the same in the template.

Once again, changing the template library from the Backbone view is just a matter of changing the template attribute.

```
template: Mustache.compile($("#library-template").html()),
```

The render method remains the same as before.

```
render: function(){
        var self = this;
        var output = self.template({'library': self.collection.toJSON()});
        self.$el.append(output);
        return self;
},
```

It's clear from the previous example that switching from Handlebars to Mustache, or vice versa, is a relatively straightforward transition.

A Quick Guide to Mustache

This section provides a brief overview of how to achieve a number of commonly used tasks within Mustache templates.

Displaying Variables

Variables are displayed by using the double curly braces syntax, just as in Handlebars.

```
{{name}}
```

Dot notation can be used to access properties of an object.

```
{{person.name}}
```

Iterating Through Lists

Blocks that will iterate through a list can be created by initializing a block with the {{#list}} syntax and closing the section using {{/list}}.

```
{{#library}}
      <li>
       <em>{{name}}</em> by {{author}}
      </li>
{{/library}}
```

The current object that has focus in the iterated list can be accessed using a single dot.

```
{{#library}}
        <p>This object {{.}}</p>
{{/library}}
```

Comments

Mustache templates can contain comment sections using the format {{! comment }}.

```
{{! Display the person name }}
{{person.name}}
```

Which Templating Library to Use?

Now that you've seen three of the leading options, deciding which templating library to use can be difficult. It really depends on your project's needs. If you are using limited or very simple templates, use Underscore. Because you will already have a dependency, using Underscore should be the very least you use. Taking advantage of any templating library will lead to a cleaner code base, with HTML nicely separated from all JavaScript code in your view.

However, if your application is likely to have many different views, it is worth considering Handlebars. The syntax of the templates is more natural, and you always have the ability to add more helpers to suit the requirements of your project. The precompilation functionality offered by Handlebars makes it a compelling choice for projects that are concerned with performance, especially those that include mobile devices as a target.

Summary

This chapter provided an overview of everything that you will need for the presentation layer of your Backbone application. We first covered Backbone.View, which provides logic and rendering capabilities for your Backbone models and collections. After looking at the simplest type of rendering, using plain HTML, we dealt with three of the major templating libraries to see how a cleaner separation of HTML and JavaScript can be achieved. From the simplicity of the included Underscore library to the power of Handlebars, the benefits of templating should now be clear.

CHAPTER 5

■ ■ ■

Routers and Events

Everything that we have constructed so far has been pretty simple, consisting of a single page with a model or collection represented in view. If you're considering using Backbone, it's unlikely that you will limit your application scope to such basic structures. Instead, your app will be composed of multiple views, which will need to communicate with each other using events. It's also quite common that you'll want to manage navigation through some type of URL scheme.

This chapter takes a look at routers and events, which will provide the glue for any substantial Backbone application.

Backbone Routers

A *route* is a bookmarkable section of your web application, usually denoted by a trailing hash identifier or fragment. Meanwhile, the router is the code that manages the routes defined within your application. Following this route should bring you to a particular portion of the overall document. Another useful analogy is to think of a router as a table of contents in a book. By referring to the table, you know where to find a particular piece of information.

Routers observe changes in the application URL to detect changes in a route using two different schemes. The first of these uses hash tags such as `http://apress.com/#myapp`, which will work across all browsers. With browsers that support HTML5 standards, the second approach is to take advantage of the History API and use more "standard" URLs such as `http://apress.com/myapp`. Either way, you won't need to worry about your target browser because Backbone will transparently fall back to the hash/fragment solution for you.

Creating a Router

Creating a router in Backbone follows the same patterns as all objects in the library, using the `.extend` method to define your custom router.

```
MyRouter = Backbone.Router.extend({
});
```

Next you will need to match particular URL patterns with functions that get invoked when that URL fragment is navigated to. This is done by passing through a `routes` hash to your `extend` function.

```
MyRouter = Backbone.Router.extend({
        routes: {'hello' : 'sayHello'},
});
```

The previous code sets up a route so that if the URL ends with #hello, a function named sayHello will be invoked. This function should be defined along with your router, like so:

```
MyRouter = Backbone.Router.extend({
        routes: {'hello' : 'sayHello'},

        sayHello: function(){
                console.log('Saying hello');
        }
});
```

To get the router listening for route changes, a new instance of the router will need to be created.

```
var router = new MyRouter();
```

Finally, to monitor changes in the hash fragments and invoke the appropriate events, you will need to initialize Backbone.history.

```
Backbone.history.start();
```

Now, when navigating to http://localhost/index.html#hello, you will see the words "Saying hello" appear in the console.

Because most Backbone applications are designed to be single-page web apps, you will need to create only one router. If you want to create separate routers for code separation or structure reasons, the main thing to watch for is that there are no route conflicts.

Now that we've seen how to create a simple router, let's take a closer look at its components and at how to build more complex routes.

Backbone.History

Backbone.history is an abstraction provided by the library that will handle hashchange events or the HTML5 pushState. When a change in URL is observed, the appropriate route is matched with the callback that you have defined in your own router.

As you saw in the example at the start of this section, Backbone.history.start() is called to start monitoring for change events. Without this, your routers will not run successfully. It's worth paying attention to the Boolean value returned from the start() function; if no route matches the current URL, it will return false.

Using pushState

If you decide to use HTML5 pushState in your application in order to provide URLs without hash fragments, you can specify this when starting your history.

```
Backbone.history.start({pushState:true});
```

However, you'll probably notice that by pasting in the example route, http://localhost/hello results in a 404 error. This is because you will need to configure the server to reroute all URLs to the index.html page to allow Backbone to deal with the routing.

You could do this by modifying the `httpd.conf` file of an Apache server to use the `mode_rewrite.c` module. This would look as follows:

```
RewriteEngine On
RewriteBase /
RewriteCond %{REQUEST_FILENAME} !-f  RewriteCond %{REQUEST_FILENAME} !-d
RewriteRule . index.html [L]
```

Alternatively, you could host your pages using Node.js and have it provide some intelligence to deal with such routes. The following is a simple example of a Node.js server that will serve your Backbone app:

```
var express = require('express');
var app = express();
app.use(express.static(__dirname));

app.use('/chapter5/hello', express.static(__dirname + "/chapter5"));
app.listen(3010);
```

Provided you have already installed the excellent `express` module, the previous code will run with the `node server.js` command. With all your client-side source in a `chapter5` directory at the same level as `server.js`, the second `app.use` rule will be used. This states that if `/chapter5/hello` is navigated to, it is served by the `chapter5` directory; this forces the application to go to `index.html`.

Because the application is not being served from the root `/` of the domain, use the `root` parameter to indicate where the Backbone application is being served from. In the case of the previous example, we are using `chapter5` as the root directory for the Backbone application:

```
Backbone.history.start({pushState:true, root:"/chapter5/"});
```

By navigating to `http://localhost:3010/chapter5/hello`, you will now see that the `sayHello` route is invoked. This may seem like a lot of work for such a simple operation, but it does lead to a cleaner URL scheme in your application.

Remember that you will need to invoke either `Backbone.history.start()` or `Backbone.history.start({pushState: true})` once all the application routers have been created to route the initial URL.

Routes for All Applications

Two routes are worth adding to all routers. One is the initial route, which is an empty string.

```
MyRouter = Backbone.Router.extend({
        routes: {'' : 'start'},
        ....
        start: function(){
                console.log('Initial route invoked');
        },
        ....
});
```

You should also provide a default route; this is invoked when a URL is used that the router has not been equipped to handle. This route is created using the pattern *default.

```
MyRouter = Backbone.Router.extend({
        routes: { '' : 'start',
                                '*default': 'defaultRoute' },
                //other router definition code
        start: function(){
                        console.log('Initial route invoked');
                },
        defaultRoute: function(){
                console.log('Router does not handle this route');
                },
                //other router definition code
});
```

Adding Parameters to Routes

The routes hash that is passed through when defining the route maps URLs within your application with functions. You can also add parameters to these mapped functions, allowing you to provide even more useful bookmarks in your Backbone app.

A route can be set up to deal with parameters in a particular pattern by using :param sections. The parameter will match a single URL component between two slashes. For example, to use the hello route created earlier to take a name parameter in the a URL like http://localhost:3010/chapter5/#hello/james, you would need to specify the route as follows. You should ensure that your defined routes are always listed before the default route.

```
routes : {'hello/:name': 'sayHello'},
```

The function definition now changes to accept the name parameter.

```
sayHello: function(name){
        console.log('Saying hello to ' + name);
}
```

Any number of these parameters can be specified in the route. You can extend this with a second parameter to deal with a URL such as #hello/james/backbone.

```
routes : {'hello/:name/:skill': 'sayHello'},
```

The function can now be updated so that it handles the extra parameter.

```
sayHello: function(name, skill){
        console.log('Saying hello to ' + name + ' ' + skill + ' author');
}
```

However, the definition of the previous route mandates that both parameters are specified in order for the route to be entered. You can also specify optional parameters by placing brackets around the parameter.

```
routes : {'hello/:name(/:skill)': 'sayHello'},
```

The previous route requires that either the #hello/james or #hello/james/backbone URL format is used. The function that the route is mapped to should then check whether any of the parameters are null.

```
sayHello: function(name, skill){
        if(skill !== null){
                console.log('Saying hello to ' + name + ' ' + skill + ' author');
        }
        else{
                console.log('Saying hello to ' + name );
        }
}
```

Note that you can prefix any of the route parameters with plain text. For example, to prefix chapter before a parameter in the URL, to form a pattern such as #hello/james/chapter5, you can use a route as shown here:

```
routes : {'hello/:name/chapter:chapterNumber': 'sayHello'},
```

This will produce two variables: name, which will be set to james, and chapterNumber, which will be set to 5.

Finally, you can pass through a splat, using *, which will match any number of URL components. This is useful if you have a path that you want to be processed. For example, the route defined here allows a URL such as #hello/james/chapter5/section1 to be used:

```
routes : {'hello/:name/*path': 'sayHello'},
```

In the case of the previous code, the path variable would evaluate to chapter5/section1.

Route Events

Any time that a routed URL is navigated to or when the back button is used in the browser, an event will get fired with the name of the mapped router function prefixed with route:. In the case of the example, this would be router:sayHello.

```
router.on("route:sayHello", function(page) {
});
```

This is useful if other objects need to listen to the changes in navigation throughout your application.

Manually Creating Routes

As well as passing through the routes as a hash when creating your router, you can manually create routes. Typically, this would be done in an initialize function that you create that gets invokes when creating a new instance of your router.

The route function takes three parameters: the route, the name, and the function that will get invoked when the route is created. To achieve the same results as our previous route examples, you could invoke the simple hello route as follows:

```
initialize: function(options){

        this.route('hello', sayHello');
},
```

However, you can do a little more with this function. The route parameter can be a routing string as in the previous examples, but you can also use regular expressions to define the route using this.route().

The second parameter is the name of the route. Typically this will be the name of the function you want to invoke. However, you can add a third callback parameter to the route. This means that the router:name that is triggered for the route event would match the second name parameter rather than the function name. The function that will get executed is the callback function and not the function that matches the route name.

```
this.route('hello', 'sayHello',
        function(){ console.log('callback invoked');
});
```

In this example, when the route is matched, the console will output "callback invoked" rather than executing the sayHello function.

Navigating Programmatically

There may be points in the application that you want to save as a URL so that the user can bookmark that point to navigate to at a later point. To do this, you can use the navigate function, provided you have already called Backbone.history.start().

The following example shows how navigate will create a new URL in the browser address bar when the showBook function is invoked:

```
function showBook(name){

        console.log('Show book ' + name);
        router.navigate('book/'+name);
}

showBook('Backbone');
```

The URL will now show the pattern #book/Backbone. Even if a route has been created to deal with this pattern, it will not be invoked with the previous code. If you do want to cause the router function to be run, all you need to do is pass through an additional trigger parameter when navigating.

```
MyRouter = Backbone.Router.extend({
        routes: {'book(/:name)' : 'displayBook' },
        ....
        displayBook: function(name){
                console.log('Displaying ' + name);
        },
        .....
});
```

With the previous route in place, the following code will now trigger the displayBook router function:

```
router.navigate('book/'+name, {trigger: true});
```

Finally, if you want to change the URL of the browser bar but prevent the program from adding an entry in the browser's history, ensure that the replace option is set to true.

```
router.navigate('book/'+name, {trigger: true, replace:true});
```

The Router as a Controller

When looking at how the Model View * pattern applies to Backbone, we mentioned that the router can perform some controller duties. There's no doubt that the router performs its main task well: dealing with changes in the URL of an application and mapping the URL to functions in the application.

The router can be utilized as an application-level controller by binding it to an application model. Because changes in the URL infer changes in the application state, the model could be updated alongside each application handler. Let's say we have a simple model that tracks the application state, in this case the current book.

```
AppModel = Backbone.Model.extend({
        defaults: {
                currentBook: 'Beginning Backbone',
        }
});
```

Change listeners could be added so that any attributes that are altered can invoke other actions or re-render a view.

```
initialize: function(){

        this.on("change", function(){
                if(this.hasChanged('currentBook')){
                        alert('Current book changed');
                }
        });
},
```

This model could now be provided as a parameter to the router on creation.

```
var appModel = new AppModel();
var router = new MyRouter({model: appModel});
```

The router's initialize function would accept this model parameter. Now, because routes are invoked in the router, the model can be informed of this application state change.

```
MyRouter = Backbone.Router.extend({
        model : null,
        routes: {'book(/:name)' : 'displayBook',
                        '' : 'start',
                        '*default': 'defaultRoute' },
        initialize: function(options){
                this.model = options.model;
        },

                ....
        displayBook: function(name){
                console.log('Displaying ' + name);

                this.model.set('currentBook', name);
        },
        ...
});
```

This provides a type of Model View Controller architecture for our application. A single application model is shared, which is passed through to both the router and an application view. The router doesn't need to know anything about the application views, and vice versa.

Of course, there are many variations that you can apply. As you'll see in the next section of this chapter, coupling an application route with events leads to several architecture possibilities.

Backbone Events

While looking at models, collections, views, and routers, we've encountered a number of different events, as Backbone allows events to be added to any object. The Backbone events module gives us the ability to bind to and trigger built-in or custom events.

All Backbone objects (`View`, `Router`, `Collection`, `Model`) have the Backbone events module included, but you can also extend any basic objects with the Backbone event capability, as follows:

```
var object = {};
_.extend(object, Backbone.Events);
```

The following section will take an in-depth look at how events work in Backbone, before enumerating the events that are built into the library.

Binding Events

Binding is where an object is set up to listen for particular events to occur. This is done using the `.on` function. This function takes three parameters: the name of the event, the function to invoke when the event is fired, and an optional context to apply this event in.

For example, in our model objects, if we want to be notified that one of the attributes has changed, the event we listen for is change.

```
var model = new Book();
model.on("change", function(){
        console.log('an attribute has been changed');
});
```

Recall that the change listener included a form that fired events based on particular attributes being changed. For example, if you wanted to listen only to changes in the author attribute, the event name would be change:author.

```
model.on("change:author", function(){
        console.log('The author attribute has been changed');
});
```

You can have the `.on` event handler deal with several different events by breaking each event name with a space. For example, to listen for changes to the author or the title of a Book object, use this:

```
model.on("change:author change:title", function(){....});
```

You can add a special listener that will monitor all events, using the all event name. This would allow you to provide one object that delegates events to the appropriate object to handle.

```
monitor.on('all', function(eventName){
        delegateObject.trigger(eventName);
});
```

Finally, it is possible to set up the event handling in a similar way to the routes in a router, providing a hash of `eventName : handler`. You can even delegate to other objects. For example, if we created a simple view that would render the book model, then we could add a function that allows the updating of the view from external objects, such as the router. XXX:

```
BookView = Backbone.View.extend({
        updateTitleView: function(){
                console.log('updating title view');
        }
});

var bookView = new BookView();
```

Now, as an instance of the Book object is created, we could pass through an events hash to the `.on` function that instructs the `updateTitleView` function to be invoked when the name attribute changes.

```
var thisBook = new Book({name : 'Beginning Backbone',
                                        author: 'James Sugrue'});

thisBook.on({ 'change:name': bookView.updateTitleView});
```

Changing the name attribute of the book will fire the event, which will in turn invoke `updateTitleView` in the `bookView` object.

```
thisBook.set('name', "Beginning Backbone.js")
```

This events hash can be a neater way of defining all the events for an object in one place, without having the callback functions inline with the event definition.

Unbinding Events

When the application state changes, it may be the case that you may no longer want to listen for particular events. Switching off listeners like this is called *unbinding* and is achieved using the `.off` function.

It is possible to unbind all handlers for a particular event. For example, if we no longer wanted to listen for changes to the name of a book in any object, the following code would unbind all listeners:

```
thisBook.off('change:name');
```

You can also unbind particular handlers. For example, if the `bookView` used earlier was no longer visible, we could unbind its handler for the name change event only, leaving any others still active.

```
thisBook.off('change:name', bookView.updateTitleView);
```

If a handler is being used for multiple events and is no longer required, it can be disassociated from all events using `null` as the event name.

```
thisBook.off(null, bookView.updateTitleView);
```

You can also remove all listeners on a particular object by using `.off` with no parameters.

```
thisBook.off();
```

This will cause all event handling, including internal Backbone events, from the object.

Listening to an Event Once

Sometimes it is adequate to listen and respond to an event once and then forget about it, without needing to go through the trouble of unbinding once the event has been dealt with.

Backbone provides the `.once` function to do this. It takes the same parameters as the `.on` handler.

```
thisBook.once({ 'change:name': bookView.updateTitleView});
```

From the console, if you execute the following, with a different name each time, you will see that it still gets handled once:

```
thisBook.set('name', 'Beginning Backbone.js')
```

You'll find this is useful for checking for events during initialization or watching for "the next time" an event fires.

Listen to Events on Other Objects

We have already seen how an event handler in a model object could invoke a function in a separate view object. It is also possible an object (the view) listen for all events on another object (the model) using the `listenTo` function.

In theory, the following lines are equivalent:

```
thisBook.on({ 'change:name': bookView.updateTitleView});
bookView.listenTo(thisBook, 'change:name', bookView.updateTitleView);
```

However, it is advantageous to use `listenTo` to keep track of events on another object, as the `stopListening` function allows the object to completely disconnect all events in one simple function call.

```
bookView.stopListening(model);
```

If the object is listening for events on a number of different objects, these can all be unregistered by passing through no parameters to the `stopListening` function.

```
bookView.stopListening()
```

For consistency, Backbone provides a way to use `listenTo` in the same way as the `.once` function, where the event is handled once, and then disconnected, using `listenToOnce`:

```
bookView.listenToOnce(thisBook, 'change:name', bookView.updateTitleView);
```

Triggering Events

So far, all the events we've investigated have been triggered internally by Backbone. It is also possible to fire events without invoking the actions that should cause them to be fired.

The .trigger function allows an event name, with a number of parameters to be passed to the event handler. You could fake a change:name event simply by using the following code:

```
thisBook.trigger('change:name',{});
```

Of course, it is also possible to fire your own events, rather than mimicking the built-in events, which we will look into later in the "Creating Custom Events" section.

Built-in Events

As we've already stated, Backbone.Event is included in every object. This includes the following:

- Backbone
- Backbone.Model
- Backbone.Collection
- Backbone.View
- Backbone.Router
- Backbone.History

Backbone provides a number of built-in events, as outlined in the following section. When the event is fired, a number of parameters are available in the callback function, which are listed in the following tables.

Collection Events

Table 5-1 describes the Backbone events available for dealing with collections.

Table 5-1. *Events for Backbone.Collection*

Event	Callback Parameters	Fired When...
add	model collection options	The model is added to the collection
remove	model collection options	The model is removed from the collection
reset	collection options	The entire contents of the collection have been replaced
sort	collection options	The collection has been re-sorted

Model Events

Table 5-2 describes the events that can be used when dealing with Backbone.Model.

Table 5-2. Events for Backbone.Model

Event	Callback Parameters	Fired When...
change	model options	Any of the attributes in the model have been changed.
change:[attribute]	model value options	A specific attribute in the model has been changed.
destroy	model collection options	The model has been destroyed.
request	model xhr options	The model has started a request to the server.
sync	model xhr options	The model has successfully synced with the server.
error	model xhr options	The model save call has failed on the server.
invalid	model error options	The model validation fails on the client side. This is usually caught when the model's save function is called when a validate function has been defined.

Router and History Events

Table 5-3 describes the events related to the Backbone.Router class.

Table 5-3. Events for Backbone.Router

Event	Callback Parameters	Fired When...
route:[name]	params	The specific route has been matched
route	router route params	Any route has been matched (fired by the history or router)

Global Events

Table 5-4 describes the events that are used globally across a Backbone application.

Table 5-4. *Global Events in a Backbone Application*

Event	Callback Parameters	Fired When...
All	eventName	Any event has been fired across the entire application

Creating Custom Events

As well as using any of the events provided by Backbone, you can create your own to allow decoupled communication between any of the objects in your application. For example, when a model is updated, you may want another model or view to act on this event.

Imagine a simple example where you want to fire a particular event if the name and author attributes of the Book model are null. The convention for event names is to use a colon-delimited identifier, such as model:useless.

The fact that events are available on the global Backbone object means you can have global listeners anywhere in your code.

```
Backbone.on('model:useless', function(){
        console.log('Model useless global invoked');
        //do more specific handling here
});
```

Triggering this global event could be dealt with in a change listener in the model that handles when either of the two attributes has been changed.

```
thisBook.on('change:name change:author', function(model, value, options){
        if(model.get('name') === null && model.get('author') === null){
                console.log('Trigger event now');
                Backbone.trigger('model:useless', {});
        }
});
```

Now, if you run the following two commands from the console, the event will be triggered:

```
thisBook.set('name', null);
thisBook.set('author', null);
```

Note that you can also pass parameters over the applications event bus. For example, the model that triggered the event could be passed.

```
Backbone.trigger('model:useless', {model:model});
```

The handler callback function could then deal with any available parameters.

```
Backbone.on('model:useless', function(data){
        console.log(data.model.get('name'));
        console.log('Model useless global');
});
```

Listening for DOM Events

As we covered in Chapter 4, we can listen to events on the DOM and bind these events to callback functions. These event keys are always defined in terms of jQuery selectors such as <event> #<elementid> or <event> .<elementclass> where event can be any interaction such as a click, mouseover, blur, or keypress.

If you are using jQuery with Backbone, you can find a complete list of the events that a view can react to by looking at the jQuery event listing: http://api.jquery.com/category/events/.

Typically, these event bindings are provided in the events hash of the view on definition.

```
LibraryView = Backbone.View.extend({
    ....

    events: {
            'click ' : 'alertBook'
    },

    ....
    alertBook: function(e){
                alert('Book clicked');
    },
    ....
});
```

Summary

In this chapter, we looked at routers and events. Using Backbone.Router along with Backbone.History, we saw how bookmarkable URLs can be provided in your application, allowing sections of the app to be revisited later.

We also learned how Backbone.Events works across all objects, handling events in one place and triggering in others. Even though Backbone already provides a rich set of built-in events, you can add your own event types to allow decoupled communication across the application. We completed the section on events by revisiting how Backbone.View can interact seamlessly with events fired from the DOM.

In the next chapter, we'll start to construct a real-world Backbone application, using all the concepts covered in the previous three chapters.

CHAPTER 6

■ ■ ■

From Start to Finish: A Complete App Example

Now that we have run through the core Backbone concepts, it's time to put everything together to create a fully functional app. This chapter will bring you through the various stages required to build an application powered by Backbone, starting at the design stages and resulting in a high-quality Twitter application. We will also introduce a more structured way of writing your application code, rather than simply inserting it between <script> tags as we have done in the previous chapters.

Designing Your Application

Before diving into the code, it's important to take a step back and identify the core functionality of the application. This allows a more structured approach to JavaScript development. Understanding the data that is being represented will inform your decisions on defining a model. Knowing which parts of the screen need to be dynamically updated, for instance, informs what views going to be required.

Our example is a Twitter-based application that will show an overview of the authenticated user's account, including the following:

- Recent tweets in the user's timeline

- The number of followers and following

- The ability to search Twitter

The wireframe diagram in Figure 6-1 identifies the main views that will be present.

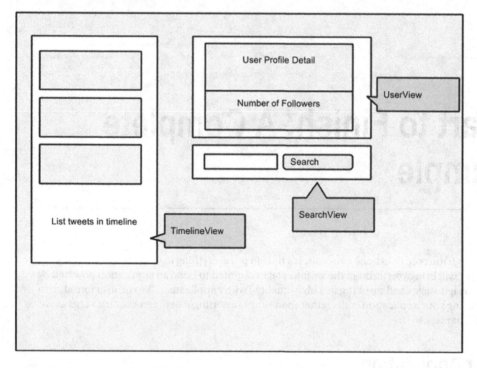

Figure 6-1. *A simple wireframe illustrating main views*

As you can see from Figure 6-1, there is one main view for the application, along with a number of subviews. It's clear that on the main page there are at least three separate view parts.

- The timeline
- The user profile data
- The search view

Although the search box is static, the functionality behind it will require building a view for the results and possibly using a router to make the search bookmarkable.

CSS Styles

To save myself from needing to work with CSS to style the application, I used the MetroUI CSS library (http://metroui.org.ua/), which gives a sharp Windows 8 look to the app. However, you can use your own custom style or another UI library such as Bootstrap (https://github.com/twbs/bootstrap).

Application Domain

I chose Twitter as the example domain for this application so that we could avoid worrying too much about the back-end service and hook into an existing API easily. The principles illustrated through this chapter hold true for any application, so don't let the focus on Twitter distract you. The main thing is to understand the interactions between views, collections, models, and routers.

Application Code Structure

Defining a clean structure to your application at the outset is essential for any nontrivial Backbone project. While it's obviously good to keep your HTML, JavaScript, and CSS in separate directories, it's also worth splitting the groups of Backbone object types. This means you would have the following type of structure for your application JavaScript, within the js/app directory.

```
app.js
view/
model/
collection/
router/
util/
```

The app.js file acts as the main entry point for the application, and the folders act as a type of package structure for the rest of your project. If you have developed in other languages such as Java or C#, this approach to structuring your code will be familiar.

Each of the objects within these folders should also be namespaced to make the code more readable and to avoid naming conflicts. For example, the TimelineView that we will create later in this chapter defines the following namespace:

```
var com = com || {};
com.apress = com.apress || {};
com.apress.view = com.apress.view || {};

com.apress.view.TimelineView = Backbone.View.extend({
```

This means when we create a new instance of the TimelineView, we can use the following code:

```
var timelineView = new com.apress.view.TimelineView();
```

As the main entry point of the application, app.js is responsible for creating the initial state of the application. Typically this will involve creating a number of views, creating a router, and starting the Backbone history.

Everything will need to be loaded in the page before the code in app.js is executed, so you will usually put the code in a block, such as jQuery's $(function(){ });. This is illustrated in the following code snippet:

```
$(function() {
        var timelineView = new com.apress.view.TimelineView(),
          router = new com.apress.router.AppRouter();
      Backbone.history.start();
});
```

External Dependencies

This project will have a number of external dependencies. As we've already seen, to use Backbone we'll be including Backbone.js, Underscore.js, and jQuery. You can also choose a templating library if you want. I usually choose Handlebars for my applications because I find the expressiveness and extensibility to be the most useful. All these external libraries are placed in the js/external directory of the application.

On the styling side, the application will also utilize modern.css from the MetroUI project. This will be included in the css directory.

Figure 6-2 shows the folder structure of the application.

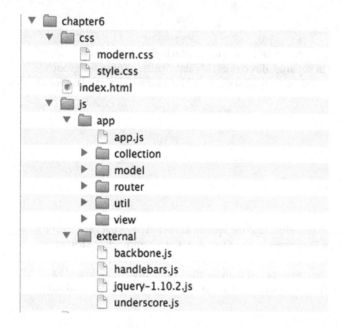

Figure 6-2. *The structure of a typical Backbone application*

Bringing It All Together

Your main HTML page will be responsible for bringing it all together, by including the stylesheets, templates, and external JavaScript libraries.

The following code shows how the code in your index page might look. You'll notice that each of the JavaScript artifacts are included individually. Later we'll look at how all these files can be merged to create one script to include. However, you'll find it's a lot easier to debug your code by including the files in their uncompressed form.

```html
<html>
<head>
    <title>Beginning Backbone Twitter Example</title>
    <link rel='stylesheet' href='css/modern.css'>
    <link rel="stylesheet" href="css/style.css">
    <!-- any other CSS here-->
</head>
<body class='metrouicss'>
<!-- HTML content and div placeholders-->
<div id='timeline' class='timeline-view'>
    <h2>My Tweets</h2>
</div>

<!-- Handlebars templates -->
<script type="text/x-handlebars-template" id="timeline-template">
 <ul class='listview'>
        {{#each tweet}}
        <li>
          <div class='icon'>
                <img src='{{user.profile_image_url}}'></img>
          </div>
```

```html
        <div class='data'>
            <h4>{{user.name}}</h4>

            <p>{{text}}</p>
        </div>
    </li>
    {{/each}}
  </ul>
</script>

<!-- External library Includes -->
<script src="js/external/jquery-1.10.2.js"></script>
<script src="js/external/underscore.js"></script>
<script src="js/external/backbone.js"></script>
<script src="js/external/handlebars.js"></script>

<!-- Model -->
<script src="js/app/model/Tweet.js"></script>
...
<!-- Collections -->
<script src="js/app/collection/Timeline.js"></script>
.....
<!-- View -->
<script src="js/app/view/TimelineView.js"></script>
.....

<!-- Router -->
<script src="js/app/router/AppRouter.js"></script>
.....

<!-- The 'main' for this app -->
<script src="js/app/app.js"></script>
</body>
</html>
```

First Steps: Dealing with Authentication

When dealing with any API, it's likely that you'll have to be able to cope with some security requirements, such as authorization on connection. This section will help you get started with authentication for clients using the Twitter API.

Getting Set Up on Twitter

Before we can have our app utilize the Twitter API, we need to do a little work on https://dev.twitter.com/apps and set up authorization for our client.

───

■ **Note**   For simplicity, our app will use application-level authentication, meaning that the developer account you run the following steps with will be seen as the current user when using the Twitter API. This means we don't need to worry about having a login flow in our client-side application.

───

Assuming that you already have a Twitter account, simply sign in and click the Create New Application button to start defining the details for your app. On the first page, you will just need to fill out some straightforward details about the application. Make sure you set up the application to use Read, Write, and Direct Messages permissions.

The next page (shown in Figure 6-3) is where you will provide the most important details for your application: the consumer key and the consumer secret.

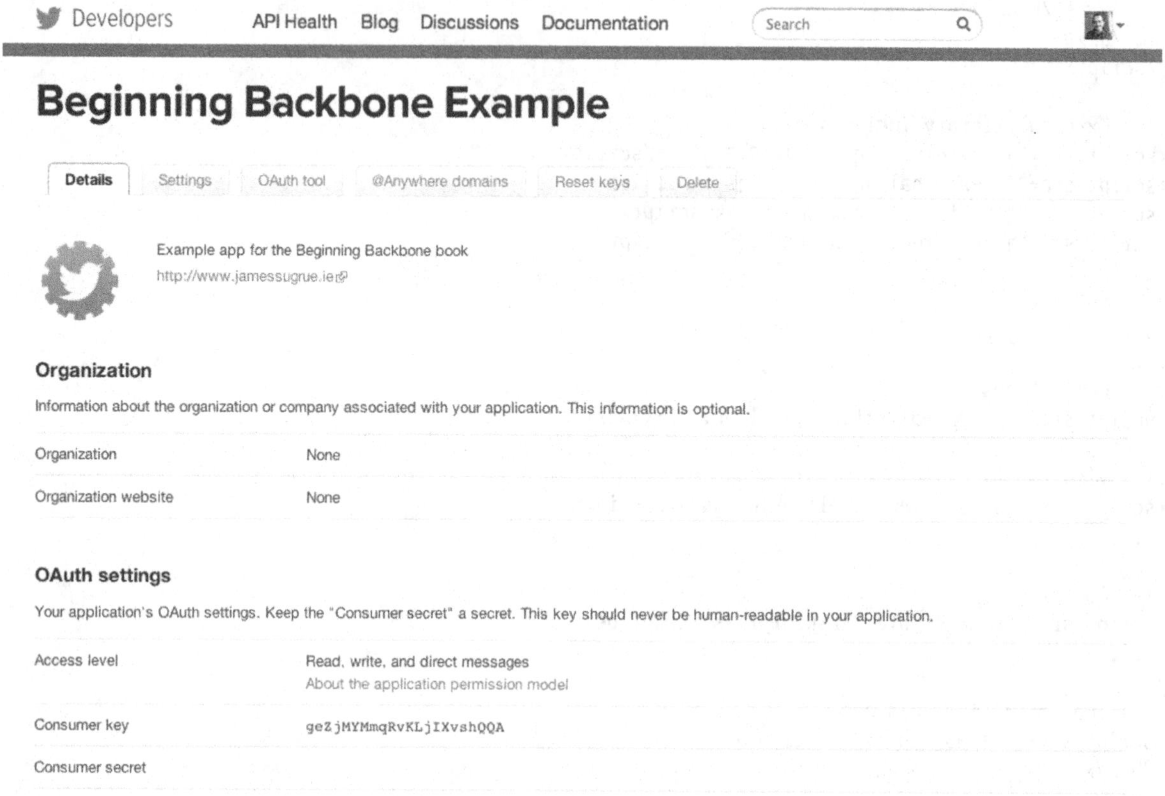

Figure 6-3. *OAuth settings from the Twitter application*

Figure 6-3 has the consumer secret blocked out because this should be kept secret. Just as I have been careful to hide the secret key in this image, you should keep it secret in your JavaScript. Anyone can view the source of a web page, so you should never have the key included in JavaScript. By selecting the "OAuth tool" tab, you'll get access to all four keys that are required for your client application to connect.

Keeping Secrets on Servers

For this application, we will have an intermediate node server running that will accept all calls from the client-side application and forward these requests to Twitter. This ensures that the secret key is stored on the server side. Figure 6-4 illustrates this pipeline.

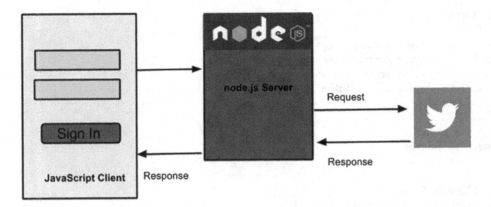

***Figure 6-4.** Illustration of the role of the node.js server*

The node.js server source will be similar to that which we created in previous chapters. However, to make dealing with the Twitter API more straightforward, I utilized Tolga Tezel's node package for Twitter (`https://github.com/ttezel/twit`). You can install the package simply by using `npm install twit`.

You'll need to include this library in your project using the `require()` function and then follow the authentication steps as listed next in the `connectToTwitter()` function.

```
var Twit = require('twit')
var client = null;

function connectToTwitter(){
   client = new Twit({
        consumer_key:          '<your consumer key>',
        consumer_secret:       '<your consumer secret>',
        access_token:          '<your access token>',
        access_token_secret:   '<your access token secret>'
   });
}
//get the app to connect to twitter.
connectToTwitter();
```

Once this code has executed, the `twitterClient` object will be set up to interact with the full Twitter API. For completeness, here is the full source code for `server.js` so far, without any handlers added for client GET and POST methods:

```
/**
 * A simple API hosted under localhost:8080/books
 */
var express = require('express');
var app = express();

var Twit = require('twit')

var client = null;
```

```
function connectToTwitter(){
    client = new Twit({
            consumer_key:            '<your consumer key>',
            consumer_secret:         '<your consumer secret>',
            access_token:            '<your access token>',
            access_token_secret:     '<your access token secret>'

    });
}
//get the app to connect to twitter.
connectToTwitter();

//additional setup to allow CORS requests
var allowCrossDomain = function(req, response, next) {
    response.header('Access-Control-Allow-Origin', "http://localhost");
    response.header('Access-Control-Allow-Methods', 'OPTIONS, GET,PUT,POST,DELETE');
    response.header('Access-Control-Allow-Headers', 'Content-Type');

    if ('OPTIONS' == req.method) {
      response.send(200);
    }
    else {
      next();
    }
};

app.configure(function() {
    app.use(allowCrossDomain);
  //Parses the JSON object given in the body request
    app.use(express.bodyParser());
});

//start up the app on port 8080
app.listen(8080);
```

We can now begin to build extra functionality on the server for the client application to hook into.

Showing the Twitter Timeline

The first thing we'll do is create a simple model and view that will allow us to see the Twitter timeline for the current user.

For a start, we'll need to set up an end point on our node.js server to respond to the timeline request. This will utilize the Twitter library to retrieve a number of "tweet objects." The following code should be placed in `server.js` for the node server:

```
/**
 * Returns the twitter timeline for the current user
 **/
app.get('/timeline', function (request, response) {

    response.header('Access-Control-Allow-Origin', '*');
      client.get('statuses/home_timeline', { },  function (err, reply) {
```

```
      if(err){
        response.send(404);
      }
      if(reply){
        response.json(reply);
      }
    });
});
```

The Data Layer

Let's focus on the model and collection that will be used to access the timeline information from our server.
The model doesn't need to have any default attributes set because they will all come from the Twitter API response.
This results in the simplest possible model class for now, although it is likely that more detail will be added to this as
we progress. The following code should be placed in Tweet.js under the model directory:

```
var com = com || {};
com.apress = com.apress || {};
com.apress.model = com.apress.model || {};

com.apress.model.Tweet = Backbone.Model.extend({

});
```

The collection will deal with connection to the server, retrieving a list of tweets, each of which will be represented
by a Tweet object. The following code should be placed in Timeline.js in the collection directory:

```
var com = com || {};
com.apress = com.apress || {};
com.apress.collection = com.apress.collection || {};

com.apress.collection.Timeline = Backbone.Collection.extend({

    //the model that this collection uses
    model: com.apress.model.Tweet,
    //the server side url to connect to for the collection
    url: 'http://localhost:8080/timeline',

    initialize: function(options){
        //anything to be defined on construction goes here
    },
});
```

The key parts of the collection are the model attribute, which states which Backbone model object to use within
this collection, and the url attribute, which defines which REST service will provide the timeline information.
Before going any further, you can test this collection by creating a new instance of it and invoking the fetch
function. For now, the following code can be placed in app.js:

```
var timeline = new com.apress.collection.Timeline();
timeline.fetch();
```

If you look at the Network tab in Chrome Developer Tools and observe the XHR requests, you'll see that the timeline collection invoked the correct service and that the service responded with data.

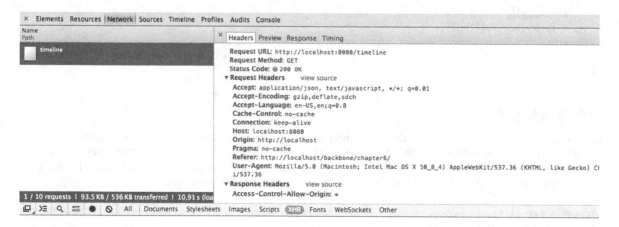

Figure 6-5. *An example of the XHR request invoked from the timeline collection*

It's worth noting the structure of the response in the Preview pane. You will receive an array of entries, and each one of these will be marshaled into the Tweet model. In Figure 6-6 you can see a listing of all the attributes that are returned.

```
× Headers  Preview  Response  Timing
▼ [{created_at:Tue Aug 27 04:38:10 +0000 2013, id:372216445989834750, id_str:372216445989834752,…},…]
  ▶ 0: {created_at:Tue Aug 27 04:38:10 +0000 2013, id:372216445989834750, id_str:372216445989834752,…}
  ▶ 1: {created_at:Tue Aug 27 04:35:31 +0000 2013, id:372215776604061700, id_str:372215776604061696,…}
  ▶ 2: {created_at:Tue Aug 27 04:33:16 +0000 2013, id:372215210183888900, id_str:372215210183888896,…}
  ▼ 3: {created_at:Tue Aug 27 04:32:09 +0000 2013, id:372214932471050240, id_str:372214932471050240,…}
      contributors: null
      coordinates: null
      created_at: "Tue Aug 27 04:32:09 +0000 2013"
    ▶ entities: {hashtags:[], symbols:[], urls:[],…}
      favorite_count: 0
      favorited: false
      geo: null
      id: 372214932471050240
      id_str: "372214932471050240"
      in_reply_to_screen_name: null
      in_reply_to_status_id: null
      in_reply_to_status_id_str: null
      in_reply_to_user_id: null
      in_reply_to_user_id_str: null
      lang: "en"
      place: null
      retweet_count: 455
      retweeted: false
    ▶ retweeted_status: {created_at:Wed Jun 12 21:36:54 +0000 2013, id:344931341378408450, id_str:344931341378408449,…}
      source: "<a href="http://twitter.com/download/android" rel="nofollow">Twitter for Android</a>"
      text: "RT @HackerNewsOnion: Enterprise CTO not impressed by pair programming.…"We often have hundreds of developers working on the same thing."
      truncated: false
    ▶ user: {id:47378354, id_str:47378354, name:Kevlin Henney, screen_name:KevlinHenney, location:⊕~1au,…}
```

Figure 6-6. *The structure of the timeline response*

Building a View for the Timeline

With the data layer under control, now it's time to build a view for this data. We'll start with getting some of the HTML ready so that we can list all the tweets in our timeline. You will usually create a div for each of your views, and the ID of this div will be used as the el variable in the Backbone view. All the following HTML code should be placed in index.html:

```
<div id='timeline' class='timeline-view'>
    <h2>My Tweets</h2>
</div>
```

We'll also create a Handlebars template for the collection. Rather than having a for loop in our JavaScript code to render each tweet individually, we can utilize Handlebars built-in helpers to iterate through the collection.

```
<script type="text/x-handlebars-template" id="timeline-template">
 <ul class='listview'>
      {{#each tweet}}
      <li>
        <div class='icon'>
               <img src='{{user.profile_image_url}}'></img>
         </div>
         <div class='data'>
             <h4>{{user.name}}</h4>

             <p>{{text}}</p>
         </div>
      </li>
      {{/each}}
   </ul>
 </script>
```

Now we can create a view that deals with the timeline. First we will hook the view in with the items that we have defined in our HTML: the div element for the view and the template that will render the collection data. The following code should be placed in TimelineView.js under the view directory.

```
var com = com || {};
com.apress = com.apress || {};
com.apress.view = com.apress.view || {};

com.apress.view.TimelineView = Backbone.View.extend({

    el: '#timeline',

    template: Handlebars.compile($("#timeline-template").html()),

    initialize: function(options){
    },
    render: function(){
    },

});
```

As we've already stated, Backbone is not an opinionated framework, which means you have a few options when using a collection with a view.

- You can initialize the collection inside your view.

- You can initialize the collection in an outer app.js, or even in your router, passing it through to the view as a parameter.

For this example, we'll actually create the collection within the view's initialize function. The collection, in this case timeline, is added as a class variable to the view so that it can be shared with different functions.

```
initialize:  function(options){
    var self = this;

    //create a collection for this view to render
    self.timeline = new com.apress.collection.Timeline();
    //initial render
    self.render();

    //force the fetch to fire a reset event
    self.timeline.fetch({reset:true});

    self.listenTo(self.timeline, 'reset', self.render);
},
```

The last two lines are critical in this initialize function. We force a fetch operation for the collection and pass through a boolean flag indicating that fetch should trigger a reset event.

The view listens for any changes to the timeline, and when it does change, the render function will be run.

The render function is quite simple; provided there are models present in the timeline collection, they are passed to the template.

```
render: function(){
    var self = this;
    if(self.timeline.models.length > 0){
        var output = self.template({tweet: self.timeline.toJSON()});

        self.$el.append(output);
    }
    return self;
},
```

Handlebars iterates through each tweet, {{#each tweet}}, so it's essential that the JSON passed to the template is named tweet. The complete code listing of this view follows:

```
var com = com || {};
com.apress = com.apress || {};
com.apress.view = com.apress.view || {};

com.apress.view.TimelineView = Backbone.View.extend({

    el: '#timeline',
```

```
    template: Handlebars.compile($("#timeline-template").html()),

    timeline: null,

    initialize:  function(options){
        var self = this;

        //create a collection for this view to render
        self.timeline = new com.apress.collection.Timeline();
        //initial render
        self.render();

        //force the fetch to fire a reset event
        self.timeline.fetch({reset:true});

        self.listenTo(self.timeline, 'reset', self.render);

    },

    render: function(){
        var self = this;
        if(self.timeline.models.length > 0){
var output = self.template({tweet: self.timeline.toJSON()});

            self.$el.append(output);
        }
        return self;
    },

});
```

Next we will set up our app.js to simply create this view. Because the view looks after the creation of the collection, there is no need to define it in the view. Also, we have no application routes set up, so we don't need to worry about the history or any routers yet.

```
var timelineView = new com.apress.view.TimelineView();
```

Provided you have included all the JavaScript created to date, navigating to your index.html page will run the entire application, showing output similar to that in Figure 6-7.

My Tweets

Rob Peck
Here's a great example of a shyster
taking advantage of parents a la my last
blog post. http://t.co/1J3HS5dyBN

Inc.
11 body language essentials for your
next negotiation http://t.co/rdTKsTuiVW

Thomas Reynolds
RT @RefreshPDX: Our next event will be
"Style Guides: Why I love them" by
@susanjrobertson on 18 September
2013! Details & tix at http://t....

Kevlin Henney
RT @HackerNewsOnion: Enterprise CTO
not impressed by pair programming.
"We often have hundreds of developers
working on the same thing."

Figure 6-7. *Result of rendering the Twitter timeline collection with TimelineView*

View Improvement: Show Timestamp

Let's look at how to improve the appearance of each tweet in our application. One thing that would be worth adding is the timestamp of each entry. However, if you look at the model, you'll see that you get a long, verbose timestamp under the created_at attribute. It would be much nicer to use the same approach as on the Twitter.com web site, where you see how long ago the tweet was created.

To do this, we can use the Moment.js (http://momentjs.com) library, which provides a user-friendly way to parse, manipulate, and format dates. First, you'll need to download the library and reference it in index.html. In this example, I have downloaded the complete Moment.js library, so it is referred to as moment.js. The default package is actually the minified version.

```
<script src="js/external/moment.js"></script>
```

Rather than adding code that will format the data within the JavaScript responsible for rendering, we can add a new attribute to the model when it is being parsed by Backbone on return from the server.

To do this, we'll extend the Tweet model with a parse function, in Tweet.js.

```
parse: function(model){

//model.created_at "Wed Aug 28 06:32:07 +0000 2013"
        var friendly = moment(model.created_at, "ddd MMM DD HH:mm:ss ZZ YYYY").fromNow();
```

```
        model.friendlyDate = friendly;

        return model;
}
```

If you inspect the model, you'll see that the format of the created_at data follows a pattern like
Wed Aug 28 06:32:07 +0000 2013. To read this date, you will need to instruct Moment.js on the format, which will
be ddd MMM DD HH:mm:ss ZZ YYYY. Once a valid date is created, Moment.js will generate a friendly strong by using its
fromNow function, which can be added to the model before the parse function returns.

One important thing to remember: if you are adding a parse implementation to you model, ensure that you
always return the model at the end.

View Improvement: Highlight Usernames

Another improvement would be to take any @username sections out of the tweet and make them links to view the
user's profile. As this will be an enhancement to how we display the tweet, rather than a change to the data, it is
acceptable to have this code present in the rendering side.

We can do this by adding a helper function to Handlebars. This allows us to have the highlighting as an
expression in the template.

First, create a new JavaScript file to contain your helper functions and save it in the util directory. Now, create
a new helper in here using the Handlebars.registerHelper function, passing through the name of helper that you
will use in the template and the parameter that it will deal with. Don't forget to include the file that you create for the
helpers in your main HTML page. In this case, I have named the file helpers.js under the utils directory.

I found a useful piece of JavaScript code that provides a regular expression for replacing @username parts with links on
Simon Whatley's blog (www.simonwhatley.co.uk/parsing-twitter-usernames-hashtags-and-urls-with-javascript).

Note that once the string is parsed, it needs to be returned as a SafeString. Any time that you add a helper that
creates its own HTML, you will probably want to use this type because it will escape the HTML code and make it
appear as expected.

```javascript
$(function() {

    Handlebars.registerHelper('format', function (str) {
        if(str){
            //highlight the @part
            str = str.replace(/[@]+[A-Za-z0-9-_]+/g,
                    function(u) {
                        var username = u.replace("@","");
                        return u.link("http://twitter.com/"+username);
                    });
            return new Handlebars.SafeString(str);
        }else{
            return str;
        }

    });

});
```

Now the template in the HTML page can be extended to deal with this simply by replacing the instance of {{text}} with {{format text}}.

```
<script type="text/x-handlebars-template" id="timeline-template">
 <ul class='listview'>
        {{#each tweet}}
        <li>
          <div class='icon'>
                  <img src='{{user.profile_image_url}}'></img>
          </div>
          <div class='data'>
              <h4>{{user.name}}</h4>

              <p>{{format text}}</p>
              <p class="timestamp"><i>{{friendlyDate}}</i></p>
          </div>
        </li>
        {{/each}}
    </ul>
 </script>
```

Adding the Profile View

The timeline is just one view in our overall application. The purpose of this example is to show how a number of views can be put together and interact to provide a better user experience. This section will show how to add more views to the application and how to deal with a single model rather than using a collection.

Profile Data Layer

The profile view will be quite simple. All we want to do is show your own profile details—full name, bio, and the number of followers—from the Twitter API. As we'll be getting just one entry, there will be no need for a collection in this instance; a model will suffice.

As with the Tweet model, the following should be placed in the model directory and have a namespace prefix of com.apress.model:

```
var com = com || {};
com.apress = com.apress || {};
com.apress.model = com.apress.model || {};

com.apress.model.Profile = Backbone.Model.extend({

    urlRoot: 'http://localhost:8080/profile',

    parse: function(model){

        return model;
    }

});
```

There is nothing more that you'll need to do with this model, as it will just return the data that is retrieved from the end point.

On your node.js server, in `server.js`, you will need to include a function that responds to the /profile request.

```
/**
 * Get the account settings for the user with the id provided.
 **/
app.get('/profile', function(request, response){

    response.header('Access-Control-Allow-Origin', '*');

    client.get('users/show', {screen_name: 'sugrue'},  function (err, reply) {

      if(err){
        console.log('Error: ' + err);
        response.send(404);

      }
      if(reply){
       /// console.log('Reply: ' + reply);
        response.json(reply);
      }

    });
});
```

To get profile details from the Twitter API, you will need to utilize the `users/show` API end point and pass a screen name. As we just want to get the details for your own profile, so pass your own Twitter handle here.

Profile View

The main page will need to be altered to make space for the profile view on the right side. We'll just use some of the grid CSS rules that are provided by MetroUI to lay out the page in a better manner.

```html
<div id="app" class="grid">
    <div class="row">
        <div class="span8">

            <div id='timeline' class='timeline-view'>
             <h2>My Tweets</h2>
            </div>
        </div>

        <div class="span4">
            <div id="profile" class="profile-view">
             <!-- Profile view here -->
            </div>
        </div>
    </div>
</div>
```

As the timeline is the most essential part of the page, that is given a span of eight columns, while the sidebar that will contain the profile view needs only four columns. We'll also make a minor change to the template used for timeline details, adding the fluid class to the `<ul>` list in order to use the extra space in the grid.

```
<script type="text/x-handlebars-template" id="timeline-template">
 <ul class='listview fluid'>
     .....
</script>
```

Before we leave `index.html`, we'll add a template to hold the profile details. The outline of this container will look something like Figure 6-8.

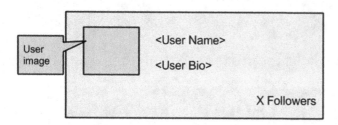

Figure 6-8. *Outline of profile view*

MetroUI has a tile class that fits this requirement well, so the template will use some of those CSS styles to achieve this appearance.

```
<!-- Template for profile -->
<script type="text/x-handlebars-template" id="profile-template">
  <div class='tiles clearfix'>
    <div class="tile double bg-color-orangeDark">
      <div class="tile-content">
        <img src="{{user.profile_image_url}}" class="place-left">
        <h3 style="margin-bottom: 5px;">{{user.name}}</h3>
        <p>{{user.description}}</p>
        <div class="brand">
            <div class="badge">{{user.followers_count}} Followers</div>
        </div>
      </div>
    </div>
  </div>
</script>
```

The badge style does need a little change: it will be too narrow for the amount of text that we want to display for followers. As in any HTML application, we can simple extend the CSS definition in `style.css`.

```
.badge{
    width: 200px!important;
    height: 24px;
}
```

This leads to the final part in the definition of the profile within the app, the Backbone view to represent the details. The code for this view is much the same as the `TimelineView`. Even though the `ProfileView` will be dealing with a model rather than a collection, the differences in the view level are minimal.

The `initialize` function will create a new instance of the `Profile` model and then request the contents from the server by invoking the `fetch` function. The following code should be placed in `ProfileView.js` under the view directory:

```
var com = com || {};
com.apress = com.apress || {};
com.apress.view = com.apress.view || {};

com.apress.view.ProfileView = Backbone.View.extend({

    el: '#profile',
    template: Handlebars.compile($("#profile-template").html()),
    model: null,

    initialize:  function(options){
        var self = this;
        //create a collection for this view to render
        self.model = new com.apress.model.Profile();

        //force the fetch to fire a reset event
        self.model.fetch({});
        self.listenTo(self.model, 'change', self.render);
    },

    render: function(){
        var self = this;
            var output = self.template({user: self.model.toJSON()});

            self.$el.html(output);

        return self;
    },
});
```

The render function resets the entire HTML for the `div` element that is to contain the profile template content, marked with the profile ID.

Putting It All Together

Just a few more steps are required in order to get the profile view properly incorporated into the application. First, `index.html` will need to be extended to include the new JavaScript source.

```
<script src="js/app/model/Profile.js"></script>
<script src="js/app/view/ProfileView.js"></script>
```

And `app.js` will need to create a new instance of the `ProfileView` when the page loads.

```
var timelineView = new com.apress.view.TimelineView(),
    profileView = new com.apress.view.ProfileView();
```

Reloading the application should now render a page similar to that in Figure 6-9.

Figure 6-9. *Twitter application with timeline and profile views*

Reusing the Profile View

Now that we have a neat view for viewing user profile details, we could improve the link that's provided on the timeline view for each mention of an @username. As well as showing how to reuse views, this section will illustrate how to add events to one of the views.

Making the Profile Model Reusable

First we'll need to parameterize the request for profile details rather than hard-coding to one particular user. This requires a change to the handler function on the server side: adding to server.js the code to handle a request parameter with the name id.

```
/**
 * Get the account settings for the user with the id provided.
 **/
app.get('/profile/:id', function(request, response){

    response.header('Access-Control-Allow-Origin', '*');

    client.get('users/show', {screen_name: request.params.id},  function (err, reply) {

      if(err){
        console.log('Error: ' + err);
        response.send(404);

      }
```

```
    if(reply){
     /// console.log('Reply: ' + reply);
       response.json(reply);
    }

  });
});
```

In Backbone, when a model has an id attribute, it is appended to the end of the urlRoot that is used to retrieve the information from the server. This means we simply need to set the id parameter for the profile model when it is created. This can be passed all the way from app.js to the constructor of the ProfileView, which then creates an instance of the Profile model.

You'll recall that any Backbone object can accept parameters to the constructor that are then used in the initialize function. In app.js, when the ProfileView is created, pass the username as follows:

```
profileView = new com.apress.view.ProfileView({user: 'sugrue'}),
```

Now the initialize function in the ProfileView class can use this new parameter.

```
initialize:  function(options){
      var self = this;
      //create a collection for this view to render
      self.model = new com.apress.model.Profile({id: options.user});
      ......
```

The application will behave the same as before, but we're now in a position where we can reuse the model to render profile details for any user.

Changing the Behavior on the Timeline

Previously, when parsing the usernames from the tweets, we created a simple link to the user's profile page. Now we'll want to detect when a profile link is clicked and display a dialog.

The Handlebars helper, helper.js, that provides this formatting will need to be updated. The link doesn't need to go to any location, but by applying a class to the link (in this case, profile), there is a way to distinguish a profile link from any other type of href.

```
Handlebars.registerHelper('format', function (str) {
      if(str){
           str = str.replace(/[@]+[A-Za-z0-9-_]+/g, function(u) {
                    var username = u.replace('@','')
                    return '<a href="#" data-user="' + username +'" class="profile">@'+username+'</a>';
           });
      }
});
```

When we click a profile link, we'll want to get the username to use for the profile. To get this passed through, we can use custom data attributes. These are attributes with prefixed with data- that allow HTML authors to add metadata to describe HTML elements further. More importantly, this can be parsed later in the JavaScript code for the view.

Adding Events to the Timeline View

Every tweet in the timeline that renders an @username link will now be identified with the profile class. We can add event handling by adding an events hash to the view.

```
events: {
    'click .profile': 'showDialog'
},
```

Now when the profile is clicked, the showDialog function will be invoked. Any view event in Backbone will include an options object, which includes a reference to the HTML element that was the source of the event. With this reference, we can get the username by using the .data() function.

```
showDialog: function(options){

    var self =this,
        $target = $(options.currentTarget),
        username = $target.data('user');
    var profileView = new com.apress.view.ProfilePopupView({user: username});

}
```

You'll notice that this creates an instance of a new view object, ProfilePopupView. We'll create this next.

Creating a Pop-up Dialog for Profiles

The source for the dialog is almost the same as that in the ProfileView. In fact, the initialize function is a direct copy, and it even reuses the same Handlebars template. The only difference is in the render function, which will create a new dialog and present that on the screen rather than appending the detail on the main page. The following code should be placed in ProfilePopupView.js in the view directory:

```
var com = com || {};
com.apress = com.apress || {};
com.apress.view = com.apress.view || {};

com.apress.view.ProfilePopupView = Backbone.View.extend({

    template: Handlebars.compile($("#profile-template").html()),
    model: null,

    initialize:  function(options){
        var self = this;

        //create a collection for this view to render
        self.model = new com.apress.model.Profile({id: options.user});
        //force the fetch to fire a reset event
        self.model.fetch({});
        self.listenTo(self.model, 'change', self.render);
    },
```

```
render: function(){
    var self = this;

    if(self.model.get('screen_name')){
        var output = self.template({user: self.model.toJSON()});

        $.Dialog({
            'title'        : '@'+self.model.get('screen_name') + 's Profile',
            'content'      : output,
            'draggable'    : true,
            'overlay'      : true,
            'closeButton'  : true,
            'buttonsAlign' : 'center',
            'keepOpened'   : true,
            'position'     : {
                'zone'     : 'left'
            },
            'buttons'      : {
                'OK'       : {
                    'action': function(){}
                }
            }
        });
    }

    return self;
},
});
```

MetroUI provides a some JavaScript for dialog creation that you will also need to include for this to function. This is hosted on GitHub at https://raw.github.com/olton/Metro-UI-CSS/master/javascript/dialog.js. To get around other errors on your page, you should also include the fonts directory.

Again, you'll need to update the includes in index.html:

```
<script src="js/external/dialog.js"></script>
<script src="js/app/view/ProfilePopupView.js"></script>
```

You should now see a screen similar to Figure 6-10 when you click an @username link.

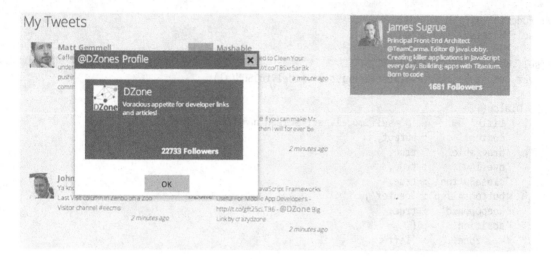

Figure 6-10. *Reuse of the profile view in a pop-up*

You should now be seeing the benefits of splitting models and views and the templates that are used in the HTML. We've added extra functionality to the application with minimal effort. The same template and styling that was done for the profile in the sidebar is available for other portions of the application that are dealing with the same model. This leads to more consistent user interfaces, along with code that is easy to follow.

Adding Search Functionality

The final part to our application screen is the addition of a search box, allowing us to run queries against the Twitter search API and render these results. In this section, we will introduce a router to the application to make the searches bookmarkable.

The Data Layer

Once again, we'll need to create an end point to serve search requests on the node.js server, in the `server.js` file. The path to the Twitter API for searching is `search/tweets`, and it takes a search term parameter (q) along with a count for the maximum number of results to return.

```
/**
 * Runs a search given a query
 **/
app.get('/search/:query', function (request, response) {

    response.header('Access-Control-Allow-Origin', '*');
    //search term is
    var searchTerm = request.params.query;
```

```
client.get('search/tweets', { q: searchTerm, count: 100 }, function(err, reply) {

    if(err){
      console.log('Error: ' + err);
      response.send(404);

    }
    if(reply){
     // console.log('Reply: ' + reply);
      response.json(reply);
    }

  });


});
```

This time we'll do something different with the model for the search. Because the search term is included as a parameter in the search URL, it will be necessary to reconstruct the end point for the model each time results are requested. To deal with this, we can override the sync method, allowing execution of some custom code before continuing to call the default Backbone sync function.

```
var com = com || {};
com.apress = com.apress || {};
com.apress.model = com.apress.model || {};

com.apress.model.Search = Backbone.Model.extend({

    url : 'http://localhost:8080/search',

    sync: function(method, model, options){
        if(this.get('query')){
            this.url = this.url + '/' + this.get('query');
        }
        Backbone.sync.call(this, method, model, options);
    },
});
```

The sync function checks whether there is a query attribute available in the mode and appends it to the URL if it exists.

Adding the Search View

The HTML representation of the search will be in a simple form. In this case, a template would be overkill because it is essentially static content.

We'll add the HTML for the search view just underneath the profile box in index.html.

```
<div class="span4">
                <div id="profile" class="profile-view">
              </div>
```

```
                    <div id="search" class="search-view">
                        <form>
                            <div class="input-control text">
                                <input type="text" id="searchbox" autofocus=""
placeholder="I'm looking for..">
                            </div>
                                <button class="bg-color-blue" id="searchbutton">Search</button>
                        </form>
                    </div>
                </div>
```

We can now create a Backbone view to deal with the search. This is required only to add a listener for the search button. This could be done in a higher-level view, but as all our views so far have had a clear division of responsibility, it makes sense to maintain the current pattern.

As you can see in the declaration of the events hash, the single event that is being dealt with is the click on the element with the ID of searchbutton. Note that we could also have a key listener for the text field that could execute the runSearch method.

Another important item to note is that the Search model object is passed to this view as a parameter, rather than having the view create the model as in previous examples. The reason for this is that the model needs to be shared between a number of objects. This will be explained in the next few paragraphs. The following code should be placed in SearchView.js in the view directory. Don't forget to include this file in your main HTML page.

```javascript
var com = com || {};
com.apress = com.apress || {};
com.apress.view = com.apress.view || {};

com.apress.view.SearchView = Backbone.View.extend({

    el: '#search',
    model: null,
    events: {
        'click #searchbutton': 'runSearch'
    },

    initialize:  function(options){
        var self = this;
        self.model = options.model;
    },

    runSearch: function(e){
        var self = this;
            query = $('#searchbox').val();

        e.preventDefault();

        console.log('Run search against  ' + query);

        //a trick to force a reset of the attribute
        self.model.set('query', '', {silent: true});
        self.model.set('query', query);
    }

});
```

There are a few points to note about the runSearch function. First, the function includes a call to e.preventDefault(), a jQuery event that will stop the default function from executing. This prevents the entire page from refreshing.

The other thing is that the view does nothing more than set the model value. The execution of search will rely on the change event for the model object. Because of this, we clear the value in the model silently first, before setting the attribute. This is purely to ensure that the change event gets fired after clicking the button. If the query value was the same as previously, the change event would not get fired.

Sharing Models Between Backbone Objects

We've already set up the SearchView to accept the search model as a parameter. The reason I have done that is so that we can have a router to deal with search URLs, making them bookmarkable. This router will also accept the model as a parameter. The changing of this shared model is what will trigger a navigation function.

The initialize function sets up the appropriate listener for changes in the query attribute of the search model. This is how the router hooks into the SearchView created in the previous section. The following code should be placed in AppRouter.js in the router directory:

```
var com = com || {};
com.apress = com.apress || {};
com.apress.router = com.apress.router || {};

com.apress.router.AppRouter = Backbone.Router.extend({

    searchModel : null,

    initialize:  function(options){

        var self = this;
        self.searchModel = options.searchModel;
        self.listenTo(self.searchModel, 'change:query', self.navigateToSearch)

    },

    navigateToSearch: function(model, options){
        //manually navigate to the search url
        this.navigate("search/" + model.get('query'), {trigger: true});
    },
});
```

The navigateToSearch function simply creates a URL that can be reused at any stage. This allows two ways to search: one from the search button and one from the URL in the browser address bar. When calling navigate, using {trigger:true} causes the route setup for this URL to be invoked.

Next we need to create the route and handler for the search. The routes hash needs to include the query parameter and will call a function named search.

```
routes: {'search/:query' : 'search'},
```

When the search function is executed, it checks whether the model already has a value set for the query attribute. When running the search from the UI, when the button is clicked, this will always be set. However, if you use the URL bar, the route will be entered without setting any attributes in the search model. This allows the function to cater for both cases.

```
search: function(query){
        var self = this;

        console.log('search for ' + query);
        if(self.searchModel.get('query') !== query){
            self.searchModel.set('query', query, {silent:true});
        }

    //now go the that view
        self.searchModel.fetch({
                success: function(model){
                    //create the results view
                    var resultsView = new com.apress.view.ResultsView({model:model});

                },
                error: function(e){
                    alert('No results available');
                }
        });
}
```

Provided that the call to the search end point is successful, the router will then create a ResultsView object to present the results.

The construction of the ResultsView class is actually similar to that of the ProfilePopupView. It's just another dialog that will reuse a Handlebars template, in this case the template for the TimelineView, to present the search results.

The search model is passed to this view before the call is made to fetch the results from the server. Once a change is detected in the model, the render function is invoked, which builds the dialog after populating the template. The results are actually stored in an array called statuses. To reuse the template, this array needs to be tagged with the name tweet. The following code should be placed in ResultsView.js in the view directory, and the file should be included with a script tag from the main HTML page:

```
var com = com || {};
com.apress = com.apress || {};
com.apress.view = com.apress.view || {};

com.apress.view.ResultsView = Backbone.View.extend({

    el: '#results',

    model: null,

    template: Handlebars.compile($("#timeline-template").html()),

    initialize: function(options){
        var self = this;
        self.model = options.model;

        self.model.fetch();
```

```
            self.listenTo(self.model,'change', self.render);

            self.render();
        },

    render: function(){

        var self = this,
            output = self.template({tweet: self.model.get('statuses')});

            $.Dialog({
                'title'        : 'Search Results',
                'content'      : output,
                'draggable'    : true,
                'overlay'      : true,
                'closeButton'  : true,
                'buttonsAlign' : 'center',
                'keepOpened'   : true,
                'position'     : {
                    'zone'     : 'left'
                },
                'buttons'      : {
                    'OK'       : {
                        'action': function(){}
                    }
                }
            });

    }

});
```

app.js will require some updates so that the search model is created at the beginning and shared between the router and the search view. All of the scripts that we have created should be included in the main HTML page using script tags.

```
$(function() {

var timelineView = new com.apress.view.TimelineView(),
profileView = new com.apress.view.ProfileView({user: 'sugrue'}),
searchModel = new com.apress.model.Search(),
searchView = new com.apress.view.SearchView({model: searchModel}),
appRouter = new com.apress.router.AppRouter({searchModel: searchModel});

    Backbone.history.start();

});
```

Now when you invoke a search, you will be presented with a dialog, as in Figure 6-11.

Figure 6-11. *A portion of the search results dialog*

Error Handling

All of our code so far has assumed that the calls to the server will be successful, returning results. However, it's important that you add error handling code to any of the calls to fetch data from the server.

You can do this by enhancing the calls to fetch to include both success and error callbacks. When an error happens, it would be useful to fire an event that can then be dealt with by an overall listener.

This listener could be added to any part of the application. Because we don't have a single view that rules over the entire app, the AppRouter class is probably best suited for this. However, the AppRouter would need to have an object shared between the views to listen for events on.

The search example allows us to do this because it is a shared object. In the initialize, the AppRouter would listen for error events.

```
self.searchModel.on('app:error', function(error){
        alert(error.message);
});
```

And in the search, when the call is made to fetch, the error handler would fire the event, along with additional parameters for the listener to use (that is, message).

```
self.model.fetch({
      error: function(e){
                  self.model.trigger("app:error", {message: 'Error retrieving timeline information'});
      },
});
```

You'll find that having a single application model to share across the application will help make the tracking of errors in application state a lot easier.

Summary

This example application has brought all the concepts that we have gone through in the previous three chapters together. You saw how to create views based on collections and models that interact with back-end services. You also saw how you can reuse models and templates across your app, reducing the amount of code necessary. External libraries were used along with Handlebar templates, and extended helper functions are added for these templates.

Finer details, such as customizations to parse and sync methods, were also made clearer, with concrete examples of where it is useful to extend this functionality in your own apps. We also built in a router and used events throughout the application.

Most importantly, you learned how to structure your Backbone application, with namespaces and directories separating concerns. This structure should provide you with a framework to use for your own apps. This chapter alone covers enough ground to show you how to create professional-quality pages powered by Backbone.

CHAPTER 7

The Backbone Ecosystem

Now that you've seen what can be built with Backbone as it exists out of the box, it's time to delve deeper into more advanced techniques that can make your application development easier and keep your code cleaner.

After just a few years, Backbone already has an impressive online community, with a number of open source projects that help address what some see as deficiencies in the library.

This chapter will take a look at these third-party components and investigate where they can help you in the development of your Backbone applications. The components are split into different purposes to make it easier to browse through the ever-increasing number of options.

At the end of this chapter you'll find a table summarizing all the third-party components discussed.

Code Samples

Each of the projects listed in this chapter have some code samples. You can access them from the GitHub repository shared at https://github.com/jamessugrue/beginning-backbone.

User Interface Components

The following plug-ins will help you when dealing with the user interface of your Backbone applications.

LayoutManager

Hosted at http://layoutmanager.org/, Tim Branyen's LayoutManager helps assemble layouts and subviews within your Backbone application. As well as helping to structure layouts, the project helps you keep in control of nested views and ensures proper memory management for views created during the life cycle of your application. On top of all of this, LayoutManager provides beforeRender() and afterRender() callbacks so that you can reliably tell when your view has completed rendering.

Let's take a look at how to integrate the project into a simple application and see how it impacts your work with views.

Why Use LayoutManager

If you have any of the following application requirements, it's likely that LayoutManager will be useful:

- You have a number of subviews within the application.
- The application layout changes frequently, with views being added and removed, and you need to ensure there are no memory leaks.
- You want to know when each view is about to render or has completed its render cycle.

127

- You want to share events across a view and its subviews.

- Managing nested views is becoming unwieldy in your app.

Configuration

You'll first need to download a version of the library to use in your application. This can be found on the project's GitHub listing as `backbone.layoutmanager.js`. As with all external libraries so far, this should be placed in the `js/external` directory, and it should be included after jQuery, Backbone, and Underscore in `index.html` because it is dependent on all those libraries.

```
<script src="js/external/jquery-1.10.2.js"></script>
<script src="js/external/underscore.js"></script>
<script src="js/external/backbone.js"></script>
<script src="js/external/handlebars.js"></script>
<script src="js/external/backbone.layoutmanager.js"></script>
```

Using LayoutManager

In our example in Chapter 7, we had a number of views on a single page. We didn't look at how subviews could be managed and instead treated each view as an individual case. LayoutManager brings in the concept of an overall layout to the application onto which the subviews are attached.

Let's first look at the creation of the simplest possible layout, which is essentially the same as a Backbone view. To illustrate the concepts, simple HTML will be used throughout this section, but remember that you can use any type of templates and views, even those created in the previous chapter.

The HTML page will need to have two parts added: a `div` that acts as the main container for the layout and a template to use in the rendering of the layout content.

```
<div class="container">
</div>

<script type="template" id="layout">
 <p>A simple layout</p>
</script>
```

As in our larger app example, we'll keep our main JavaScript source in a separate `app.js` file.

```
<script src="js/app/app.js"></script>
```

The creation of the layout requires two attributes to be set: the main element that the layout is contained within (the `div` with the container class) and the template to render the content with (the script with an ID of `layout`).

```
$(function() {
        var layout = new Backbone.Layout({
    el : '.container',

    template: '#layout'
});
layout.render();
});
```

The final call to the layout's render function will complete the building of the HTML page and display it on the browser.

Adding Subviews

The real power of LayoutManager comes with the addition of subviews within the layout. First let's add an element where we expect to place the subview in the layout template's HTML, as shown here:

```
<script type="template" id="layout">
        <p>A simple layout</p>
        <div id="subview"></div>
</script>
```

A template for the subview itself should also be made available.

```
<!-- View template -->
<script type="template" id="view">
  <i>This is the sub view content…</i>
</script>
```

Back in app.js, the view needs to be defined before the layout is used.

```
var SimpleSubview = Backbone.Layout.extend({
    template: "#view"
});
```

To append views to the layout, a views hash is used, in a similar way to the events and routes definitions from previous chapters. This hash identifies the element that should contain the view on the left side, with a reference to the Backbone View object on the right, binding the nested view to the layout.

```
var layout = new Backbone.Layout({
    el : '.container',
    template: '#layout',
    views: {
        '#subview' : new SimpleSubview()
    }
});
layout.render();
```

The result of this code is the rendering of the layout as before along with the subview content.

Advantages of LayoutManager

This approach to structuring your views affords a number of advantages to your application.

Event listeners can be declared at the layout level, in the same way as in a normal view. However, as you have references to all the subviews, these events can be considered global view events.

The layout life cycle can be properly tracked with the addition of a callback for beforeRender and afterRender to the Layout object:

```
var layout = new Backbone.Layout({
    //other layout definition

    beforeRender: function(){
        console.log('About to render');
    },

    afterRender: function(){
        console.log('Render completed');
    }
});
```

Finally, all views that you have already created can be augmented to act as layouts themselves, by declaring the following line at application-level scope (typically at the start of app.js):

```
Backbone.Layout.configure({ manage: true });
```

This can be a great way to alter existing Backbone apps to use the improved view mechanics that are provided by LayoutManager.

Backgrid

Backgrid.js (http://backgridjs.com/) provides a set of user interface elements that are dedicated to displaying data sets in a tabular fashion. The project also provides the ability to sort and edit this data, which comes from your Backbone collections and models.

Why Use Backgrid

If your application is data heavy and you require the ability to display, edit, and sort this data in tables, Backgrid is a great option. It reduces the amount of custom code required to provide editing in tables, which can only be a good thing.

Configuration

As with most Backbone extensions, you will need to ensure you have the trio of Backbone, Underscore. and jQuery available on your page before including backgrid.js. The source can be downloaded from https://github.com/wyuenho/backgrid, under the lib directory.

```
<script src="js/external/backgrid.js"></script>
```

As this library provides a number of features for the presentation layer, you will also need to include backgrid.css on your page.

```
<link rel="stylesheet" href="css/backgrid.css">
```

Using Backgrid

Before you can see the Backgrid in action, you'll need to get a model and collection defined to use in the construction of the grid. Here we'll create a simple collection for use, but in your real-world applications, you'll be able to use any existing collection.

```
//Model and Collection definitions
var Book = Backbone.Model.extend({});
var Library = Backbone.Collection.extend({});

//define contents
var backboneBook = new Book({name: 'Beginning Backbone', author: 'James Sugrue', year:
'2013-12-24'});
var nodeBook = new Book({name: 'Pro Node.js for Developers', author: 'Colin J. Ihrig', year:
'2013-11-01'});
var proJavascriptBook = new Book({name: 'Pro JavaScript Techniques', author: 'John Resig',
year: '2006-02-01'});

//create collection
var myLibrary = new Library();
myLibrary.set([backboneBook, nodeBook, proJavascriptBook]);
```

Once the collection is in place, you can then define which columns to display. Each column object has a name attribute, which maps the column to a particular attribute in the model, as well as a display label and a cell type.

```
var columns = [ {
  name: "name",
  label: "Name",
  cell: "string"
}, {
  name: "author",
  label: "Author",
  cell: "string"
}, {
  name: "year",
  label: "Year",
  editable: false,
  cell: "date",
}];
```

The creation of the grid simply accepts two parameters: the collection and the columns.

```
// Initialize a new Grid instance
var grid = new Backgrid.Grid({
  columns: columns,
  collection: myLibrary
});
```

From there the final step is to render the grid onto the HTML page. The following example assumes that you have an element with the container class available:

```
<div class="container"></div>
```

The grid is then simply appended onto this element.

```
$(".container").append(grid.render().$el);
```

Running the previous example provides a table view of all your data; that is, it can be sorted by clicking the table header. Each element that is marked editable can be edited in place on the table. With a minimal amount of coding, you have a complete data grid available in your application.

Pagination is possible by utilizing other third-party components. Along with the ten built-in cell types, a number of additional extensions are available for more complex grids.

Backbone UI

BackboneUI, hosted at `http://perka.github.io/backbone-ui/`, adds the data binding that other MV* libraries provided. This means that models and collections can be represented as UI components, and this data is passed differently to the parts of the HTML page.

Why Use Backbone UI

If the model and collection objects that are used in your app can be closely bound to simple UI elements such as menus, buttons, and tables, it can be worth looking at Backbone UI to reduce the number of templates and custom HTML required.

Configuration

As well as the usual dependencies for Backbone-related projects, you will need to add the Laconic library, shared at `https://github.com/joestelmach/laconic`.

```
<script src="js/external/laconic.js"></script>
```

The source distribution of Backbone UI contains two files, which you will need to include in your HTML page: `backbone-ui.js` and `backbone-ui.css`.

```
<link rel="stylesheet" href="css/backbone-ui.css">
......
<script src="js/external/backbone-ui.js"></script>
```

With this simple configuration in place, you're ready to use Backbone UI in your own application.

Using Backbone UI

Once you have your models and collections in place, using Backbone UI couldn't be simpler. In a similar fashion to Backgrid, UI components are built-in JavaScript and appended to particular elements on the DOM of your HTML page.

For example, to create a button that displays the name of the book object as its text, a `Button` object is created with the instance of the model that is being used, along with the mapping of the model property to the user interface, using the `content` attribute.

```
var button = new Backbone.UI.Button({
  model: backboneBook,
  content: 'name'
}).render();
```

Once an element with the container class can be found in the HTML page, the following would render a button with the text *Beginning Backbone*:

```
$(".container").append(button.el);
```

The previous example assumes the same model and collection is being used as in the Backgrid code example. Backbone UI contains a number of other UI widgets that can be bound to models, including the following:

- Calendar (requires Moment.js)
- Checkbox
- Date Picker (requires Moment.js)
- Link
- Text Area
- Text Field
- Time Picker

There are also a number of components that can be bound to models with alternatives, a term used to identify a collection that is used to present other values. These widgets are multivalue widgets such as menus and drop-down lists.

For example, you may want to create a menu widget to allow the selection of one of the books from the library. In this case, the model property continues to point to a particular book instance, while the alternatives property is mapped to the myLibrary collection.

```
var menu = new Backbone.UI.Menu({
  model: backboneBook,
  content: 'name',
  alternatives: myLibrary,
  altLabelContent: 'name'
}).render();
```

```
$(".container").append(menu.el);
```

The other multiselect input elements provided in Backbone UI are as follows:

- Menu
- Pulldown
- RadioGroup
- ListView
- TableView

The library also provides a number of widgets, Scroller and TabSet, that are do not bind to a model. To give you complete control over the look and feel of your application, Backbone UI provides an option to use your own custom skin, a collection of CSS, and image files.

Backbone.stickit

One of the major complaints that people have about Backbone is that you need to look after a lot of the boilerplate code between the models and views so that when the model changes, you need to update the view accordingly. While the event handling system that we have seen in use across the previous chapters is useful, Backbone.stickit (http://nytimes.github.io/backbone.stickit/) provides a complete binding.

The library works without any additional markup in your HTML and even promises to make your templates cleaner because there is less need to interpolate variables while the view is rendering.

Why Use Backbone.stickit

If you find the wiring of model attribute changes to refreshes of a view's data to be too cumbersome, Backbone.stickit is one of the best alternatives. It blends into the life cycle of a Backbone view seamlessly, with some simple code. JavaScript developers who have used Knockout or Ember may be more comfortable with the binding support that is provided by Backbone.stickit.

Configuration

Integrating Backbone.stickit into your application is a painless process. Just download the source from http://nytimes.github.io/backbone.stickit/ and include the library in your HTML page.

```
<script src="js/external/backbone.stickit.js"></script>
```

Using Backbone.stickit

First you will need to have a model prepared to visualize in a Backbone view. Once again, we'll use the simple Book model from previous chapters.

```
var Book = Backbone.Model.extend({});
//define contents
var backboneBook = new Book({name: 'Beginning Backbone', author: 'James Sugrue', year: '2013-12-24'});
```

Before we move into creating the view, the other thing that will be required in this sample is a div with a particular class, in this case container, on the HTML page.

```
<div class="container">
</div>
```

When creating a view that utilizes Backbone.stickit bindings, you will need to define a bindings hash in the model. Each binding takes a pair of strings; the first is the CSS selector for the section of the template that will store the variable, and the second is the attribute in the model that is being bound to. In the following example, the binding for the name attribute in the model is to an element with the ID title in the view's HTML.

```
//Define the Library View
MyView = Backbone.View.extend({
```

```
        el : '.container',
In
    bindings: {
        "#title" : 'name',
        '#author' : 'author'
    },
    model : null,
    content: null,
    initialize: function(options){
        this.model = options.model;
    },

    render: function(){
        var self = this;
        self.$el.html('<div id="title"/> <input id="author" type="text">');
        self.stickit();
        return self;
    },
});
```

The second important part to notice is that the render calls a `self.stickit()` function, which enforces the binding.

When the view is created, with the model passed through as a parameter, it displays the values as expected.

```
var view1 = new MyView({model: backboneBook});
view1.render();

backboneBook.set('name', 'Beginning Backbone.js');
```

However, the real power of `Backbone.stickit()` is in how, with any change to the bound model attributes, the view will automatically update. The following piece of code will update the model every six seconds. By inserting this code, notice how the HTML updates automatically.

```
var count = 1;
setInterval(function(e){
        count++;
        backboneBook.set('name', 'New Name ' + count);
}, 6000);
```

When the view is being disposed, you can remove all bindings by calling `view.unstickit()`. There are also a number of callback functions that can be added when defining your bindings that allow more control over whether the view gets updated, as well as functions that can be invoked when the update of the view is complete.

Backbone.Notifications

Backbone.Notifications (https://github.com/fatiherikli/backbone-notifications) is a global notification system for your Backbone app. The library provides the CSS and JavaScript required for notifications dealing with pop-ups (flash), loading, and progress bars.

Why Use Backbone.Notifications

When building an application from scratch, adding in notifications for error and success conditions can be a little cumbersome and is often ignored by developers. However, with such a simple library available that looks after both the logic and presentation of notifications to the user, it's difficult to resist adding Backbone.Notifications.

You can see a complete list of sample notifications at the project web site, hosted at http://fatiherikli.github.io/backbone-notifications/.

Configuration

Once you have downloaded the source from https://github.com/fatiherikli/backbone-notifications, simply include the CSS and JavaScript files from the src directory.

```
<link rel="stylesheet" href="css/backbone-ui.css">
.....
<script src="js/external/backbone-ui.js"></script>
```

The CSS is an important inclusion here because it deals with the presentation of the notifications on the screen. Of course, you can change these styles to fit in with your application easily.

Using Backbone.Notifications

Backbone.Notifications will work with any Backbone objects because they already have the Events functionality included. However, if you want to use the library on non-Backbone objects, you can extend the object with Backbone.Events, as described in the following code snippet:

```
var notifications  {};
_.extend(notifications, Backbone.Events);
```

To keep things clear, the example we'll implement here will use one of the model objects that we have already created.

```
var Book = Backbone.Model.extend({});
var backboneBook = new Book({name: 'Beginning Backbone', author: 'James Sugrue', year: '2013-12-24'});
```

Before you can trigger any notifications, you will need to create a new Notifier object and append that to an element in the HTML page, usually the body. When creating the Notifier, you will need to specify which object will trigger the notification, in this case, backboneBook.

```
new Notifier({
        model: backboneBook
    }).render().$el.appendTo("body");
```

Any time you want to trigger an event, such as a save complete or error, you can simply cause a notification to be displayed by calling the trigger function on the object.

```
backboneBook.trigger("success", "Book saved");
```

The first parameter of this function is the type of notification to use, such as `start:loader`, `end:loader`, `start:progress`, `end:progress`, `update:progress`, `error`, `success`, or `flash`.

At the least, this library provides a consistent and simple way to build notifications into your Backbone application.

Models and Collection Extensions

So far, we've considered extensions available specifically for display and input purposes, but there are also many options available for extending the functionality of models and collections.

Backbone.trackit

Backbone.trackit (`https://github.com/NYTimes/backbone.trackit`) is another project from the *New York Times* that manages changes in Backbone models, providing the ability to undo previous changes and trigger events when there are unsaved changes.

Why Use Backbone.trackit

As you've already seen in Chapter 3, Backbone keeps a record of only the current and previous sets of values for the attributes. While useful, this functionality doesn't go far enough for apps with more complex user interactions, where you want to record multiple changes. This is where Backbone.trackit comes in.

It's worth noting that this does not provide a complete undo/redo stack. For such an extension, check out Backbone.memento.

Configuration

To include Backbone.trackit in your application, simply download `backbone.trackit.js` from the `dist` folder on `https://github.com/NYTimes/backbone.trackit`, and include the script in your HTML page.

```
<script src="js/external/backbone.trackit.js"></script>
```

Using Backbone.trackit

Once again, the simple Book model will be used to illustrate Backbone.trackit.

```
var Book = Backbone.Model.extend({
    urlRoot: 'http://localhost:8080/books/',
});
//define contents
var backboneBook = new Book({name: 'Beginning Backbone', author: 'James Sugrue', year: '2013-12-24'});
```

Rather than being a cross-application configuration, Backbone.trackit can be applied to individual model objects, using the `startTracking` function.

```
backboneBook.startTracking();
```

Once tracking has started, the unsavedAttributes function will return the attributes in the model that have not yet been saved. The log statements in the following piece of code will continue to accrue the set of attributes that have been changed:

```
backboneBook.set('name', 'Beginning Backbone.js');
console.log(backboneBook.unsavedAttributes());

backboneBook.set('author', 'J Sugrue');
console.log(backboneBook.unsavedAttributes());
```

However, once a successful save has occurred, the call to unsavedAttributes() will return false. If you want to reset the attributes to avoid saving the changes, call the resetAttributes() function.

```
console.log('Author is ' + backboneBook.get('author'));
backboneBook.resetAttributes();
console.log('Author is ' + backboneBook.get('author'));
```

The previous code performs a complete reset of the attribute changes made since tracking started or the last successful save was made.

Backbone.memento

Derick Bailey's Backbone.memento extension (https://github.com/derickbailey/backbone.memento) provides a stack to push and pop changes to Backbone models and collections. This provides a more complete undo/redo stack for your Backbone apps.

Why Use Backbone.memento

While Backbone.trackit can be useful for keeping track of model changes, more complex web apps, such as document editing systems, may require the ability to perform multiple undo or redo operations. This is exactly what Backbone. memento can provide.

Configuration

Simply download backbone.memento.js from the GitHub project page, https://github.com/derickbailey/ backbone.memento, and include the script in your own HTML page.

```
<script src="js/external/backbone.memento.js"></script>
```

Using Backbone.memento

For each model or collection that you want to add undo/redo support to, you need to extend the initialize method with two extra lines to add Backbone.memento to the object.

```
var Book = Backbone.Model.extend({
    urlRoot: 'http://localhost:8080/books/',
    initialize: function(){
        var memento = new Backbone.memento(this);
        _.extend(this, memento);
    }

});
```

While the previous code deals with models, the same syntax can be applied to a collection. You can also have the Backbone.memento plug-in ignore changes made to particular attributes and not include them in the stack using an ignore array.

Every time you want to save the state of the model to the stack, a store function can be called for the model; to reset to a previous state, the restore function can be used. The following code example illustrates this flow:

```
//define contents
var backboneBook = new Book({name: 'Beginning Backbone', author: 'James Sugrue', year: '2013-12-24'});

console.log('Before set: ' + backboneBook.get('name'));
backboneBook.set('name', 'Beginning Backbone.js');
backboneBook.store();
console.log('After store: ' + backboneBook.get('name'));

backboneBook.set('name', 'Beginning Backbone')
console.log('After set: ' + backboneBook.get('name'));
backboneBook.restore();
console.log('After restore: ' + backboneBook.get('name'));
```

The result of the execution will be as follows:

```
Before set: Beginning Backbone
After store: Beginning Backbone.js
After set: Beginning Backbone
After restore: Beginning Backbone.js
```

As you can see, even after changing the name of the book after the first call to store, the restore call reverts the change.

Backbone.localStorage

Everything that we've covered so far has assumed that the model/collection data gets stored on a server, over a REST interface. Backbone.localStorage (https://github.com/jeromegn/Backbone.localStorage) overrides Backbone. Sync to allow you to use HTML5 local storage as the data store.

Why Use Backbone.localStorage

Not every application will need to save all data to a server. You may want some collections to save to a local database on the client machine to store items such as preferences. With Backbone.localStorage you can target specific collections to use this local storage, while allowing other collections to use the standard sync method of HTTP.

Configuration

Including Backbone.localStorage in your application is as simple as downloading the latest version of backbone. localStorage.js from the GitHub repository, https://github.com/jeromegn/Backbone.localStorage, and including the JavaScript in your HTML page.

```
<script src="js/external/backbone.localStoage.js"></script>
```

Using Backbone.localStorage

Backbone.localStorage is an unintrusive plug-in that just requires you to create collections that target HTML5 local storage instead of remote server storage. To do this, the definition of your collection will need a new localStorage parameter.

```
localStorage : new Backbone.LocalStorage("libraryapp:MyLibrary"),
```

The string parameter used when creating the new LocalStorage instance is the unique identifier for your application contents.

```
var Book = Backbone.Model.extend({});
var Library = Backbone.Collection.extend({
    model: Book,
    localStorage : new Backbone.LocalStorage("MyLibrary"),
});

//define contents
var backboneBook = new Book({name: 'Beginning Backbone', author: 'James Sugrue',
year: '2013-12-24'});
var nodeBook = new Book({name: 'Pro Node.js for Developers', author: 'Colin J. Ihrig',
year: '2013-11-01'});
var proJavascriptBook = new Book({name: 'Pro JavaScript Techniques', author: 'John Resig',
year: '2006-02-01'});
//create collection
var myLibrary = new Library();
```

Note that, at the time of writing, for your model items to be correctly stored in local storage, you need to use the create function of the collection rather than the set function.

```
myLibrary.create(backboneBook);
myLibrary.create(nodeBook);
```

Now when you inspect the local storage of your application through Chrome Developer Tools, on the Resources tab, you should find the details of the two books you have added to the collection, as in Figure 7-1.

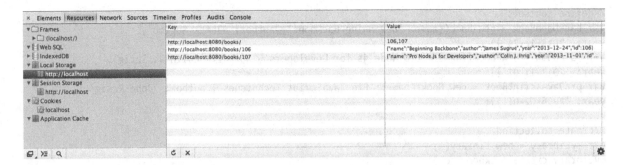

Figure 7-1. *The local storage of the application following execution of the previous example*

Backbone.dualStorage

Backbone.dualStorage (`https://github.com/nilbus/Backbone.dualStorage`) goes a step further than Backbone. localStorage, providing a local caching mechanism for your data so that if your app goes offline, data continues to be stored and can be synced with the server when connectivity is restored.

Why Use Backbone.dualStorage

This plug-in is particularly useful for mobile apps built on Backbone, because connectivity can be an issue. If you are finding that data is being lost as a result of dropped connections or server downtime, this can be a relatively painless way of dealing with the problem. Also, this allows users to have a complete application experience at all times. For users roaming between countries, this can be an essential mobile feature.

Configuration

To include Backbone.dualStorage in your application, simply download the library from `https://github.com/nilbus/Backbone.dualStorage` and include it in your HTML page.

```
<script src="js/external/backbone.dualstorage.js"></script>
```

Using Backbone.dualStorage

Backbone.dualStorage is one of the easiest of all the Backbone plug-ins to use in your project because its default behavior requires no code changes.

```
//Model and Collection definitions
var Book = Backbone.Model.extend({});
var Library = Backbone.Collection.extend({
    model: Book,
    url: 'http://localhost:8080/books/',
});
```

```
//define contents
var backboneBook = new Book({name: 'Beginning Backbone', author: 'James Sugrue',
year: '2013-12-24'});
var nodeBook = new Book({name: 'Pro Node.js for Developers', author: 'Colin J. Ihrig',
year: '2013-11-01'});
var proJavascriptBook = new Book({name: 'Pro JavaScript Techniques', author: 'John Resig',
year: '2006-02-01'});

//create collection
var myLibrary = new Library();
myLibrary.create(backboneBook);
myLibrary.create(nodeBook);
```

Running the previous code results in a cached copy appearing in the local storage for your app. Once again, check Chrome Developer Tools for proof of this, as in Figure 7-2.

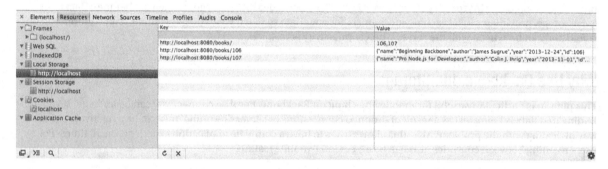

Figure 7-2. *Chrome Developer Tools showing the locally cached items*

If you detect that the client and server are out of sync, you can call a special synchronization function on the collection to send all local changes to the server.

```
myLibrary.syncDirtyAndDestroyed();
```

Note that you will need to write your own code to detect the loss and reestablishment of connections.

If you require some collections to act differently, you can set them to be never cached by using the remote: true parameter on creation. You can also set the collection to only save changes locally by using the local: true parameter.

Backbone.ViewModel

Backbone.ViewModel, available from http://github.com/tommyh/backbone-view-model, allows you to create a model that can deal with more complex views. If you had your model change attributes just for the view, these attributes could be synced to the server. So, it makes sense to have a separation of your view model to the persistent model.

Why Use Backbone.ViewModel

When the views in your application require a lot of conversion from what is stored in the real persistence model before it is displayed, a proper separation of concerns may be necessary.

Configuration

Backbone.ViewModel is just a single JavaScript file that contains a different type of model definition. This can be downloaded from https://github.com/tommyh/backbone-view-model and just needs to be included in your HTML page.

```
<script src="js/external/view-model.js"></script>
```

Using Backbone.ViewModel

Backbone.ViewModel will extend a normal model that you have created, allowing you to specify a set of computed attributes that will be used for the view. First let's create a simple model that will be the basis for the view.

```
var Book = Backbone.Model.extend({});
var backboneBook = new Book({name: 'Beginning Backbone', author: 'James Sugrue', year: '2013-12-24'});
```

The ViewModel will be based on this model, which gets stored as an attribute in the ViewModel object as source_model. When creating a ViewModel object, the computed_attributes hash allows you to create functions that will transform the representation of the properties in the source_model attribute.

```
var BookViewModel = Backbone.ViewModel.extend({
    'truncated_book_title' : function(){
      return this.get('source_model').get('name').substring(0, 10) + '...';
    },
    'author' : function(){
        return this.get('source_model').get('author');}
    }
});
```

While this is useful for the truncation of the book title, you will also need to expose variables from the original model that you need displayed in the view.

Notice in the render function of the view, you are now dealing with the attributes that appear in the ViewModel.

```
//Define the Library View
MyView = Backbone.View.extend({

 el : '.container',

 model : null,
 content: null,

 initialize: function(options){
   this.model = options.model;
 },

 render: function(){
   var self = this;
   self.$el.html('Author is  ' + this.model.get('author') + ' Title is ' +
this.model.get('truncated_book_title'));

   return self;
   },
});
```

143

When creating the instance of the view, the ViewModel is passed through as the model rather than backboneBook, which itself is a parameter to the ViewModel.

```
var backboneBookViewModel = new BookViewModel({source_model: backboneBook});

var view1 = new MyView({model: backboneBookViewModel});
view1.render();
```

While this can make your code a little more complex, some applications may want to enforce the separation of persistence and view models in such a way. I prefer to use Handlebars helpers to modify the attributes at render time.

Backbone-Validator

A number of extensions are available to help you validate your models beyond the built-in Backbone validate() function. One of these is Backbone-Validator (https://github.com/fantactuka/backbone-validator), which provides model validation as well as allowing events to be bound to views to display validation errors if required.

Why Use Backbone-Validator

When applications need a lot of validation and the view needs to display any validation errors, this plug-in removes a large amount of custom code that would be required when using standard Backbone JavaScript code. Form-based applications are the most obvious beneficiaries of this plug-in.

Configuration

Backbone-Validator just needs to be downloaded from https://github.com/fantactuka/backbone-validator and included in your HTML page.

```
<script src="js/external/backbon-validator.js"></script>
```

Using Backbone-Validator

Any model can be extended to use Backbone-Validator -by passing through a validation hash, which includes the attribute name to validate along with a number of validation settings, such as whether it can be blank, what format it should use, and what message to display when the validation fails.

The following example adds this validation to the Book model:

```
//Model and Collection definitions
var Book = Backbone.Model.extend({
 validation:
 {
   name: {
     blank: false,
     message: 'Every book needs a name'
   },

 }
});
```

This can be easily tested by creating a Book object without setting the name attribute.

```
var backboneBook = new Book();
console.log('Is this valid? ' + backboneBook.isValid());
```

The result of the previous log statement would return `false`. Additionally, if you force a `set` function to use validation, you will force the `validationError` array of the object to be populated.

```
backboneBook.set({name: ''}, {validate: true});
console.log(backboneBook.validationError);
```

Most importantly, you can have your view bind `callbacks` that deal with invalid fields quite easily, by adding a call to `bindValidation` in the `initialize` function for the view.

```
//Define the Library View
MyView = Backbone.View.extend({

 el : '.container',

 model : null,
 content: null,

 initialize: function(options){
   this.model = options.model;
   this.bindValidation();
 },

 onInvalidField: function(attrName, attrValue, errors, model){
   alert(attrName + ' has an invalid value');
 },

 render: function(){
   var self = this;
   self.$el.html('Author is  ' + this.model.get('author') + ' Book title is  '  this.model.
get('name'));
   return self;
   },
});

var view1 = new MyView({model: backboneBook});
view1.render();
```

The previous code will result in an alert displaying when an invalid field is used in the model passed to the view. The extension includes a number of validators, covering formats, lengths, and whether a value is required.

Query Engine

While it is easy to find variables in small collections, for more complex real-world applications you may need a little more power in searching and filtering for larger collections. Query Engine (`https://github.com/bevry/query-engine`) provides these capabilities out of the box, even supporting NoSQL queries, and will run on a node.js server as well as your browser.

Why Use Query Engine

If you are dealing with large collections and need to provide a lot of search, filter, and query functionality in your application, Query Engine will make your code easier to follow and will probably perform better than a custom-made solution. It would make sense to use this library if you are building an application that provides searching of databases and you don't want to defer all filtering to the server side.

Configuration

To include QueryEngine in your project, you just need to download the `query-engine.js` file from `https://github.com/bevry/query-engine/blob/master/out/lib/query-engine.js` and include it in your HTML page.

```
<script src="js/external/query-engine.js"></script>
```

Using QueryEngine

QueryEngine provides two states for the custom `QueryCollection` class: standard and live. Live collections will listen out for collection events so that any change made in the collection causes any related query to be rerun.

Rather than creating a standard `Backbone.Collection`, you will need to create a `QueryCollection`, using `queryEngine.QueryCollection.extend`, as in the following code:

```
//Model and Collection definitions
var Book = Backbone.Model.extend({
});
var Library = queryEngine.QueryCollection.extend({
 model: Book,
});
```

With this setup, any of the `QueryCollection` functions are now available. For example, the following piece of code sets up the collection to contain four books:

```
//define contents
var backboneBook = new Book({name: 'Beginning Backbone', author: 'James Sugrue', year: '2013-12-24'});
var nodeBook = new Book({name: 'Pro Node.js for Developers', author: 'Colin J. Ihrig',
year: '2013-11-01'});
var proJavascriptBook = new Book({name: 'Pro JavaScript Techniques', author: 'John Resig',
year: '2006-02-01'});
var backboneBook2 = new Book({name: 'Backbone: The Sequel', author: 'James Sugrue', year: '2014-12-01'});

//create collection
var myLibrary = new Library();
myLibrary.set([backboneBook, nodeBook, proJavascriptBook, backboneBook2]);
```

Now to find all books with a particular author, the `findAll` function can be used, with the appropriate filter attributes:

```
var results = myLibrary.findAll({author: 'James Sugrue'});
console.log('Returned ' + results.length + ' results');
```

In the results variable, there will be two models included that correlate to the books with the author James Sugrue.

ModelAttrs

ModelAttrs (https://github.com/rhysbrettbowen/Backbone.ModelAttrs) is a simple Backbone plug-in that allows you to retrieve and set attributes with a more concise, jQuery-like format.

Why Use ModelAttrs

If you find the model.set('attribute name', 'attribute value') type of syntax too verbose and would rather use a more concise format, ModelAttrs can be a simple alteration to your project code.

Configuration

ModelAttrs is a really small JavaScript file that can be downloaded from https://github.com/rhysbrettbowen/ Backbone.ModelAttrs and included in your HTML page.

```
<script src="js/external/attrs.js"></script>
```

Using ModelAttrs

To use ModelAttrs, you will need to convert your model object to a ModelAttrs object using the toAttrs function that is provided with the library.

```
toAttrs(<model>)
```

The following code shows how to get a variable from an existing Backbone model using the library:

```
//Model definition
var Book = Backbone.Model.extend({
});

//define contents
var backboneBook = new Book({name: 'Beginning Backbone', author: 'James Sugrue', year: '2013-12-24'});

var backboneAttrs = toAttrs(backboneBook);

console.log(backboneAttrs.name());
```

Now you are able to get the name of the book by calling the .name() function rather than using backboneBook.get('name').

Setting a variable is just as simple, and most importantly, setting the variable will be reflected in the original model object, as in the following code:

```
backboneAttrs.name('Beginning Backbone.js');
console.log(backboneAttrs.name());
console.log(backboneBook.get('name'));
```

Developer Tools and Utilities

The Backbone ecosystem isn't limited just to extensions to the library. With the power of the developer tools available in Chrome and Firefox, you may think that there is no need for anything more. However, there is an add-on available for Firefox named Backbone Eye (http://dhruvaray.github.io/spa-eye/) that helps developers understand the behavior of a Backbone application without the need to debug JavaScript.

The add-on extends Firebug, so once you have both the Firebug and Backbone Eye add-ons installed, you will see a new tab in your Firebug browser, as in Figure 7-3.

Figure 7-3. *Backbone Eye add-on in action*

Figure 7-3 is the result of inspecting the example used for the LayoutManager plug-in using Eye. Models, collections, and views are all enumerated within the tool. However, the most important view is the Zombies aspect, which gives a listing of objects that are still in use, even after being removed from the application using Backbone's remove or destroy calls.

The Interaction Tools view draws sequence diagrams illustrating the interaction flows between the views, models, and applications in your project.

Backbone Eye can be a really useful tool when new developers join a project and need to get an understanding of the code base. It can also be a great way of zeroing in on memory leaks.

Quick Reference

Table 7-1 describes all the projects listed in this chapter. All projects are licensed under the MIT license.

Table 7-1. *Quick Reference of Projects Mentioned in This Chapter*

Project	Description
LayoutManager	Provides management of views and subviews within Backbone apps.
Backgrid	Provides data grid user interface elements, such as tables.
BackboneUI	Offers a number of widgets that provide full data binding between the widget and model.
Backbone.stickit	Dynamically updates Backbone views when a model changes without any additional code.
Backbone.Notifications	Provides global notifications on the user interface with minimal code.
Backbone.trackit	Allows multiple changes in model attributes to be tracked.
Backbone.memento	Provides full undo/redo stack for changes in the model during the application life cycle.
Backbone.localStorage	Provides the option to store collection data in local HTML5 storage instead of on the server.
Backbone.dualStorage	Provides an adapter that caches changes in local storage, allowing for offline use of a Backbone app.
Backbone.ViewModel	Creates a separation between the persisted model and that used for the view.
Backbone.Validator	Enhanced validation for models, including view bindings for any validation errors.
QueryEngine	Powerful search and filtering functions for Backbone collections.
ModelAttrs	More concise setting and getting of attribute values from Backbone models.

Summary

In this chapter, we looked at a number of projects that can help to strengthen your Backbone applications. Some great extensions exist for both the view and model layers, allowing Backbone to achieve additional capabilities that some feel are missing in the basic Backbone offering.

This chapter has only scratched the surface of what is available throughout the Backbone community. There are often multiple projects that will help solve similar problems, so if a library described here doesn't quite fit your requirements, you should take a look at some alternatives. For a comprehensive listing of community projects, check out Jeremy Ashkenas' listing at `https://github.com/jashkenas/backbone/wiki/Extensions,-Plugins,-Resources`.

■ ■ ■

Testing Your Backbone.js Application

Testing is one of the most essential development activities that you will undertake in large-scale JavaScript applications. Within the vast JavaScript ecosystem, there are a number of options for testing applications, which means there is no longer any excuse for not testing your JavaScript code. This chapter will take a look at the leading testing frameworks available and how creating testable code will not only improve the stability of your application but lead to a cleaner architecture. This chapter also examines some of the key reasons to apply Test-Driven Development to your JavaScript code.

The Advantages of Test-Driven Development

Introduced with a number of concepts from Extreme Programming, Test-Driven Development (TDD) describes a process where the developer is required to write tests while developing application code. Ideally, the test is written first so that it initially fails. Then the code is written so that the next time the test is run, it passes. Then the code is refactored if any more tests are failing. The whole process is an iterative one, as described in Figure 8-1.

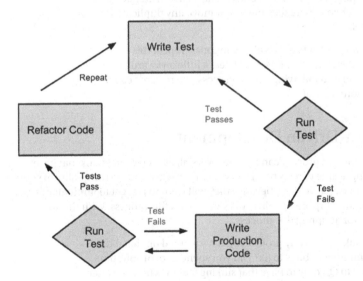

Figure 8-1. *The iterative nature of Test-Driven Development*

When adhering to Test-Driven Development in the strictest way possible, you will want to follow the steps in this order:

1. *Write test*: Before you write any new code, you are expected to write a test that fails first. Of course, it is impossible that the test could pass because the feature that is being implemented does not exist yet. The benefit of this is that it forces you to consider how the new code should act in certain conditions. You will need to have a good understanding of the requirements before you embark on this process.

2. *Run test expecting failure*: The next step is to execute your newly written test case, expecting the result to be a failure. This is an important step because it checks that the test is correctly included in your test suite, which is the collection of all test cases for the application. It also ensures that the test will not pass without the code for the feature being in place. With the failing test in place, you can be reasonably confident that you are testing for the correct behavior.

3. *Write production code*: With the failing test case in place, you can move onto your development work. The focus of this coding now shifts from coding in general to get the feature in place to specifically getting the failing test case to pass. This makes the coding process much more deliberate and scientific.

   It will be tempting to add some code that covers the requirements but does not apply to this test case. This should be avoided, and instead you should take the opportunity to iterate through this process again, starting with a failing test case for such functionality.

4. *Run test suite*: You are now ready to rerun your test suite, which is expected to pass at this point. If this fails, you may need to rework some of your production code. And once it passes, you can move on to the refactor step.

5. *Refactor code*: Refactoring describes the process of refining your code so that it is cleaner and of higher quality in general. It is quite likely that the code you have just written to get the test passing isn't ideal. A common theme in refactoring is to remove any duplicated code into shared functions or utility classes.

6. *Repeat*: As you move on to the next requirements, you will continuously repeat this process. If you're new to Test-Driven Development, this will all feel a little awkward and slow. But if you can afford to invest time into following such a process, the rewards can be great, and the process starts to feel more natural.

Putting Forward the Case for Test-Driven Development

As you can imagine, enforcing such a strict development process can be controversial, especially in teams that have established little or no testing. It's clear that having a suite of tests that grows over time will enhance the quality of your project, but it can seem like a long road to developers, particularly because they will want to just get to implementing features. The project manager might find that the initial speed of delivery is slower with this process. With this in mind, the following list highlights the main cases for adopting this process:

- *You will save time in the long run*: Think back to any project you have worked on that didn't have unit tests. Did you have a high number of bugs to fix? Did you spend a lot of your time debugging? Did you deliver your code to QA only to have that sinking feeling when bug after bug was logged against the code? Did you wish you had written more tests and understood the goal of your development better before delivering?

If some or all of these issues apply to you, don't worry—you're not alone. In fact, the array of testing frameworks in existence is testament to this. The effort in building up such libraries would have been unnecessary if every developer didn't have these issues.

There is a cost to writing your tests up front. There will be an infrastructure to get together first, where you'll need to choose a testing framework. You will also need to set up some kind of continuous integration system, which we will discuss in a later chapter. But this cost is a fraction of the penalty you need to pay for untested code.

Writing unit tests along with your production code will lead to fewer bugs coming back from QA. Even when bugs do get logged against your build, you will start to get into a process of writing a test to replicate the bug first, before following the TDD process to get the bug cleared. This will reduce the chance of any regression in functionality because your automated test suite will always check for the presence of the issue in question.

Taking the Test-Driven Development approach will result in a calmer end to the project when you are about to deliver to a customer. It will avoid those late-night bug-fixing marathons that can be all too common in software development projects, making you feel better in the long run. Instead of wasting time addressing bugs that should never have happened, you'll free up your time to continually work on the development of new features. And what developer wouldn't want that?

- *Executing test cases will be fast*: There can be a perception that if you have a large code base, and, hence, a large number of unit tests, the execution of the test suite will take a long time. There might have been a time when that was true, but in this day and age, there are a number of test frameworks that allow for lightning-fast test execution, even when the UI in the browser is being testing. You'll see later in this chapter how PhantomJS has revolutionized the speed of UI tests for web applications.

  Some legacy systems may have issues with the scale and volume of data in the back end. The interaction with this data may take time, particularly with REST calls that return large amounts of data. However, you have the option to create a "mock server" for your unit tests, which will return data faster in a predictable and repeated fashion. By replacing any real-world systems that execute slowly with these mock versions, you can speed up your unit tests almost effortlessly.

- *Code will be better understood*: When joining a project, getting your head around the code can take a while, especially where there is little or no documentation. Test cases can act as valuable documentation around existing code. The tests show how to invoke objects, what the code is expected to do, and how it interacts with the server and other classes. Writing tests can actually decrease the amount of time required for new developers to get up to speed with your project.

  Additionally, following the TDD approach ensures that the requirements are well understood and tested before handing the build to the QA team. Although you may not understand the requirements during your first few iterations of Test-Driven Development, you will undoubtedly get better at it. As you release better-quality code with fewer bugs, you will increase your reputation as a mature developer with your QA department and management team.

- *The resulting code will be well structured*: Without needing to run your code in isolation, within a test harness, you have free reign over how to structure your code. It can be as tightly coupled as you want, with model code residing inside your view classes and other such antipatterns. You'll find that you are forced to adhere to the MV* paradigm, with models, views, and logic neatly separated to enable easier testing.

- *The frameworks exist; you should use them*: A common argument against testing JavaScript code is that it's too difficult. Sure, JavaScript still feels like a "new" language, and without the type-safety that exists in languages such as Java and C#, it may seem chaotic. Throughout this book we have seen how Backbone enforces a new level of discipline in your code structure: controlled, object-oriented JavaScript is possible. With all the effort that has been put into building the thriving JavaScript ecosystem, a number of testing frameworks have risen to ensure the quality is as high as you would expect.

  As a Backbone user, you would be pretty disappointed if something didn't work as advertised. Just as the Backbone development team has included a high number of tests (check `https://github.com/jashkenas/backbone/tree/master/test` if you don't believe me!), you should take the same pride in your own code delivery. In this chapter, you'll see how easy it is to incorporate these testing frameworks into your project. And when something this easy gives you so much respect, it's difficult to resist.

Dealing with Legacy Codebases

Test-Driven Development always sounds like a great idea in greenfield projects where no production code is in place. However, in reality, you will be dealing with existing code that will probably have no existing tests. Bringing in the discipline of unit testing JavaScript code at this point in a project life cycle can be challenging.

The widely accepted rule of thumb to deal with this situation is to add tests incrementally, rather than just diving head first into months of arduous unit testing with little return to show for the investment. Instead, it's worth identifying some key areas where adding tests can be of benefit.

- Any new features that are being added to the project can benefit.

- If areas of code are being refactored, it is worth writing tests first to ensure the code acts that same before and after the refactor.

- Every application has trouble spots where most bugs arise from. It is worth identifying these, in sets of a manageable number (such as three), and adding comprehensive tests to each area.

- Apply the Boy Scout rule, as listed in Robert Martins' *Clean Code* book, where code is "left in a better state than how you found it." If you are adding some code to a JavaScript file, take the time to add an additional test to increase the test coverage.

Test Automation

Before moving onto the various testing frameworks that are available in the JavaScript world, it's worth noting that in an ideal world, all your test cases would be run in an automated fashion anytime that the code base changes. This ensures that test failures are caught as soon as possible and removes the responsibility for ensuring the tests are always run from the developer. The next chapter will cover this form of continuous integration, along with other build processes for JavaScript using the Grunt task runner. While the main focus of this chapter will be on writing tests with QUnit, we will also take a look at Jasmine and Selenium.

Testing with QUnit

QUnit (`www.qunitjs.com`) can be considered the default test framework of choice for JavaScript developers. Originally developed by Jörn Zaefferer as part of jQuery, in order to test the framework, it became a stand-alone project in 2009 and is now used across the most popular JavaScript libraries, not least of which is Backbone. This section will take a look at how you can get started using QUnit, with a focus on testing the code written in Chapter 6.

Getting Started with QUnit

Incorporating QUnit into your project is amazingly simple. First include both the JS and CSS files from http://qunitjs.com, as in Figure 8-2.

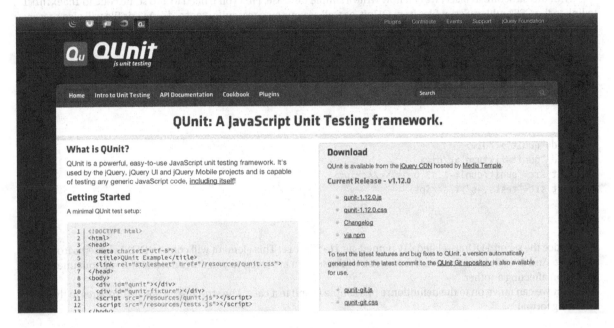

Figure 8-2. *QUnitjs.com*

The structure of your code base is essential: you won't want your production and test code to be mixed up, so it is wise to create a separate test folder. Because the aim of this chapter is to test the code written in Chapter 6, we can simply make a copy of this folder and place a folder named `test` adjacent to the app directory. As we will be using other test libraries, the JavaScript and CSS files for QUnit should be placed in a `qunit` directory. Finally, we'll include an `index.html` file to act as the test driver and a `tests.js` file to contain our test suite. The directory structure should now look like Figure 8-3.

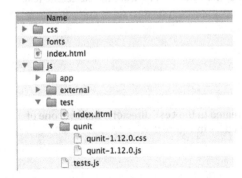

Figure 8-3. *Directory structure for QUnit tests*

■ Note   You can also include the files from the jQuery content delivery network (CDN) at `http://code.jquery.com/`.

With this structure in place, we can now write a simple test case. First you'll need to add some code to index.html to link to the CSS and JavaScript files from QUnit, as well as your own test suite, tests.js. As this file will also present the results of the test execution, you should include a div with the ID qunit to which the results will be appended.

```
<html>
<head>
 <title>Chapter 8: QUnit</title>
 <link rel="stylesheet" href="qunit/qunit-1.12.0.css">
</head>
<body>
 <div id="qunit"></div>
 <div id="qunit-fixture"></div>
 <script src="qunit/qunit-1.12.0.js"></script>
 <script src="tests.js"></script>
</body>
</html>
```

Notice the second QUnit-related div named qunit-fixture. This element will contain DOM elements from each test. And as each test executes, the contents of the section are reset, so you don't need to worry about one test's execution affecting another.

Now we can move on to the definitionre of a simple QUnit test case. The structure of any test adheres to the following format:

```
test( "testname", function() {
    //assertions
});
```

The first argument that is passed through is the name of the test, which should be as descriptive as possible. The second parameter is the function that runs the actual code for the test. This will contain one or more assertions to check for certain behavior.

The following test case contains two assertions, one of which will fail. The ok() assertion checks whether the first argument is true, and if it is, the test will pass. Both assertions are checking similar functionality by checking the two equality operators. However, because the second assertion checks that the value and type are the same, the test will fail.

```
test( "Simple Equality Tests", function() {
 ok( 1 == "1", 'Passed simple equals check');
 ok( 1=== "1", 'Passed really equals check')
});
```

Executing this test case is achieved by opening the index.html file created in the test directory. Because one of the tests has failed, the results will report that one test passed and one failed, as in Figure 8-4.

Figure 8-4. *QUnit test results*

To get the test to pass, simply change the second statement so that it returns true.

```
ok( 1 !== "1", 'Passed really equals check');
```

Table 8-1 lists all the assertions available in QUnit.

Table 8-1. *QUnit Assertions*

Assertion	Purpose
deepEqual(actual, expected, message)	Performs a deep recursive comparison assertion working on all primitive types, arrays, objects, regular expressions, dates, and functions
equal(actual, expected, message)	Performs a nonstrict comparison
notDeepEqual(actual, expected, message)	The inverse of deepEqual(), running a deep recursive comparison and returning a success if the objects are not equal
notEqual(actual, expected, message)	The inverse of equal(), running a nonstrict comparison return success if the objects are unequal
notStrictEqual(actual, expected, message)	The inverse of strictEqual, using value and type comparisons with the !== conditional
ok(condition, message)	Performs a boolean assertion, returning true if the first parameter returns true
strictEqual(actual, expected, message)	Performs a strict value and type assertion, similar to === in normal JavaScript conditions
throws()	Asserts that a callback throws an exception when run
expect(number)	Defines how many assertions to expect during the course of this text execution

Breaking Tests into Modules

It can be useful to organize your test suite into modules of tests. QUnit allows for this with the module() function, which takes a String parameter to denote the module name. This should be placed before each set of test declarations that are part of the module, as shown in the following code snippet:

```
module('Equality Tests');

test( "Simple Equality Tests", function() {
 ok( 1 == '1', 'Passed simple equals check');
 ok( 1 !== '1', 'Passed really equals check')
 notEqual(1, '2', 'Not Equal');
});

test('More simple tests', function(){
 expect(2);
 equal(true, true, 'Simple true == true test');
 strictEqual(true, true, 'Simple true === true test');
});

module('Another module of tests');

test('Name tests', function(){
 var name = 'James';
 equal(name, 'James', 'Name check test complete');
});
```

When the previous test suite is run, the output should match that in Figure 8-5. Note how each set of tests is prefixed with the module that it is part of. There is also a useful drop-down box to select results from only one of the modules presented on the top-right side.

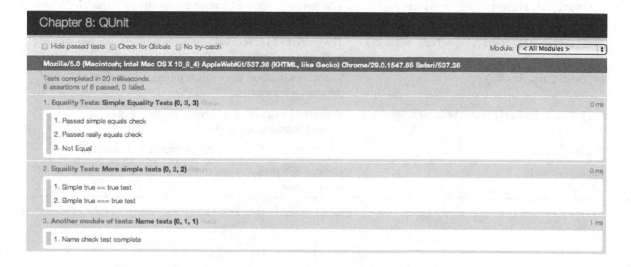

Figure 8-5. *QUnit test results with modules*

Testing Asynchronous Functions

You will undoubtedly come across asynchronous functions that you need to test within your code base. QUnit provides a really useful way of expressing that a test run has such a function under test with the asyncTest() function.

```
module('Asynchronous Tests');

asyncTest('asyncTest', function() {
  expect(1);
  var actual = true;
  setTimeout(function() {
    ok(actual, 'Simple test to prove async');
    start();
  }, 1000);
});
```

The use of the call to start() is essential in running this test case because it restarts the test runner, which would have been waiting for the timeout of one second to pass before executing the test. Without this, the test would just have appeared to stall. Note that the inclusion of asynchronous tests will increase the execution time of your test suite.

QUnit Callbacks

QUnit has a number of callbacks available so that you can execute code at the beginning of the test suite, before a module has been run, or after a test case completes. This can be useful if you need to do any setup or teardown of data at specific points in the test suite or if you just want to capture the test results using your own custom build monitoring and reporting tools.

Table 8-2 lists the callbacks available for QUnit test suites, with sample code snippets for each.

Table 8-2. Listing of QUnit Callbacks

Callback Purpose	Code Snippet
Runs at the beginning of a QUnit test suite run	`QUnit.begin = function(){};`
Runs at the end of the QUnit test suite, providing the total number of assertions and the number of failures as parameters	`QUnit.done = function(failures, total){` `};`
Runs after each assertion, providing the result of the test case (either log or error) along with the message	`QUnit.log = function(results, message){` `};`
Runs before each test, with the name of the test included as a parameter	`QUnit.testStart = function(name){` `};`
Runs after each test, with the test name, number of assertions, and number of failures provided as parameters	`QUnit.testDone = function(name, failures, total){` `};`
Runs before each module, providing the module name as a parameter	`QUnit.moduleStart = function(name){` `};`
Runs after each module, providing the name of the module, a count of the failed assertions, and the total number of assertions as parameters	`QUnit.moduleDone = function(name, failures, total){` `};`

Setting Up and Clearing Down During Test Execution

A common requirement in unit test cases is to have two phases that happen between the tests: a setup, where certain data can be added or variables can be set up, and a teardown, where the cleanup after test execution occurs, ensuring that all tests are independent and no data interferes with another test run.

Rather than being defined per test, the setup and teardown functions are defined as part of the module and will apply to each test that executes within that module. For example, the following code would run setup before each of the two tests in the module and run the teardown logic as each test completes:

```
module('Equality Tests', {
 setup: function(){
   console.log('setting things up');
 },
 teardown: function(){
   console.log('clearing things down');
 }
});

test( "Simple Equality Tests", function() {
 ok( 1 == '1', 'Passed simple equals check');
 ok( 1 !== '1', 'Passed really equals check')
 notEqual(1, '2', 'Not Equal');
});

test('More simple tests', function(){
 expect(2);
 equal(true, true, 'Simple true == true test');
 strictEqual(true, true, 'Simple true === true test');
});
```

Testing DOM Interaction with Fixtures

As well as testing JavaScript logic, you will likely want to write tests that ensure any DOM manipulation is working as expected. The first step in preparing for this is to ensure you have a div with an identifier named qunit-fixture present on the HTML page where your QUnit tests reside.

```
<div id="qunit-fixture"></div>
```

As each test executes, QUnit will automatically reset the HTML within this qunit-fixture, saving you from needing to worry about it. Also, ensure that you have jQuery included in your HTML page because it is most likely that you will utilizing it for searching and manipulating the DOM.

```
<script src="../external/jquery-1.10.2.js"></script>
```

Let's see how fixtures can work now, by creating a simple test that will add elements to the fixture, and test to ensure they have been successfully appended to the DOM.

First let's ensure that the correct content is included in the fixture when the test suite begins. Rather than adding this to the HTML statically, we can add it to the page using the begin callback.

```
var fixtureEl = null;

QUnit.begin = function() {
 fixtureEl = $('#qunit-fixture');
 fixtureEl.append('<p id=\'myparagraph\'>New Paragraph</p>');
};
```

Note that using the callbacks, the HTML could be set up at any point, such as before a module or before each test. We'll now provide a module that includes one test to check for the presence of this paragraph.

```
//tests for DOM manipulation
module('Fixture Test');

test('Check for paragraph', function(){

 var results = fixtureEl.find('#myparagraph').length;
 console.log(fixtureEl);
 console.log(results);
 ok(results === 1, 'Found the correct paragraph');

});
```

As you can see, it's pretty straightforward to have JavaScript tests that validate the integrity of your DOM.

Recording QUnit Results

If you are running your tests on a continuous integration server, as we will look at in the next chapter, you will need to have the capability of recording the results of your tests without the need to refresh the HTML page that runs the tests.

While you can roll out your own solution based around the QUnit callbacks, there are plug-ins available that provide the ability to store the results in the most common format across continuous integration systems: JUnit style. As the leading unit test framework in the Java world, JUnits report style became the de facto standard. To incorporate this reporting into your own test suite, you'll just need to add another include in your suite.

First, download qunit-reporter-junit.js from https://github.com/jquery/qunit-reporter-junit and include this in the index.html file that holds your other QUnit scripts. You should include this after the main QUnit script.

```
<script src="../external/jquery-1.10.2.js"></script>
<script src="qunit/qunit-1.12.0.js"></script>
<script src="../external/qunit-reporter-junit.js"></script>
<script src="tests.js"></script>
```

Now all that's left to do is add a new handler for jUnitReports in the test.js file. The report object contains the results of the test run in JUnit format. From there, you can write them out to a file or upload them to a server.

```
QUnit.jUnitReport = function(report) {
    console.log(report.xml);
};
```

One important thing to note is that your previous QUnit.Begin definition will override the same that exists in the qunit-report plug-in. To avoid this, I moved some code around so that my fixture definition happens in the setup function of my DOM tests module.

```
QUnit.jUnitReport = function(report) {
    console.log(report.xml);
};
//tests for DOM manipulation
'Fixture Test', {'Fixture Test', {
 setup: function(){
  fixtureEl = $('#qunit-fixture');
  fixtureEl.append('<p id=\'myparagraph\'>New Paragraph</p>');
 }
});
test('Check for paragraph', function(){
 var results = fixtureEl.find('#myparagraph').length;
 console.log(fixtureEl);
 console.log(results);
 ok(results === 1, 'Found the correct paragraph');
});
```

As we explore build systems in the next chapter, we will discover some other approaches for reporting your test results.

Running QUnit Without a Browser

If you are running your tests in the background, whether on a nightly build machine or on a continuous integration system, you will want the ability to execute the suite without requiring a browser to be open, especially when you don't have a monitor.

PhantomJS (http://phantomjs.org) is considered the best solution for such tasks. The library provides you with a headless WebKit browser and a complete JavaScript API. As well as allowing you to run your tests in headless mode (in other words, without rendering the user interface elements), PhantomJS even has the ability to take screenshots of the browser at any particular time.

Installation instructions for PhantomJS are available on the project web site under http://phantomjs.org/download.html, as illustrated in Figure 8-6, where you will be instructed to download the appropriate installer for your operating system. However, if you are already using Node.js, you can use the Node Package Manager to install PhantomJS by using the following command:

```
npm install phantomjs
```

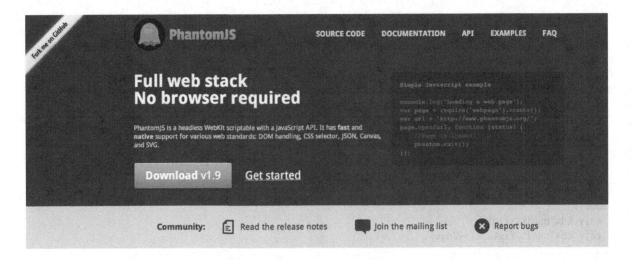

Figure 8-6. PhantomJS web site at `http://phantomjs.org`

Now that you have PhantomJS installed, you will need to obtain the PhantomJS Runner plug-in for QUnit, `runner.js`, from `https://github.com/jquery/qunit/tree/master/addons/phantomjs`. Unlike other scripts, we have downloaded throughout this book, `runner.js` will be executed from the command line. Because of this, you can place the file at the same level as `index.html`.

PhantomJS is used from the command line, taking the URL of the test suite as the key parameter:

```
phantomjs runner.js [url-of-your-qunit-testsuite] [timeout-in-seconds]
```

To run the test suite, execute the following command from the directory where you saved `runner.js`, ignoring the timeout parameter for now.

```
phantomjs runner.js http://localhost/backbone/chapter8/js/test/index.html
```

As the tests are executing, everything that you had previously placed in `console.log` will appear printed on the console. Additionally, a final line will be printed to the screen with the summarized results of the test suite.

```
Took 1034ms to run 8 tests. 8 passed, 0 failed.
```

With a combination of PhantomJS and some custom test recording as mentioned in the previous section, you can easily create your own continuous testing system. Don't forget that we'll approach this very topic in Chapter 9.

A Simple Backbone Model Test

Now that we have a solid understanding of how QUnit works, let's create a simple test to exercise one of the Backbone models created in Chapter 6.

Because these are separate tests, we will create a different HTML page to hold the suite, named app.html. We are testing Backbone objects, so we will need to include the usual scripts for such applications (Backbone, Underscore) as well as any of the files that contain the objects we want to test.

```html
<html>
<head>
 <title>Chapter 8: QUnit Application Tests</title>
 <link rel="stylesheet" href="qunit/qunit-1.12.0.css">
</head>
<body>
 <div id="qunit"></div>
 <div id="qunit-fixture"></div>

<!-- General Includes -->
<script src="../external/underscore.js"></script>
<script src="../external/backbone.js"></script>
<script src="../external/moment.js"></script>

<!-- Model -->
<script src="../app/model/Tweet.js"></script>
<script src="../app/model/Profile.js"></script>

<script src="../external/jquery-1.10.2.js"></script>
<script src="qunit/qunit-1.12.0.js"></script>
<script src="apptests.js"></script>

</body>
</html>
```

The test suite will reside in a file named apptests.js and will just have one module of tests that checks that the variables set when creating a new instance of the model are correct.

```javascript
//tests for DOM manipulation
module('Model Tests: Tweet');

test('Check initialization parameters', function(){

 expect(2);

 //create a new instance of a Tweet model
 var user = {name: 'James'};
 var tweet = new com.apress.model.Tweet({user: user, text: 'Hello World'});

 equal(tweet.get("text"), "Hello World", "Tweet text set correctly");
 equal(tweet.get("user").name, "James", "User name object set correctly");
});
```

When the test suite has completed, you should see a 100 percent pass rate. These tests are not very complex, however, and do not test the full extent of the system. The ideal suite of unit tests would build from this foundation to a more complete set of tests.

A Simple Backbone View Test

As well as testing your Backbone models, you will want to write some tests to ensure any views you have created are working correctly. This can also be easily achieved in QUnit, albeit with some convoluted setup.

First you will need to ensure the complete set of scripts that are included for Handlebars and jQuery are also included in the test HTML page, and you should also include the appropriate CSS files. In practice, if you are testing views with QUnit, the HTML will be similar to the actual app, with the inclusion of QUnit.

Each of the divs that contain the views should reside within the QUnit fixture element, as in the following example:

```html
<html>
<head>
 <title>Chapter 8: QUnit Application Tests</title>
 <link rel="stylesheet" href="qunit/qunit-1.12.0.css">
  <link rel='stylesheet' href='../../css/modern.css'>
  <link rel="stylesheet" href="../../css/style.css">
</head>
<body>
 <div id="qunit"></div>
 <div id="qunit-fixture">

<div id="app" class="grid">
    <div class="row">
        <div class="span8">

            <div id='timeline' class='timeline-view'>
              <h2>My Tweets</h2>
            </div>
        </div>

        <div class="span4">
            <div id="profile" class="profile-view">
                <!-- This would be the template -->
            </div>
            <div id="search" class="search-view">
              <form>
                    <div class="input-control text">
                        <input type="text" id="searchbox" autofocus="" placeholder="I'm looking for..">
                    </div>
                        <button class="bg-color-blue" id="searchbutton">Search</button>
              </form>
            </div>
        </div>
    </div>
  </div>
</div>
```

```
<!-- Template for profile -->
<script type="text/x-handlebars-template" id="profile-template">
<div class='tiles clearfix'>
    <div class="tile double bg-color-orangeDark">
      <div class="tile-content">
          <img src="{{user.profile_image_url}}" class="place-left">
          <h3 style="margin-bottom: 5px;">{{user.name}}</h3>
          <p>{{user.description}}</p>
          <div class="brand">
              <div class="badge">{{user.followers_count}} Followers</div>
          </div>
      </div>
    </div>
 </div>
</script>

<!-- General Includes -->
<script src="../external/jquery-1.10.2.js"></script>
<script src="../external/underscore.js"></script>
<script src="../external/backbone.js"></script>
<script src="../external/moment.js"></script>
<!-- General Includes -->
<script src="../external/handlebars.js"></script>
<script src="../external/moment.js"></script>
<script src="../external/dialog.js"></script>

<!-- Model -->
<script src="../app/model/Tweet.js"></script>
<script src="../app/model/Profile.js"></script>

<!-- View -->
<script src="../app/view/ProfileView.js"></script>

<script src="qunit/qunit-1.12.0.js"></script>
<script src="apptests.js"></script>
</body>
</html>
```

As all of the views used in the application are populated with content from the server that we created in Chapter 6, you will need to ensure that the server is running for these tests. More importantly, because each view needs to wait for a response before it renders, the tests will need to be written as asynchronous tests. The following code snippet tests that the profile view contains the correct text in the name section, within the h3 tags:

```
module('View Tests: Profile');
asyncTest( "asynchronous view tests", function() {
 expect( 1 );
 var profileView = new com.apress.view.ProfileView({user: 'sugrue'});
 profileView.render();
```

```
setTimeout(function() {

  equal(profileView.$('h3').text(), "James Sugrue", "Profile view rendered with correct name");
  start();
}, 1000);
});
```

Sinon.JS

When running unit tests, it's not always convenient to have a full server running in the background to respond to API requests. While this does provide the most complete set of testing because it uses the real-world system, it can be difficult to test how the code reacts under error conditions.

Sinon.JS (http://sinonjs.org/) is a library that is compatible with any JavaScript testing framework that allows you to create mock objects. A mock object is used when you want to simulate the dependencies that a piece of code might have without the overhead of creating the real objects, including server requests, resulting in higher test coverage for the various conditions that may occur in the system.

To integrate Sinon.JS with QUnit, you will need to include the basis Sinon library from http://sinonjs.org. To make the integration a little smoother, you can also using the Sinon-QUnit plug-in from http://sinonjs.org/qunit/. The following code snippet shows the additions that will be required in your test HTML:

```
<script src="sinon.js"></script>
<script src="sinon-qunit-1.0.0.js"></script>
```

Sinon has a number of useful additions to make testing easier, such as test spies, stubs, mocks, and fake servers. We'll look at each of these in turn and see how they help improve the quality of our Backbone tests.

■ **Note**   At the time of writing, including the Sinon-QUnit plug-in breaks any async tests because the plug-in includes fake timers. To get around this, add a declaration to restore the clock, `this.clock.restore();`, to the beginning of any async tests.

Test Spies

Test spies are used to test callbacks and functions throughout your code. You can use spies to track how many times a particular function has been executed.

The following artificial example tracks that the render call has actually run for the profile view. However, the ideal use of spies is to check that "deeper" functions in the call stack have been run, such as utility methods that the render function may require.

The spy is created using the spy function, which takes two parameters: the object under test and the function that is being tracked.

```
module('View Tests: Profile');
asyncTest( "asynchronous view tests", function() {

  this.clock.restore();
  expect( 2 );
```

```
var profileView = new com.apress.view.ProfileView({user: 'sugrue'});

this.spy(profileView, 'render');
profileView.render();

ok(profileView.render.calledOnce, 'Profile view render function
                                             executed once');

setTimeout(function() {

    equal(profileView.$('h3').text(), "James Sugrue",
                "Profile view rendered with correct name");
    start();
}, 1000);
});
```

As well as providing the simple calledOnce assertion, which returns a boolean value, there are a number of other functions available in the Spy interface. These include the ability to check the arguments of the call, by using the calledWith assertion. In our case, the usefulness is limited because the render function takes no parameters.

```
ok(profileView.render.calledWith(), 'Profile view render called with no parameters');
```

Typically, the parameters that are expected to be used with the function are included in the parameter list of the calledWith function. Additional inspection functions include the ability to check the order of function calls (using calledBefore/calledAfter) and callCount, which returns the number of times a particular function has been called.

Along with standard debugging techniques using Chrome Developer Tools, these inspection techniques can be another useful way of ensuring that objects are used correctly throughout your app. In general, you'll use spies when you have event handlers that are fired when a particular function is executed.

Test Stubs and Mocks

Stubs are used to replace the behavior of a function or to simulate error conditions easily. In fact, if you are following the Test-Driven Development approach strictly, you should probably start with building stubs.

The following simple example shows how you could stub a new save function for the Tweet model object through Sinon. First, the stub is created in the module setup, and from there, the save function is made available to the Tweet object when it is under test.

```
module('Sinon Stubs', {

  setup:function() {
    this.tweetModel = new com.apress.model.Tweet({user: {name: 'James'}, text: 'Hello World'});
    sinon.stub(this.tweetModel, 'save',
    function(cb){ //SAVE STUB HERE
    });
  }

});

test('Use a stubbed save function', function(){
 expect(0);
 console.log(this.tweetModel.save());
});
```

However, you will probably find the mock functionality in Sinon more useful for your applications. The difference between mocks and stubs is that when you create a mock, you will be setting up expectations for one or more of the functions in the object. These expectations must all be met for the test to pass.

The following test simply mocks the collection that is being used. Because all functions that we have created in the collection so far are called on initialization, let's add an extra function to Timeline.js first. Even though this does nothing useful, it will be enough to provide a mocking example.

```
com.apress.collection.Timeline = Backbone.Collection.extend({
    //Previous Timeline collection code here

    organizeCollection: function(){
        console.log('organizing');
    }

});
```

Creating a mock is as simple as using Sinon's built-in mock function, which takes the object you want to mock as a parameter. You can then set a set of expectations on functions within the mock object. In this case, we expect the organiseCollection function to be executed at least once during the course of this test suite.

```
module('Sinon Mocks', {

});

test('Use a mock collection', function(){
 expect(1);

 var collection = new com.apress.collection.Timeline();
 //mock the collection
 var mock = sinon.mock(collection);
 mock.expects('organizeCollection').atLeast(1);

 collection.organizeCollection();

 mock.verify();
});
```

In this example, the test will pass as we call the organiseCollection function directly in the test. Typically these mocked objects would be called from other objects within your test script, rather than calling them directly.

Using Fake Servers

One of the most useful parts of Sinon is the ability to use a fake server to respond to XHR (XMLHttpRequest) instances. This is useful when you need to check that your code can handle bad requests from the server, such as 404 responses, as well as ensuring that the happy path can be verified.

First you need to create a fake server, using this.sandbox.useFakeServer(). Once this is called, all requests will be intercepted by Sinon. You then need to prime the server to respond with particular content. After a request is made to the server, you then need to force a response before the test can complete.

This is all illustrated in the following code snippet where the request for the timeline contents is simulated:

```
module('Fake server');

test('Use fake server', function(){

    expect(2);
    //set up a fake server
    var server = this.sandbox.useFakeServer();
    var timeline = new com.apress.collection.Timeline();
    //prepare reponse text
    var timelineResponse = '[{"created_at": "Tue Sep 24 06:23:09 +0000 2013", "text" :
    "a simulated tweet"},{"created_at": "Tue Sep 24 04:23:09 +0000 2013", "text" :
    "another simulated tweet"}]';
    //prime the server to respond with particular text on a certain URL
    server.respondWith("GET", "/test", [200, {"Content-Type":
    "application/json"},timelineResponse]);
    //change the url of the collection
    timeline.url = '/test';
    //fetch collection contents
    timeline.fetch({reset: true});
    //force the server to respond
    server.respond();

    console.log('Timeline has ' + timeline.length);

    ok(timeline.length === 2, 'Correct size of collection');
    ok(timeline.at(0).get('text') === 'a simulated tweet', 'Correct text in tweet');
});
```

Note that the URL of the collection is changed from the default (http://localhost:8080/timeline) to /test to match with what was set up on the fake server. Strictly speaking, this is necessary only when you have two different requests to handle in a test run. However, it does make the test more explicit and easier to read.

If you use Sinon for only one part of unit testing the Backbone application, it's likely that the fake server functionality would be your choice.

Testing with Jasmine

While QUnit provides a more traditional style of unit testing, typically described as xUnit in the software industry, Pivotal Labs Jasmine library (http://pivotal.github.io/jasmine/) follows an approach known as Behavior-Driven Development (BDD).

BDD builds on the techniques of Test-Driven Development and opens the ability to write and understand tests to a wider group. This means that business analysts, requirement engineers, and QA personnel can be included in the testing effort, rather than being able to include only developers who are fluent in JavaScript.

In this section, we will provide a brief overview of Jasmine's syntax and how it can be used to test your Backbone application.

Getting Started with Jasmine

Just as with QUnit, including Jasmine in your project is pretty simple. You will need to download Jasmine from `https://github.com/pivotal/jasmine/downloads`, as illustrated in Figure 8-7. This comes in the form of a ZIP file with everything you need to get started. You should copy this into the `test` directory, where we had the QUnit tests from the previous section. The distribution already has the main runner file, `SpecRunner.html`, included. To make sure everything is in place, navigate to `http://localhost/backbone/chapter8/js/test/jasmine/SpecRunner.html` to see the results of a sample test runner. Once your directory structure looks like Figure 8-8, this URL should work.

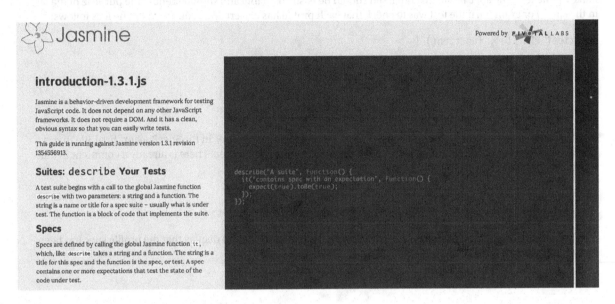

Figure 8-7. *Jasmine web site http://pivotal.github.io/jasmine/*

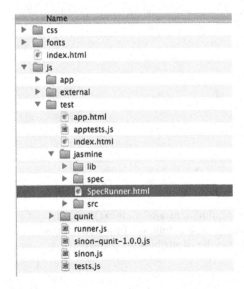

Figure 8-8. *HTML application structure following inclusion of Jasmine*

Your Jasmine tests will be comprised of suites and specs. A suite is a grouping of tests, which should focus on a particular scenario. The suite is defined using the describe function, which takes a test name and a function that will contain the specs. A test suite focused on profiles could be defined as follows:

```
describe('Profile', function() {
});
```

A spec is defined with the it function, which takes a spec name and a function that contains the assertions that make up the test. The spec name that is passed should be easily readable and should identify the purpose of the tests in the spec. For example, if the test was to check that each profile has a username, you could define it as follows:

```
describe('Profile', function() {

    it('should have a user name', function(){

    });
});
```

If you save the previous code snippet in AppSpec.js and include that spec in the SpecRunner.html file that is packaged in the Jasmine distribution, you will have your first real Jasmine spec. There is already a comment in that HTML file that shows where you should place your include declarations.

```
<!-- include spec files here... -->
 <script type="text/javascript" src="spec/ProfileSpec.js"></script>
```

Even though our spec contains no assertions, running the HTML should display that the profile spec has been run, as in Figure 8-9.

Figure 8-9. *Output from a simple Jasmine test run*

Expectations

To build a complete test, each spec should contain a number of expectations, similar to assertions in QUnit. An expectation is constructed using the expect function, which will take the actual result, followed by a matcher that takes the expected value. The following test ensures that the profile object has the id attribute set correctly:

```
describe('Profile', function() {
    it('should have an id', function(){
        var profile = new com.apress.model.Profile({id: 'sugrue'});
```

```
      expect(profile.get('id')).toBe('sugrue');
      expect(profile.get('id')).not.toBe('james'
  });
});
```

Note that any matcher can be prefixed with not in order to do a negative check, as illustrated in the second check.

Now that we have brought in dependencies to our own objects, as well as Backbone, the spec runner will need a more complete list of includes.

```
<!DOCTYPE HTML PUBLIC "-//W3C//DTD HTML 4.01 Transitional//EN"
 "http://www.w3.org/TR/html4/loose.dtd">
<html>
<head>
 <title>Jasmine Spec Runner</title>

 <link rel="shortcut icon" type="image/png" href="lib/jasmine-1.3.1/jasmine_favicon.png">
 <link rel="stylesheet" type="text/css" href="lib/jasmine-1.3.1/jasmine.css">
 <script type="text/javascript" src="lib/jasmine-1.3.1/jasmine.js"></script>
 <script type="text/javascript" src="lib/jasmine-1.3.1/jasmine-html.js"></script>

 <!-- include source files here... -->
 <!-- General Includes -->
 <script src="../../external/jquery-1.10.2.js"></script>
 <script src="../../external/underscore.js"></script>
 <script src="../../external/backbone.js"></script>
 <script src="../../external/moment.js"></script>
 <!-- General Includes -->
 <script src="../../external/handlebars.js"></script>
 <script src="../../external/moment.js"></script>
 <script src="../../external/dialog.js"></script>
 <script src="../../app/model/Profile.js"></script>

 <!-- include spec files here... -->
 <script type="text/javascript" src="spec/ProfileSpec.js"></script>

 <script type="text/javascript">
   (function() {
     var jasmineEnv = jasmine.getEnv();
     jasmineEnv.updateInterval = 1000;

     var htmlReporter = new jasmine.HtmlReporter();

     jasmineEnv.addReporter(htmlReporter);

     jasmineEnv.specFilter = function(spec) {
       return htmlReporter.specFilter(spec);
     };

     var currentWindowOnload = window.onload;
```

```
    window.onload = function() {
      if (currentWindowOnload) {
        currentWindowOnload();
      }
      execJasmine();
    };

    function execJasmine() {
      jasmineEnv.execute();
    }

  })();
  </script>

</head>
<body>
</body>
</html>
```

As you can imagine, there are a number of matchers available in Jasmine, and there is also the ability to create your own. Table 8-3 lists the set of included matchers.

Table 8-3. The Matchers Available in Jasmine

Matcher	Purpose
toBe(value)	Compares using the === function (strict equals)
toEqual(value)	Equality check for simple literals and variables
toMatch(regularExpression)	Matcher for regular expressions
toBeDefined()	Checks that the variable is not undefined
toBeUndefined()	Checks that the variable is undefined
toBeNull()	Checks that the variable is null
toBeTruthy()	Checks that a boolean evaluates to true
toBeFalsy()	Checks that a boolean evaluates to false
toContain(value)	Finds an item within an array
toBeLessThan(value)	Checks that the result is less than the value parameter
toBeGreaterThan(value)	Checks that the result is greater than the value parameter
toBeCloseTo(e, value)	Precision mathematical comparison for float values
toThrow()	Checks that the function throws an exception

Setup and Teardown

As well as containing one or more specs, a suite may also contain a beforeEach function that gets executed before each spec, along with an afterEach function that will clean up after the spec has completed. Note that the objects set up in these functions are made available by prefixing with the this reference.

```
describe("Profile", function() {

    beforeEach(function(){
        console.log('Any code required for setup');
        this.profile = new com.apress.model.Profile({id: 'sugrue'});
    });

    it('should have an id', function(){
        expect(this.profile.get('id')).toBe('sugrue');
        expect(this.profile.get('id')).not.toBe('james');
    });

    afterEach(function(){
        console.log('Cleanup code...');
    });

});
```

Testing Views

Jasmine has a useful plug-in available that allows you to execute matchers using jQuery syntax. The Jasmine-jQuery plug-in can be downloaded from https://github.com/velesin/jasmine-jquery. To use the plug-in, download the jasmine-jquery.js file from the lib directory, and include it in your spec runner, just after the other Jasmine-related includes. However, make sure that jQuery is included first because the plug-in depends on it.

```
<script src="../../external/jquery-1.10.2.js"></script>
 <script type="text/javascript" src="lib/jasmine-1.3.1/jasmine.js"></script>
 <script type="text/javascript" src="lib/jasmine-1.3.1/jasmine-html.js"></script>
 <script type="text/javascript" src="lib/jasmine-jquery.js"></script>
```

Rather than including fixture HTML within the specRunner.html page, you can actually include the required HTML separately with the loadFixture function, which accepts the path to the HTML as a parameter. Even though there is no path passed, the HTML file should reside in spec/javascripts/fixtures. You can also use a URL if your fixture HTML is hosted on a server.

The content of the HTML file will just be the inner HTML used in the real app, without the templates. Any Handlebars templates should be included in the specRunner.html file, before the view that requires them is loaded.

The follow spec ensures that the ProfileView renders on the page:

```
it('should have a view', function(){
  loadFixtures('./app-fixture.html');
  var profileView = new com.apress.view.ProfileView({user: 'sugrue'});
  expect(profileView.render().$el).toExist();

});
```

Table 8-4 lists the matchers that are available as part of the plug-in.

Table 8-4. *Jasmine-jQuery Matchers*

Matcher	Purpose
toBe(jQuerySelector)	Checks that an element on the page is correctly rendered
toBeChecked(.)	For tags with a checked attribute, such as a check box
toBeEmpty()	Checks that there is no DOM elements or text
toBeHidden()	Checks that an element is hidden
toHaveCss(css)	Checks for CSS styles applied to the element
toBeSelected()	For tags with a selected attribute, such as option
toBeVisible()	Checks that an element is visible (i.e., takes up space in the document)
toContain(jQuerySelector)	Checks the internals of an element for the presence of other elements
toBeMatchedBy(jQuerySelector)	Checks that the element can be found using a given selector
toExist()	Checks that an element exists
toHaveAttr(name, value)	Checks that an element has an attribute with a particular name and value
toHaveProp (name, value)	Checks that an element has a property with the given value
toHaveBeenTriggeredOn (selector)	Checks that an event has been triggered on the element with the given selector
toHaveBeenTriggered()	Checks whether an event was triggered on the element
toHaveBeenTriggeredOnAndWith (selector, params)	Checks whether an event has been triggered on the element that matches the selector, with the parameters in the params hash
toHaveClass(className)	Checks that the element is using the given CSS class
toHaveData (key, value)	Checks that the element has data attributes included
toHaveHtml(string)	Check that the element has particular HTML
toContainHTML(string)	Checks that the element contains some HTML string
toContainText (string)	Checks that the element has the supplied string data included
toHaveId(id)	Checks that the element has a particular ID
toHaveText(string)	Checks that the element contains the given string, which can also be a regular expression
toHaveValue(value)	For tags with value attributes, such as input
toHaveLength(value)	Checks the number of elements returned, for example the number of inputs or list items
toBeDisabled()	Checks whether a form element is disabled
toBeFocused()	Checks whether an element has focus
toHandle(event)	Checks that an element has a handler for a particular event type
toHandleWith(event, handler)	Checks that an element handles an event with a specific handler

As you can see, this plug-in provides you with a vast number of matchers that make testing views more straightforward. If your application is view-heavy, Jasmine, along with this plug-in, could be a better choice.

Fake Server

Just as with QUnit, the ability to create a fake server is enabled by including Sinon.js in your tests. All you need to do is include the sinon.js file in your SpecRunner, and then you're ready to go.

The following code snippet shows a separate test suite that is focused on testing the Timeline collection and will use the Sinons fake server to accomplish this. If you've already read the section on Sinon.js, this should be familiar.

```
describe("Timeline", function(){

beforeEach(function(){
        this.server = sinon.fakeServer.create();
    });

afterEach(function(){
    this.server.restore();
});

it ('Should return some tweets', function(){

    var timeline = new com.apress.collection.Timeline();
    //prepare reponse text
    var timelineResponse = '[{"created_at": "Tue Sep 24 06:23:09 +0000 2013",
"text" : "a simulated tweet"},{"created_at": "Tue Sep 24 04:23:09 +0000 2013",
"text" : "another simulated tweet"}]';
    //prime the server to respond with particular text on a certain URL
    this.server.respondWith("GET", "/test", [200, {"Content-Type":
"application/json"},timelineResponse]);
    //change the url of the collection
    timeline.url = '/test';
    //fetch collection contents
    timeline.fetch({reset: true});
    //force the server to respond
    this.server.respond();

    console.log('Timeline has ' + timeline.length);
    expect(timeline.length).toBe(2);
    });

});
```

The suite takes advantage of the beforeEach and afterEach functions to set up the server and clear it down after each spec has completed.

Running from the Command Line

To complete the overview of Jasmine, let's take a look at how to run your tests from the console using PhantomJS, just as we did with QUnit. Provided you've already followed the steps to install PhantomJS as detailed in the QUnit section, you'll just need to get the Jasmine runner script that is included in the examples directory on PhantomJS's GitHub repository at https://raw.github.com/ariya/phantomjs/master/examples/run-jasmine.js.

To run your tests, simply execute the following from the command line, in the directory where you stored the run-jasmine.js script:

```
phantomjs run-jasmine.js http://localhost/backbone/chapter8/js/test/jasmine/SpecRunner.html
```

Summary

In this chapter, we looked at one of the most important disciplines in any software development project: unit testing. QUnit is the most accessible of all unit test libraries and has a number of plug-ins that take the pain out of dealing with test results. We saw how PhantomJS can reduce the need for a standard browser to be used during the test run, allowing tests to run seamlessly in the background.

Paired with Sinon.JS, we saw how QUnit tests could include mock objects and spies. More importantly, we discussed how API calls can be simulated using the fake server functionality provided by Sinon.

We took a brief look at Jasmine, a behavior-driven test framework, which makes it easier to describe test cases in what is a much more understandable syntax. We also integrated Sinon's fake server to our Jasmine tests, as well as using PhantomJS to run the tests from the command line.

Both QUnit and Jasmine are quite powerful, and the library you choose will depend on your preferred syntax. More traditional developers will want to follow the QUnit approach, while the curious may want to use Jasmine's BDD approach.

CHAPTER 9

■ ■ ■

Using Grunt for Your Build Process

A key factor behind the success of any language is the amount of tooling that is available to automate repetitive tasks. C has makefiles, Java has Ant and Maven, and Ruby has rakefiles. It was only a matter of time before the right tool came along for JavaScript, and that seems to be Grunt. In this chapter, we'll introduce you to Grunt and explain how you can use it to improve quality, generate production-ready code, and much more. Continuing from the previous chapter, you will also see how you can automate the execution of your unit tests with Grunt.

An Introduction to Grunt

The aim of continuous integration is to improve software quality and reduce the time it takes to deliver production-ready applications by ensuring tests are executed as code changes. Of course, many other tasks happen in a continuous process, but running unit tests is considered the most important.

Grunt (`http://gruntjs.com`, see Figure 9-1), created by Ben Alman in 2012, has become the default continuous integration tool for JavaScript web applications. Rather than writing your own custom build scripts to execute from the shell or adopting another languages' build tools, Grunt scripts are written in JavaScript. It is a task-based system that is simply executed from the command line. The only dependency it has is Node.js.

Figure 9-1. Grunt web site at `http://gruntjs.com`

There is already a huge ecosystem of plug-ins available so that you can run almost any task you need from Grunt. If you find it lacking any functionality, you can even write your own, custom tasks.

Some Reasons to Choose Grunt

There are a number of good reasons to use Grunt, besides that you get to use JavaScript to define your build scripts.

Grunt follows a philosophy of using configuration over scripting, meaning you create your tasks in a declarative way, rather than needing to use any low-level JavaScript. However, if you prefer, writing your own tasks will allow you to use a scripting approach. This is the type of freedom that every developer would like to enjoy.

The plug-in ecosystem is huge, and as you'll see later in this chapter, there is a plug-in available for everything that you'd want to do in a web project. With so many packages available in the Node.js ecosystem to help with web-related tasks, Grunt makes it easy to wrap these packages and have the functionality available as a Grunt task.

Even if you don't download additional plug-ins, there are enough built-in tasks to cover the basic continuous integration requirements for a JavaScript project.

Throughout this chapter you will see how Grunt can revolutionize the way you write and deliver your web applications.

Installing Grunt

If you want to use Grunt, you will need to install Node.js first. If you've been following the examples in this book, you will already have Node.js installed. If you haven't, go to `http://nodejs.org` and follow the installation steps for your operating system.

The Grunt command-line interface (CLI) is installed through the Node Package Manager by executing the following on the command line, using the -g flag to ensure it is installed globally. Note that you will need to execute this with admin rights; on Mac OS X this means prefixing the command with sudo.

```
npm install -g grunt-cli
```

To check that it has successfully installed, run grunt --help from the command line.

Adding Grunt to Existing Projects

Running the grunt command from your terminal will result in an error message stating that the Gruntfile could not be found. This file, Gruntfile.js, is the main build script for your project. Written in JavaScript (or CoffeeScript), it will contain the tasks that are required in your build.

Let's see an example of using Grunt for our Twitter application. Because we already have unit tests available from the previous chapters source, we can just make a copy of that directory.

Next, create a file named Gruntfile.js in the root of that directory, alongside the index.html file used for the app. The structure of this file should look as follows:

```
module.exports = function(grunt) {
    //All grunt tasks here..
};
```

This is known as a *wrapper function*, and every Gruntfile you create will need to use this format. We'll add some tasks to this throughout this chapter.

Specifying Dependencies

Every project should have a package.json file that lists the dependencies for the script. At a minimum, this should contain the project name, the version, and a dependency on the Grunt package. At the time of writing, the current version of Grunt is 0.4.1, so that is used in the package.json code here:

```
{
  "name": "Beginning_Backbone",
  "version": "0.1.0",
  "devDependencies": {
    "grunt": "~0.4.1"
  }
}
```

Node.js will look after installing all the dependencies for your project if you run the following from the command line, in the same directory as package.json:

```
npm install
```

This script reads the contents of package.json and installs all the packages listed in devDependencies locally. As new tasks are added to the Gruntfile, you should add an entry in the devDependencies section of this file.

Note that you can also use the --saveDev flag in the install command to have a plug-in downloaded locally and also have its name and version saved along with the other dependencies in your package.json. The following command adds the appropriate entry for the latest version of Grunt to the .json file:

```
npm install grunt --save-dev
```

This can be a useful way to both install plug-ins locally and update the dependency configuration for other developers in your team in one simple command. If using a version control system, you will typically want to exclude the node_modules folder, leaving other developers who check out your code to reinstall the modules locally.

Project Configuration

As well as providing details on the dependencies, any other project-related attributes can be stored in package.json. Usually, this file is read as a JSON object during the initialization of the Grunt script.

All of this initial configuration takes place in the grunt.initConfig function, which is also used for task configuration, as we'll see shortly. The attributes stored in this file, especially the version, may also be useful for your build script. Grunt provides a file API to allow you to easily read the JSON into your script.

```
module.exports = function(grunt) {

 grunt.initConfig({
    pkg: grunt.file.readJSON('package.json'),
 });

};
```

We're still not at a place where the Gruntfile will execute properly. If you run grunt from the command line now, you'll be informed that you are missing a default task.

```
Warning: Task "default" not found. Use --force to continue.
```

Adding a Task

Let's now look at how to add a default task for our build script to execute. We'll use the same sample as at http://gruntjs.org, which uses the JavaScript uglify plug-in. The uglify plug-in provides the ability to minify (compress) all your JavaScript source into one file. Any of the scripts that you have downloaded from third parties will usually have such a version, appended with .min.js, named as the production version.

The uglify task is available from GitHub at https://github.com/gruntjs/grunt-contrib-uglify. It provides the instructions you need to get started, but let's go through this step-by-step.

First you will need to install the uglify task using the Node Package Manager, with the --save-dev flag.

```
npm install grunt-contrib-uglify --save-dev
```

This results in package.json being updated as follows, with the addition of uglify in the dependencies:

```
{
 "name": "Beginning_Backbone",
 "version": "0.1.0",
 "devDependencies": {
    "grunt": "~0.4.1",
    "grunt-contrib-uglify": "~0.2.4"
 }
}
```

Now that the task is available, it needs to be loaded in the Gruntfile. Any task contained in a node module can be loaded using the grunt.loadNpmTasks function, as in the following code snippet:

```
// Load the plugin that provides the "uglify" task.
grunt.loadNpmTasks('grunt-contrib-uglify');
```

The next step is to set up the configuration for the uglify task. This, along with the configuration for any task, takes place in the initConfig block. There are lots of different configuration options for the uglify task, but we'll just use the simplest.

First the uglify plug-in's configuration object needs to be included in the initConfig, with an options property, which defines the banner (comment) to use in the minified file. All tasks allow an options property to be included to override any built-in defaults.

Note how the <%= %> tag allows configuration properties to be included in the task. In this case, pkg.name is read from package.json. Meanwhile, Grunt provides other configuration variables such a grunt.template.today to print a formatted date.

The build object contains details of the source files to use with the src property, in this case all JavaScript files stored within js/app. It also contains a dest property, which defines where the output file will go.

```
grunt.initConfig({
    pkg: grunt.file.readJSON('package.json'),
    uglify: {
      options: {
        banner: '/*! <%= pkg.name %> <%= grunt.template.today("yyyy-mm-dd") %> */\n'
      },
      build: {
        src: 'js/app/**/*.js',
        dest: 'build/<%= pkg.name %>.min.js'
      }
    }
});
```

Every task you encounter will have different configuration objects. If you define a property that is not required, it will just be ignored by the script. You can even add complete JavaScript to the configuration, if you find that simple properties do not suffice.

The bare minimum of any Gruntfile dictates that a default task must exist. This can be added using the grunt.registerTask function, which takes the name of the task and takes an array of subtasks that will be executed as part of the task. In this case, there is just one task to include: uglify.

```
grunt.registerTask('default', ['uglify']);
```

The complete listing of the Gruntfile is now as follows:

```
module.exports = function(grunt) {
        grunt.initConfig({
            pkg: grunt.file.readJSON('package.json'),
            uglify: {
              options: {
                banner: '/*! <%= pkg.name %> <%= grunt.template.today("yyyy-mm-dd") %> */\n'
              },
```

```
                    build: {
                      src: 'js/app/**/*.js',
                      dest: 'build/<%= pkg.name %>.min.js'
                    }
      }
});

// Load the plugin that provides the "uglify" task.
grunt.loadNpmTasks('grunt-contrib-uglify');

// Default task(s).
grunt.registerTask('default', ['uglify']);

};
```

Executing grunt on the command line will now execute the uglify task, generating a file named Beginning_Backbone.min.js in the build directory. Throughout this chapter we will continue to extend this Gruntfile to create a complete build script for continuous integration.

Task Configuration

We've already covered the basics of task configuration, including the definition of an options object. You might find that you need to have different targets available in each task. This can be achieved by defining additional subtasks as properties in the configuration object. To illustrate this, let's add a subtask to the uglify target.

For example, let's imagine \ we want to minify just one single JavaScript file, app.js. We could define a new property within the uglify task for this.

```
grunt.initConfig({
   pkg: grunt.file.readJSON('package.json'),
   uglify: {
     options: {
       banner: '/*! <%= pkg.name %> <%= grunt.template.today("yyyy-mm-dd") %> */\n'
     },
     build: {
       src: 'js/app/**/*.js',
       dest: 'build/<%= pkg.name %>.min.js'
     },
     singleFile: {

       src: 'js/app/app.js',
       dest: 'build/appmin.js'
     }
   }
});
```

If we wanted to call only the uglify subtask, we could register the task as follows:

```
grunt.registerTask('default', ['uglify:singleFile']);
```

This will run only the subtask, but if we had used the old uglify target instead when registering the task, both the build and singleFile targets would have been executed.

Dealing with Files

Given the nature of continuous integration, most of the tasks you use in Grunt will have some interaction with the file system. The most common pattern is to have source and destination file mappings, which can be expressed in a number of ways. Source files appear after the `src` property, and destination files appear after the `dest` property.

Compact Format

The compact format is when both the `src` and `dest` properties are expressed as an array of files. Here's an example using the `uglify` task to compress two particular files:

```
models: {
    src: ['js/model/Profile.js','js/model/Tweet.js'],
    dest: ['build/models.min.js']
}
```

File Object Format

This is used in cases where you need multiple `src`-`dest` mappings for a target. The list of files is put into a `files` property, which contains an array of mappings between a destination file and an array of source files.

An example of this could be used when you want to explicitly create a different file for each of the models, views, and collections in the application during the `uglify` task.

```
uglify: {
    options: {
      banner: '/*! <%= pkg.name %> <%= grunt.template.today("yyyy-mm-dd") %> */\n'
    },
    individuals: {
      files : {
        'build/models.min.js'       : ['js/app/model/Profile.js', 'js/app/model/Tweet.js',
'js/app/Search.js'],
        'build/collections.min.js'  : ['js/app/collection/Timeline.js'],
        'build/views.min.js'        : ['js/app/view/ProfilePopupView.js',
'js/app/view/ProfileView.js', 'js/app/view/ResultsView.js', 'js/app/view/SearchView.js',
'js/app/view/TimeView.js'],
        'build/routers.min.js'js/app/router/AppRouter.js'], /app/router/AppRouter.js'],
        'build/util.min.js'         : ['js/app/util/Helpers.js']
      }
    }
}
```

A number of destination files are created, each of which takes a list of source files. Note that you cannot use additional properties, which we will cover shortly, with this format.

File Array Format

This format is quite similar to the previous object format, except in place of a string per mapping, there is an object containing a list of `src` files and a list of `dest` files. Each entry is an object rather than a string, with the `src` and `dest` properties explicitly tagged.

```
uglify: {
    options: {
      banner: '/*! <%= pkg.name %> <%= grunt.template.today("yyyy-mm-dd") %> */\n'
    },
    individuals: {
      files : {
{dest:'build/models.min.js', src:['js/app/model/Profile.js', 'js/app/model/Tweet.js',
'js/app/Search.js']},
{dest: 'build/collections.min.js', src: ['js/app/collection/Timeline.js']}
      }
    }
}
```

Additional Properties

You can add a number of properties to a file listing, in both the compact and files array formats, that help focus in on which files to use. These are listed in Table 9-1.

Table 9-1. *Additional File Properties in Grunt*

Property	Description
filter	Accepts a function that accepts the src filepath and returns true or false. Usually an fs.Stats method name is used, which can include the following: isFile isDirectory
nonull	When a match is not found, returns a list containing the pattern itself. This is useful for debugging filepath issues when the script is executed with the --verbose flag.
dot	Allows a pattern to match filenames that are prefixed with a dot.
expand	When set to true, allows you to build the file object dynamically, as described in Table 9-2.

Using the expand property allows a number of other optional parameters to be set, giving even more control over file objects, as listed in Table 9-2.

Table 9-2. *Properties That Can Be Used When expand = true*

Property	Description
cwd	A path that any src files will need to be relative to.
src	The pattern to match, relative to the cwd setting.
dest	Destination path.
ext	The extension to use in the destination files. If used, this will replace any extension that has already been defined for the dest file.
flatten	Removes all path parts from the dest paths.
rename	A function that can be used to rename the files. This will execute after the ext and flatten parts are complete.

Wildcards

Rather than listing all the files you need to work with individually, Grunt allows wildcards to find sets of files. This is also known as *globbing*. The original build target that we specified used one of these patterns in the src property.

```
build: {
    src: 'js/app/**/*.js',
    dest: 'build/<%= pkg.name %>.min.js'
},
```

Table 9-3 lists the most common patterns that are available.

Table 9-3. *Globbing Patterns for Files in Grunt*

Pattern	Description
*	Matches any number of characters, but not /. For example, js/app/model/*.js would accept all JS files within the model package.
?	Matches a single character but not /.
**	Matches any number of characters, including /. For example, js/app/**/*.js would accept all JS files in the app directory and its subdirectories.
{}	Allows for a comma-separated set of patterns.
!	Negates the match.

Using Grunt for Your Project

Now that we've looked at the basics behind Grunt, we can put together a more comprehensive build script for our project. At a minimum, you will want the following steps to happen continuously in your Backbone project:

1. Run static analysis on the code using a lint plug-in.

2. Minify your JavaScript and CSS source.

3. Automate your unit tests against the resulting source code.

Adding Static Analysis Tools

JSHint (www.jshint.com) is a static analysis tool that helps detect potential errors in your JavaScript code. The tool is a fork of Douglas Crockford's JSLint tool and is maintained by the community. The belief behind the JSHint project is that it deals with errors that might actually break your code, rather than the stricter enforcement that is applied by JSLint.

By running JSHint on your source code, you will avoid any typos or syntax errors. Any such quality checks are worth it, especially when creating production code. You can find the Grunt plug-in for JSHint at https://github.com/gruntjs/grunt-contrib-jshint.

The Importance of Static Analysis

As JavaScript has matured over the years, most browsers have added measures that make them more lenient and make them accept "bad" code. Because JavaScript is a dynamic language, there is a high chance of unruly code that might cause problems hidden to code reviewers and inexperienced developers. Most mature languages have static analysis tools, and with JavaScript it's even more important, given the chance of sloppy code. By adding an automated check, you can help ensure that your code is given every chance to shine. Although sometimes the errors that static analysis uncovers may be uncomfortable to address at first, you will end up with a much cleaner code base by using a lint tool.

Installation and Configuration

To install JSHint and add the dependency to your project, run the following from the command line:

```
npm install grunt-contrib-jshint --save-dev
```

Now, in the Gruntfile we'll need to load the node module for JSHint.

```
grunt.loadNpmTasks('grunt-contrib-jshint');
```

The configuration of the `jshint` task takes place mostly in the `options` configuration object, which accepts a number of different lint checks to carry out. Any checks that you want to carry out should be set to `true`. Table 9-4 lists some of the most commonly used JSHint checks. A complete list of these checks is available at www.jshint.com/docs/options/.

Table 9-4. *Commonly Used JSHint Checks*

Option	Purpose
curly	Requires curly braces are placed around blocks in loops and conditionals
eqeqeq	Requires that all equality operations are carried out using precision equals (=== or !==)
eqnull	When true, suppresses warnings about == null comparisons
browser	Defines globals exposed by modern browsers, such as window, document, and navigator
globals	A list of <library>:<expose> pairs that defines that libraries have globals defined, including jQuery, MooTools, Phantom, and more
latedef	Prohibits use of a variable before it is defined
plusplus	Prohibits use of ++ or --
undef	Prohibits use of undeclared variables; can be very useful for spotting typos
unused	Prohibits use of variables that are defined but never used in the source
maxdepth	Accepts a number of how many levels of nesting should be allowed; can be useful to manage complicated code

The options for this task also include an `ignores` attribute, where you can specify a list of files to ignore. Typically, you will ignore any external libraries you have included in your project.

The `initConfig` section should now include a JSHint task defined similar to the following. Note that not all of the checks listed earlier have been enforced.

```
grunt.initConfig({
    pkg: grunt.file.readJSON('package.json'),

    jshint: {
        options: {
            curly: true,
```

```
      eqeqeq: true,
      eqnull: true,
      browser: false,
      globals: {
        jQuery: true
      },
      ignores: ['js/external/**/.*.js']
    },
    files: {
      src: ['js/app/**/*.js']
    },
  },
});
```

Finally, the task needs to be added to the default task. The `registerTask` function takes two parameters: the alias for the task and an array of tasks that will be executed under that alias.

```
grunt.registerTask('default', ['jshint']);
```

Some formatting errors may appear in your source such as mixed spaces and tabs. You have the choice to fix them by using a JavaScript source formatter, such as JSFormat in Sublime Text. You can also just choose to remove the check from your JSHint configuration.

After formatting the source code, you might still have some remaining errors, which will get output to the console, as in Figure 9-2. Most of the errors that JSHint throws up are pretty easy to follow, but if you have any trouble, you can find explanations at http://jslinterrors.com/.

```
James-Sugrues-MacBook-Pro:chapter9 james.sugrue$ grunt
Running "jshint:files" (jshint) task
Linting js/app/router/AppRouter.js ...ERROR
[L17:C79] W033: Missing semicolon.
    self.listenTo(self.searchModel, 'change:query', self.navigateToSearch)
Linting js/app/util/Helpers.js ...ERROR
[L9:C43] W033: Missing semicolon.
        var username = u.replace('@', '')

Warning: Task "jshint:files" failed. Use --force to continue.

Aborted due to warnings.
James-Sugrues-MacBook-Pro:chapter9 james.sugrue$
```

Figure 9-2. *Output from JSHint*

If you are running on your local machine, printing to the console is OK. However, when running on continuous integration servers, it is more desirable to have the output go to a file. Naturally, the task has a configuration option for this eventuality, by using the `reporterOutput` attribute that takes a filepath as its parameter.

```
jshint: {
  options: {
    curly: true,
    eqeqeq: true,
    eqnull: true,
      browser: false,
      globals: {
        jQuery: true
      },
      ignores: ['js/external/**/.*.js'],
      reporterOutput : 'reports/jshint.txt'
    },
    files: {
      src: ['js/app/**/*.js']
    },
```

The previous code snippet shows how the report of the JSHint run will now be written to a jshint.txt file in the reports directory.

Minifying JavaScript Source

A number of plug-ins are available to help you to minify your JavaScript source. As we mentioned earlier in this chapter, *minification* is the process of merging all your JavaScript into one file to reduce the overhead when loading the script. Because we used Uglify earlier, we'll stick with that choice here. As part of its compression flow, UglifyJS (http://lisperator.net/uglifyjs/) removes whitespace and shortens variables names.

The Grunt plug-in for Uglify is at https://github.com/gruntjs/grunt-contrib-uglify.

The Importance of Code Compression

While running your JavaScript code on your development machine, your focus is on getting everything working. There's nothing wrong with this, but when your code goes into production, you will need to take performance into consideration. Running tools such as YSlow (http://developer.yahoo.com/yslow/) will analyze your web app for any performance issues and give you suggestions on how to fix these issues.

One of the most common problems is the inclusion of too many external JavaScript scripts. Each of the HTTP requests required to load one of these scripts takes time. As well as the network overhead, uncompressed JavaScript will also mean more data is being transferred. By minifying your JavaScript, you ensure that you are avoiding one of the most common performance issues in web apps.

Installation and Configuration

To install uglify and add the dependency to your project, run the following from the command line:

```
npm install grunt-contrib-uglify --save-dev
```

Now, in the Gruntfile we'll need to load the node module for uglify:

```
grunt.loadNpmTasks('grunt-contrib-uglify');
```

Table 9-5 lists some of the options available when configuring the uglify task.

Table 9-5. *UglifyJS Task Configuration Options*

Option	Purpose
banner	The string that will be prepended to the top of the minified file.
mangle	Turns mangling, the process of shortening variable names, on or off.
report	Reports the results of the uglify process. Possible values include false (default), min (minification results), and gzip (gzip results).
preserveComments	Specifies whether comments should be discarded. Possible values include false (default; strips all comments), all (preserves all comments), and some (preserves comments that start with !).
wrap	Wraps all of the code in a closure to ensure nothing is leaking.
footer	A string to be appended to the end of the minified output.

To ensure your minification is successful, you will first need to consider the order in which the uncompressed scripts are loaded. In our app example, all the external scripts were loaded first, in a particular order, before we loaded our own Backbone code.

While you can choose to use minified versions of the external libraries, we'll include them in a separate minified file. This results in the number of scripts loaded going from 18, as in the following code snippet, to 2.

```
<!-- General Includes -->
<script src="js/external/jquery-1.10.2.js"></script>
<script src="js/external/underscore.js"></script>
<script src="js/external/backbone.js"></script>
<script src="js/external/handlebars.js"></script>
<script src="js/external/moment.js"></script>
<script src="js/external/dialog.js"></script>

<!-- Model -->
<script src="js/app/model/Tweet.js"></script>
<script src="js/app/model/Profile.js"></script>
<script src="js/app/model/Search.js"></script>
<!-- Collections -->
<script src="js/app/collection/Timeline.js"></script>
<!-- View -->
<script src="js/app/view/TimelineView.js"></script>
<script src="js/app/view/ProfileView.js"></script>
<script src="js/app/view/ProfilePopupView.js"></script>
<script src="js/app/view/SearchView.js"></script>
<script src="js/app/view/ResultsView.js"></script>
<!-- Router -->
<script src="js/app/router/AppRouter.js"></script>
<!-- Util -->
<script src="js/app/util/Helpers.js"></script>
<!-- The 'main' for this app -->
<script src="js/app/app.js"></script>
```

As we can create subtasks within any of our tasks, we'll split uglify into two: one for external scripts and one for our own JavaScript source.

```
uglify: {
    options: {
      banner: '/*! <%= pkg.name %> <%= grunt.template.today("yyyy-mm-dd") %> */\n'
    },
    externalLibraries: {
      //WILL DEAL WITH EXTERNAL
        },
    individuals: {
      //WILL DEAL WITH OUR SOURCE
        }
    }
}
```

The file listing to be used for the externalLibraries section should be explicit to ensure that the source files are minified in the order that they are loaded. All of these files are minified into external.min.js in the build directory.

```
externalLibraries: {
      files:{
        'build/external.min.js' : ['js/external/jquery-1.10.2.js',
                                  'js/external/underscore.js',
                                  'js/external/backbone.js',
                                  'js/external/handlebars.js',
                                  'js/external/moment.js',
                                  'js/external/dialog.js']
      }
    },
```

The minification task for our own source code can be slightly different. There are no interdependencies between the files that exist in the same subdirectory. For example, no model object depends on another. Therefore, we can using the ** pattern to include all the files, one subdirectory at a time.

```
app: {
      files : {
        'build/app.min.js'         : ['js/app/model/*.js', 'js/app/collection/*.js',
                                     'js/app/view/*.js', 'js/app/router/*.js',
                                     'js/app/util/.*.js', 'js/app/*.js' ],
      }
    }
```

Now the uglify task needs to be included to the list of default tasks.

```
grunt.registerTask('default', ['jshint','uglify' ]);
```

Once run, you can change the index.html file of your app to use the minified files. The following should be the only script includes required by the application:

```
<script src="build/external.min.js"></script>
<script src="build/app.min.js"></script>
```

As you try your application with the minified scripts, you may find some JavaScript errors happen during loading. Ensure that you have included all the required files in the correct order if this happens.

For reference, the complete code listing for the uglify task should look as follows:

```
uglify: {
    options: {
        banner: '/*! <%= pkg.name %> <%= grunt.template.today("yyyy-mm-dd") %> */\n',
        report: 'min'
    },

    externalLibraries: {
        files:{
            'build/external.min.js' : ['js/external/jquery-1.10.2.js',
                                        'js/external/underscore.js',
                                        'js/external/backbone.js',
                                        'js/external/handlebars.js',
                                        'js/external/moment.js',
                                        'js/external/dialog.js']
        }
    },
    app: {
        files : {
            'build/app.min.js'        : ['js/app/model/*.js', 'js/app/collection/*.js',
                                         'js/app/view/*.js', 'js/app/router/*.js',
                                         'js/app/util/.*.js', 'js/app/*.js' ],
        }
    }
}
```

Note the addition of the report property in the options of the task. This results in the minification savings being printed to the console after the task executed. Figure 9-3 shows the savings made by running uglify on our source.

```
James-Sugrues-MacBook-Pro:chapter9 james.sugrue$ grunt
Running "jshint:files" (jshint) task
>> Report "reports/jshint.txt" created.

Running "uglify:externalLibraries" (uglify) task
File "build/external.min.js" created.
Original: 510249 bytes.
Minified: 186705 bytes.

Running "uglify:app" (uglify) task
File "build/app.min.js" created.
Original: 8651 bytes.
Minified: 5443 bytes.

Done, without errors.
James-Sugrues-MacBook-Pro:chapter9 james.sugrue$
```

Figure 9-3. *Output of the uglify Grunt task*

Minifying CSS

Just as it's important to minify your JavaScript code, it is worth minifying the CSS in your application for the same reasons. Again, a number of plug-ins are available to achieve this. CSSMin (https://github.com/gruntjs/grunt-contrib-cssmin) is one such plug-in.

Installation and Configuration

To install CSSMin and add the dependency to your project, run the following from the command line:

```
npm install grunt-contrib-cssmin --save-dev
```

Now, in the Gruntfile we'll need to load the node module.

```
grunt.loadNpmTasks('grunt-contrib-cssmin');
```

CSSMin is a simple tool, so just a few options are available for the configuration of the task. Table 9-6 lists some of the options available when configuring the CSSMin task.

Table 9-6. CSSMin Task Configuration Options

Option	Purpose
banner	Prefixes the compressed source with a particular banner.
report	Reports the results of the uglify process. Possible values include false (default), min (minification results), and gzip (gzip results).
keepSpecialComments	Keeps or removes special comments. By default special comments are kept. Using 1 as the value will keep the first one, and 0 will remove all of them.

The application we have created has a limited amount of CSS included, but it's still worth compressing in order to make the files smaller, and reduce the loading overhead. Currently index.html includes references to two style sheets.

```
<link rel='stylesheet' href='css/modern.css'>
<link rel="stylesheet" href="css/style.css">
```

The Grunt task configuration is quite simple, containing a combine object with the list of files that needs to be included to generate the app.min.css file.

```
cssmin:{
    combine:{
        files: {
            'build/app.min.css' : ['css/**.css']
        }
    }
}
```

Now the CSSMin task needs to be included in the list of default tasks.

```
grunt.registerTask('default', ['jshint','uglify','cssmin' ])
```

Following the minification process, the two CSS files can be replaced by this single minified CSS:

```
<link rel='stylesheet' href='css/app.min.css'>
```

Automating Your Test Suite

In the previous chapter, we covered two test libraries, QUnit and Jasmine. The following section will show how you can add a task for each of these.

QUnit Task

The QUnit Grunt plug-in (https://github.com/gruntjs/grunt-contrib-qunit) allows you to automate the execution of the QUnit test suite created in the previous chapter. When you download the plug-in, it will automatically download PhantomJS as a dependency. This means that the task can run in the background without a standard browser.

Installation and Configuration

To install QUnit and add the dependency to your project, run the following from the command line:

```
npm install grunt-contrib-qunit --save-dev
```

Now, in the Gruntfile we'll need to load the node module for QUnit.

```
grunt.loadNpmTasks('grunt-contrib-qunit');
```

The configuration of our QUnit task is quite simple. All that is really required is to pass the URL of the QUnit test suite to the urls property.

```
qunit:{
    all: {
      options: {
        urls: ['http://localhost/backbone/chapter9/js/test/app.html']
      }
    }
}
```

Table 9-7 lists other configuration options for the QUnit task. Finally, the QUnit task needs to be included as part of the default task.

```
grunt.registerTask('default', ['jshint', 'uglify', 'cssmin', 'qunit']);
```

Table 9-7. *QUnit Task Configuration Options*

Option	Purpose
timeout	Time in milliseconds that Grunt will wait for a QUnit start() before failing the task. The default is 5,000 milliseconds.
urls	The test suite URLs to be passed to PhantomJS.
force	When set to true, this allows the task to ignore failures and continue running. The default is false.

Running the script will end with the QUnit tests being executed, with the results of the tests being written to console. Figure 9-4 shows the results of the updated Grunt script.

```
James-Sugrues-MacBook-Pro:chapter9 james.sugrue$ grunt
Running "jshint:files" (jshint) task
>> Report "reports/jshint.txt" created.

Running "uglify:externalLibraries" (uglify) task
File "build/external.min.js" created.
Original: 510249 bytes.
Minified: 186705 bytes.

Running "uglify:app" (uglify) task
File "build/app.min.js" created.
Original: 8557 bytes.
Minified: 5361 bytes.

Running "cssmin:combine" (cssmin) task
File build/app.min.css created.

Running "qunit:all" (qunit) task
Testing http://localhost/backbone/chapter9/js/test/app.html .undefined
....OK
>> 8 assertions passed (1072ms)

Done, without errors.
```

Figure 9-4. *Output from Grunt script following the addition of QUnit tests*

Note that it would be useful to amend the test script to load the minified versions of your tests rather than the developer versions.

Generating QUnit Reports

Continuous integration servers such as Hudson and Jenkins allow you to schedule builds to run nightly or at a particular elapsed time after code has been committed to source control. These systems also allow you to view your unit test results, provided the reports are generated in a particular format. Just as we covered in the previous chapter on testing, the JUnit report format is considered the standard.

Although the QUnit task has no report configuration included, there is a separate task available to create these reports, called QUnit-JUnit (https://github.com/sbrandwoo/grunt-qunit-junit).

To install the plug-in, just run the usual command.

```
npm install grunt-qunit-junit --save-dev
```

In your Gruntfile, load the npm task.

```
grunt.loadNpmTasks('grunt-qunit-junit');
```

Now you can create a configuration for the reporting task in the initConfig block. The main parameter is the destination to save the reports to.

```
//qunit reports
    qunit_junit: {
            options: {
                //the location to generate reports to
                dest: 'reports/'
            }
    }
```

The task needs to be executed ahead of the QUnit testing task itself. This is so that the reporting listens for any tests.

```
grunt.registerTask('default', ['jshint', 'uglify', 'cssmin', 'qunit_junit', 'qunit']);
```

When you run your script, all the test results should be in a TEST-app.xml file within the reports directory. This report file should be easily processed by any continuous integration system.

Jasmine Task

In the previous chapter, we also explored using Jasmine to write your tests, as an alternative to QUnit. A grunt task exists to execute Jasmine tests (see https://github.com/gruntjs/grunt-contrib-jasmine). Just as with the QUnit task, Jasmine has a dependency on PhantomJS and will install it if required.

Installation and Configuration

To install the Jasmine plug-in and add the dependency to your project, run the following from the command line:

```
npm install grunt-contrib-jasmine --save-dev
```

Now, in the Gruntfile we'll need to load the node module for Jasmine.

```
grunt.loadNpmTasks('grunt-contrib-jasmine');
```

In your Gruntfile, load the jasmine task.

```
grunt.loadNpmTasks('grunt-contrib-jasmine');
```

Now you can configure your Jasmine test run. Because we're not using the SpecRunner created in the previous chapter, you'll need to put a bit of extra work into this configuration.

We'll only pass through the source files that were under test and also use the vendor property to load the additional external libraries such as Sinon, our compressed external dependencies, and jasmine-jquery. A full list f configuration options is listed in Table 9-8.

Table 9-8. Jasmine Task Configuration Options

Option	Purpose
src	A string or array of files that are being tested.
specs	A string or array of files pointing to the specs that are being used. This should be the .js specs rather than the SpecRunner.html ones.
vendor	A string or array of third-party libraries that should be loaded before the tests execute.
junit.path	The path to output the JUnit XML to.
junit.consolidate	Whether to consolidate all JUnit XML into one file.
host	The host to run the tests against.
template	Custom template used to generate your SpecRunner, parsed as Underscore.js templates.

You'll notice that we've left out ProfileView.js. The reason for this is that views are a little more complex to get tested from the Jasmine plug-in, so it's easier to focus on the data tests.

```
//jasmine tests
jasmine: {
  main: {
  src: ['js/app/model/Profile.js', 'js/app/model/Tweet.js', 'js/app/collection/Timeline.js'],

  options: {
      specs: 'js/test/jasmine/spec/ProfileSpec.js',
      vendor : ['js/test/sinon.js', 'build/external.min.js', 'js/test/jasmine/lib/jasmine-jquery.js'],
      junit :{
       path: 'reports/'
      }
    }
   }
}
```

We've also added the path for the JUnit reports to be exported to. These will all be named according to the suite, so in this case we'll have two suites.

Finally, we just need to add the task to our default list.

```
grunt.registerTask('default', ['jshint', 'uglify', 'cssmin', 'qunit_junit', 'qunit', 'jasmine']);
```

Creating Different Task Sets

The additional tasks we have created are not always suitable for all machines. A developer workspace will need to run a different set of tasks to an continuous integration server. This can be controlled quite simply with the registerTask function in Grunt.

For example, let's say the developers would run grunt dev on the command line, while the continuous integration server would run grunt build. We'll create two different task sets for each of these.

```
grunt.registerTask('dev', ['jshint',  'qunit_junit', 'qunit', 'jasmine']);
grunt.registerTask('build', ['jshint',  'uglify', 'cssmin', 'qunit_junit', 'qunit', 'jasmine']);
grunt.registerTask('default', ['jshint', 'uglify', 'cssmin', 'qunit_junit', 'qunit', 'jasmine']);
```

On developer machines, the static analysis and test tasks are run, while the build machine will also run the minification tasks. This way of running tasks can be extremely useful because different users of the build file will have different targets.

Project Scaffolding

Grunt has excellent support for starting up a new project using its grunt-init module. Rather than needing to write a lot of boilerplate code, you can simply take advantage of this functionality.

To get started, you'll need to install the grunt-init plug-in through the Node Package Manager. It's useful to do this globally using the -g flag.

```
npm install -g grunt-init
```

When running grunt-init, you'll need to provide a template to use for the project. There are a number of templates available, including a standard jQuery plug-in template at https://github.com/gruntjs/grunt-init-jquery. You can download the source, or you can clone the Git repository using the following command:

```
git clone https://github.com/gruntjs/grunt-init-jquery.git ~/.grunt-init/jquery
```

The template is now available and can be used by the grunt-init task by using the following:

```
grunt-init   ~/.grunt-init/jquery
```

After following a series of questions, you'll have a complete starting template for a jQuery plug-in ready. Figure 9-5 shows the output after running the previous code.

```
[?] Version (0.1.0) 1.01
error:  Invalid input for Version
error:  Must be a valid semantic version (semver.org).
[?] Version (0.1.0) 1.0.1
[?] Project git repository (git://github.com/james.sugrue/test.git)
[?] Project homepage (https://github.com/james.sugrue/test)
[?] Project issues tracker (https://github.com/james.sugrue/test/issues)
[?] Licenses (MIT)
[?] Author name (James Sugrue)
[?] Author email (james.sugrue@avego.com)
[?] Author url (none)
[?] Required jQuery version (*)
[?] Do you need to make any changes to the above before continuing? (y/N) n

Writing .gitignore...OK
Writing .jshintrc...OK
Writing CONTRIBUTING.md...OK
Writing Gruntfile.js...OK
Writing README.md...OK
Writing libs/jquery-loader.js...OK
Writing libs/jquery/jquery.js...OK
Writing libs/qunit/qunit.css...OK
Writing libs/qunit/qunit.js...OK
Writing src/.jshintrc...OK
Writing src/MyProject.js...OK
Writing test/.jshintrc...OK
Writing test/MyProject.html...OK
Writing test/MyProject_test.js...OK
Writing LICENSE-MIT...OK
Writing package.json...OK
Writing MyProject.jquery.json...OK

Initialized from template "jquery".
You should now install project dependencies with npm install. After that, you
may execute project tasks with grunt. For more information about installing
and configuring Grunt, please see the Getting Started guide:

http://gruntjs.com/getting-started

Done, without errors.
James-Sugrues-MacBook-Pro:test james.sugrue$ ls
CONTRIBUTING.md         LICENSE-MIT        README.md      package.json      test
Gruntfile.js            MyProject.jquery.json  libs          src
James-Sugrues-MacBook-Pro:test james.sugrue$ █
```

Figure 9-5. Output following grunt-init task

Of course, there are many templates to help get started with Backbone projects, including https://bitbucket.org/
nicopigelet/grunt-init-backbone. To download the template, run the following command to clone the Git repository:

```
git clone https://bitbucket.org/nicopigelet/grunt-init-backbone.git ~/.grunt-init/backbone
```

Then all you need to do is run the following command to create the basics that you need to build your
Backbone project.

```
grunt-init backbone
```

Some Useful Grunt Plug-Ins

This chapter just barely scratched the surface of the wide array of plug-ins that are available. Table 9-9 describes some other plug-ins you might find useful.

Table 9-9. *Useful Grunt Plug-Ins*

Plugin	Description
Grunt Watch Task (`https://github.com/gruntjs/grunt-contrib-watch`)	Watches a set of files for changes on your machine and runs Grunt tasks when changes are detected. This can also force a live reload on your browser so changes are immediately visible.
SAAS Preprocessor (`https://github.com/gruntjs/grunt-contrib-sass`)	CSS preprocessor task to convert SASS files in to CSS. SASS allows you to define styles for your application in a less verbose way than plain CSS.
Handlbars (`https://github.com/gruntjs/grunt-contrib-handlebars`)	Grunt task for precompilation of Handlebars templates. Template precompilation, paired with the use of the Handlebars engine library (rather than the complete version), can greatly improve application performance.
Backbone Boilerplate (`https://github.com/backbone-boilerplate/grunt-bbb`)	Pairs with grunt-init to help generate all boilerplate code and structure required for a Backbone project.

Summary

This chapter introduced the Grunt task runner system and explained how it can help add huge levels of quality to your project by enabling continuous integration. The typical tasks for any JavaScript project were covered including compression and minification of JavaScript and CSS source, unit testing, and static analysis. The Grunt ecosystem is huge, and there will always be a task available for any given problem. I really encourage adopting Grunt for your application, even if you are already using another build system. Because the tasks and configuration are all written in pure JavaScript, it reduces the learning curve.

CHAPTER 10

■ ■ ■

Extending Backbone with Marionette and Thorax

For small projects, the approach that we've taken to building Backbone applications works fine. However, as the scale of your Backbone.js application increases, it might be time to consider using either Marionette or Thorax to make the code base more manageable and to reduce the amount of boilerplate code. This chapter will introduce both of these add-ons and show the difference that they can make to how you write your applications.

Marionette

Marionette (http://marionettejs.com, Figure 10-1) was created by Derick Bailey to simplify the construction of large-scale Backbone applications. It is a collection of the patterns he has found while building Backbone applications.

Figure 10-1. Marionette web site at http://marionettejs.com

The framework deals with the fact that Backbone is an unopinionated framework, which provides the developer with all the parts they need without strictly prescribing how they should be put together. Two of the key problem areas that developers find themselves in with Backbone are view management and memory management. Marionette aims to alleviate these concerns in your applications.

Even though Marionette has a rich set of features, you can still choose which ones to use in your Backbone application. This gives you the freedom to gradually migrate an app to using Marionette, rather than having to face a big application overhaul.

Getting Started with Marionette

When you visit http://marionettejs.com, you will be presented with a couple of different download options, including a prepackaged zip that contains Marionette, Backbone, jQuery, and all other dependencies. There is also a bundled version that leaves out the main third-party libraries but still includes some other Marionette dependencies. Finally, there is a simple core, which just includes the standard backbone.marionette.js file.

The prepackaged zip is perfect for those starting off with a new application, but as we'll be extending our application with Marionette, it's best to take the bundled version. Download this version of backbone.marionette.js and add it to the external directory of your application. Provided you are building on the example from Chapter 6, your source directory should look like Figure 10-2.

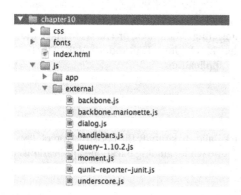

Figure 10-2. *Application structure with backbone.marionette.js included*

Marionette Feature Set

A few key pieces form the basis of Marionette.

Application Infrastructure

Marionette applications are built around modules and submodules that allow greater reuse and composability. At the center of all of this is the Marionette.Application object, which organizes your entire app. There is also a dedicated Controller object, which controls the workflow and process of modules and therefore the entire application.

Views

Marionette introduces some specific view objects to cater for the differing requirements in applications. An ItemView is provided for rendering single items, and a CollectionView iterates over a collection and renders individual ItemView instances. The Layout object allows complex user interfaces to be laid out into a set of Region objects.

View Management

A number of mechanisms are available to manage regions and subviews within the framework. There is also a renderer, which allows templates to be rendered in a consistent manner. Your views can also be sped up by utilizing the `TemplateCache`.

Messaging

Marionette provides a request-response framework and a command execution framework to allow better decoupling of application code. Both of these components allow one part of the application to request work to be done without needing to be tied to the component that performs the work.

Put together, the features that Marionette provides brings Backbone into a new league. Developers with a background in more traditional languages and web application frameworks will find these features more familiar, and it makes the JavaScript code more manageable.

A Simple Marionette Application

This section will take you through the creation of a Marionette-based application step-by-step.

To create the app, you can make a copy of `index.html` and name it `m.html`. We'll include a different `app.js` to manage the application using Marionette rather than plain Backbone. This will be stored in a directory named `Marionette` under the `js` directory.

The main `m.html` page will need to include your Marionette download, as well as this new `app.js`.

```
<!-- General Includes -->
<script src="js/external/jquery-1.10.2.js"></script>
<script src="js/external/underscore.js"></script>
<script src="js/external/backbone.js"></script>
<script src="js/external/handlebars.js"></script>
<script src="js/external/moment.js"></script>
<script src="js/external/dialog.js"></script>
<script src="js/external/backbone.marionette.js"></script>

<!-- The 'main' for this app -->
<script src="js/marionette/app.js"></script>
```

Create an Application

The `Backbone.Marionette.Application` object is at the center of any Marionette app. This application is the first thing that is created and can be extended with many options if you want. The simplest invocation of this object is as follows:

```
$(function() {

    //create a new Marionette Application
    MApp = new Backbone.Marionette.Application();
});
```

From here, you will be able to add regions, set up initializers to prepare the application in a particular way, or set up application-level event listeners.

Adding Regions

The `Marionette.Region` object provides functions to manage your views within your application. Regions can be added in any one of three forms: by using a jQuery selector, by creating your own custom `Region` object, or by using a combination of both methods.

An application can contain multiple `Region` objects, and later we'll see how `Layout` objects can be added to encapsulate a number of regions.

To add the main content area of the page as a region to this application, simply add the following lines:

```
MApp.addRegions({
    mainRegion: '#app'
});
```

An equivalent way to achieve this would be to create your own `Region` object and set the root element for that `Region`.

```
AppRegion = Marionette.Region.extend({
el: '#app'
});
MApp.addRegions({
    mainRegion: AppRegion
});
```

Both of the following code snippets will create a `Region` as part of the application, using a div with an ID of content as the area to render within.

The region can be accessed through the `Backbone.Marionette.Application` reference, by using the region name (in this case `mainRegion`). You can access the region directly as an attribute.

```
var region = MApp.mainRegion;
```

Alternatively, you can use the `getRegion` function.

```
var region = MApp.getRegion('mainRegion');
```

Adding Views to a Region

Marionette has a number of different view types defined, including `ItemView`, which is ideally used to render a single item, and `CollectionView`, which should be used to render a number of `ItemView`s when dealing with collections.

For a simple example, the `TimelineView` that was previously defined as a `Backbone.View` could be refactored to extend `Backbone.Marionette.ItemView`. A copy of the original `Timeline.js` can be renamed to `MarionetteTimeline` and adjusted as follows:

```
var com = com || {};
com.apress = com.apress || {};
com.apress.view = com.apress.view || {};

com.apress.view.MarionetteTimelineView = Backbone.Marionette.ItemView.extend({
```

This new view needs to be included in the list of scripts on the main HTML page.

```
<script src="js/app/view/MarionetteTimelineView.js"></script>
```

Finally, the view can be added to the Region. There are two ways to do this; one is to include the view when creating the region by using the currentView attribute.

```
var timelineView = new com.apress.view.MarionetteTimelineView();
AppRegion = Marionette.Region.extend({
    el: '#app',
    currentView: timelineView

});
```

This causes the view to be rendered as soon as the Region is displayed. You can also attach a view after the Region has been created using the attachView function.

```
var timelineView = new com.apress.view.MarionetteTimelineView();
MApp.mainRegion.attachView(timelineView);
```

As Region objects manage views, it follows that there are methods available to show or hide a particular view. A Region also has the benefit of including a reset function that will completely clear all views that have been displayed within.

```
MApp.getRegion('mainRegion').reset();
```

You can also close individual views within a Region using the close function.

```
MApp.mainRegion.close(timelineView);
```

Region Events

When calling show() or close() on Marionette views, events are fired that the Region can listen to and react if necessary. The listeners can be added to the Region as follows:

```
MApp.mainRegion.on("show", function(view){
    console.log( ' View has been displayed ');
});
MApp.mainRegion.on("close", function(view){
    console.log( ' View has been closed ');
});
```

Executing code to show or close the view will now trigger the appropriate function.

```
MApp.mainRegion.show(timelineView);
MApp.mainRegion.close(timelineView);
```

Additionally, both Region and View classes can have onShow and onClose functions defined to handle these events.

```
AppRegion = Marionette.Region.extend({
    el: '#app',
    onShow: function(view){
        console.log('View is shown');
    },

    onClose: function(view){
        console.log('View is closed');
    }
});
```

Marionette CollectionView

Strictly speaking, it would be better to utilize the CollectionView as the type of Marionette view because the Twitter timeline is really a series of Tweet objects. In the previous section when we used ItemView, the same render function from Chapter 6 was still in use, so Marionette's rendering was not used.

Marionette actually provides a default rendering for ItemViews, based on their templates, and the Model object that can be provided from its collection. Figure 10-3 illustrates how the CollectionView and ItemView can be used together.

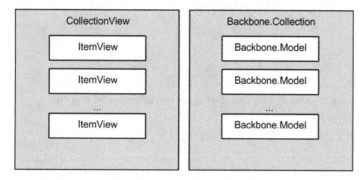

Figure 10-3. *An illustration of the relationship between CollectionView, ItemView, Backbone.Collection, and Backbone.Model*

As you can see from Figure 10-3, a CollectionView represents a single Backbone.Collection. For each of the Backbone.Model objects present in that collection, an ItemView is created to render that model.

Creating an ItemView is usually a simple task, where the template required is passed, with no rendering function required. The showProfile event listener and handler from Chapter 6 are also added to the ItemView because it is an event that relates to each of these subviews.

To represent the model objects correctly, you can create a new JavaScript file in the view directory named TimelineItemView.

Note that the template parameter, which is required in all ItemViews, references the compiled version of our Handlebars template. If your Marionette application is utilizing Underscore templates, this would not be necessary. Instead, you could pass the ID of that Underscore template.

```
var com = com || {};
com.apress = com.apress || {};
com.apress.view = com.apress.view || {};
```

```
com.apress.view.TimelineItemView = Backbone.Marionette.ItemView.extend({

    template: Handlebars.compile($("#timeline-item-template").html()),

    events: {
        'click .profile': 'showDialog'
    },

    showDialog: function(options) {
        var self = this,
            $target = $(options.currentTarget),
            username = $target.data('user');

        var profileView = new com.apress.view.ProfilePopupView({
            user: username
        });
    }
});
```

Previously the template that was being used to render timeline information iterated over an entire collection. We are now dealing with individual items, so the template will need to reflect this in the main HTML page, m.html.

```html
<!-- Template for timeline items -->
    <script type="text/x-handlebars-template" id="timeline-item-template">
        <li>
            <div class='icon'>
                <img src='{{user.profile_image_url}}'></img>
            </div>
            <div class='data'>
                <h4>{{user.name}}</h4>

                <p>{{format text}}</p>
                <p class="timestamp"><i>{{friendlyDate}}</i></p>
            </div>
        </li>
    </script>
```

While in the HTML page, we should update the root element of the timeline to be a ul tag by adding this under the div with the timeline identifier.

```html
<div id='timeline' class='timeline-view'>
<h2>My Tweets</h2>
                <ul id='timeline-list' class='listview fluid'>
                </ul>
</div>
```

The next step is to build a CollectionView that will use the newly created TimelineItemView. Once again, the amount of refactoring required from the previous TimelineView, which utilized the Backbone.View class, will be minimal. To remove any ambiguity, this JavaScript object should be named MarionetteTimelineView. It can also be placed in the view directory of the application.

Rather than extending Backbone.View, it will need to extend Backbone.Marionette.CollectionView.

```
var com = com || {};
com.apress = com.apress || {};
com.apress.view = com.apress.view || {};

    com.apress.view.MarionetteTimelineView = Backbone.Marionette.CollectionView.extend({
});
```

The most important attribute in a CollectionView is the ItemView that is used to render the Model objects.

```
com.apress.view.MarionetteTimelineView = Backbone.Marionette.CollectionView.extend({

    itemView : com.apress.view.TimelineItemView,
});
```

Note that the itemView refers to the class that is used rather than an instance of the view that would be created using the new operator. It is essential that you refer to the ItemView in this manner to avoid confusing errors in your application.

The other important attribute in the CollectionView is the collection attribute, which refers to the Backbone.Collection to use. The initalize function that previously existed can be kept because all it was responsible for was fetching the collection and calling render when the collection reset. If you wanted, you could build the Backbone.Collection outside of this view and pass it as a parameter.

The event handlers for clicking a user's profile link have been moved to the TimelineItemView, and the root element has been updated to the ul identified with timeline-list, rather than using the higher-level div element.

```
var com = com || {};
com.apress = com.apress || {};
com.apress.view = com.apress.view || {};

com.apress.view.MarionetteTimelineView = Backbone.Marionette.CollectionView.extend({

    el: '#timeline-list',
    itemView : com.apress.view.TimelineItemView,

    initialize: function(options) {
        var self = this;
        //create a collection for this view to render
        self.collection = new com.apress.collection.Timeline();

        //force the fetch to fire a reset event
        self.collection.fetch({
            reset: true
        });
        self.listenTo(self.collection, 'reset', self.render);
    }

});
```

To get everything running, ensure that the new view is included correctly in the main HTML page.

```
<script src="js/app/view/TimelineItemView.js"></script>
<script src="js/app/view/MarionetteTimelineView.js"></script>
```

Now, in `app.js`, the region can use the `MarionetteTimelineView` in place of the old view.

```
var timelineView = new com.apress.view.MarionetteTimelineView();
MApp.mainRegion.show(timelineView);
```

When the application is run, you should see the Twitter timeline rendered once again, as in Figure 10-4.

Figure 10-4. *Using a CollectionView to render the Twitter timeline*

Later in this chapter when we look at the Marionette Layout object, we will see how to incorporate the profile view that appeared on the right side in the Chapter 6 example.

Marionette Composite View

Marionette has one other type of view, in addition to `ItemView` and `CollectionView`, named `CompositeView`. This view extends the functionality that is provided by `CollectionView`. For more complex user interfaces that require collections, this can be a good choice because it allows you to provide a template to be used for the overall collection as well as using a template for the individual model objects in the collection.

To illustrate this, let's take a look at the previous example where CollectionView was used to render the collection contents. The HTML had to be altered to include the ul container tags for the list of TimelineItemView objects to be rendered. The following code snippet shows how this looks in our main HTML page:

```
<div id='timeline' class='timeline-view'>
        <h2>My Tweets</h2>
            <ul id='timeline-list' class='listview fluid'>
                </ul>
</div>
```

Using the CompositeView, we can get rid of this additional ul declaration and move it into a template, to be used only when the collection is being rendered.

```
<script type="text/x-handlebars-template" id="timeline-template">
 <ul id='timeline-list' class='listview fluid'>
 </ul>
</script>
```

This results in the timeline div returning to a simpler form.

```
<div id='timeline' class='timeline-view'>
        <h2>My Tweets</h2>
 </div>
```

To utilize this change, a new CompositeView version of the previous MarionetteTimelineView will need to be created. In this example, we'll call this MarionetteCompositeTimelineView. Start by making a copy of MarionetteTimelineView, and change the declaration to use the correct view.

```
var com = com || {};
com.apress = com.apress || {};
com.apress.view = com.apress.view || {};

com.apress.view.MarionetteCompositeTimelineView = Backbone.Marionette.CompositeView.extend({
});
```

You can also add a template attribute that will use the new timeline-template created previously. The root element attribute, el, will need to change to the higher-level timeline div, but the itemView can stay the same.

```
com.apress.view.MarionetteCompositeTimelineView = Backbone.Marionette.CompositeView.extend({
    el: '#timeline',
    template: Handlebars.compile($("#timeline-template").html()),
    itemView : com.apress.view.TimelineItemView,
}
```

Finally, the appendHtml function should be overridden so that each item that is added to the view is placed under the ul tag. The default implementation would have added it to the root el instead, which would have resulted in incorrect rendering in our case.

```
appendHtml: function(compositeView, itemView){
    compositeView.$('#timeline-list').append(itemView.el);
}
```

The complete code listing for MarionetteCompositeView would look as follows:

```
var com = com || {};
com.apress = com.apress || {};
com.apress.view = com.apress.view || {};

com.apress.view.MarionetteCompositeTimelineView = Backbone.Marionette.CompositeView.extend({
    el: '#timeline',
    template: Handlebars.compile($("#timeline-template").html()),

    itemView : com.apress.view.TimelineItemView,

    initialize: function(options) {
        var self = this;

        self.itemView =  com.apress.view.TimelineItemView;

        //create a collection for this view to render
        self.collection = new com.apress.collection.Timeline();
        //initial render
        //self.render();

        //force the fetch to fire a reset event
        self.collection.fetch({
            reset: true
        });

        self.listenTo(self.collection, 'reset', self.render);
    },

    appendHtml: function(compositeView, itemView){
        compositeView.$('#timeline-list').append(itemView.el);
    }
});
```

There are two minor changes required to have this work with the TimelineItemView object. First, add a tagName attribute to TimelineItemView with the value li. This instructs Backbone to wrap the HTML for this view in an li tag. Without this, the default would have been to wrap the HTML in a div.

```
com.apress.view.TimelineItemView = Backbone.Marionette.ItemView.extend({

  //el: '#timeline',
  template: Handlebars.compile($("#timeline-item-template").html()),
  tagName: 'li',

  //other TimelineItemView source
});
```

This will require the timeline-item-template to be changed so that it no longer contains the li tag.

```html
<!-- Template for timeline -->
<script type="text/x-handlebars-template" id="timeline-item-template">
        <div class='icon'>
                <img src='{{user.profile_image_url}}'></img>
        </div>
          <div class='data'>
               <h4>{{user.name}}</h4>

               <p>{{format text}}</p>
               <p class="timestamp"><i>{{friendlyDate}}</i></p>
          </div>
</script>
```

Finally, to use this new view in the application, simply change the declaration of timelineView in app.js to use the new MarionetteCompositeView.

```javascript
var timelineView = new com.apress.view.MarionetteCompositeTimelineView();
MApp.mainRegion.attachView(timelineView);
```

Depending on your preference, either the simpler CollectionView or the CompositeView can be used in the application. In our application example, to switch between both, you just need to remember to set up that initial ul within the timeline div.

Marionette Views in More Detail

All views in Marionette extend a base Marionette.View class, although you will never use this view directly. Instead, it provides common functionality to be used across all three view types.

General View Events

A few events are common across all views. When any Marionette view is closed, the following sequence of events occur on the view being closed:

1. The onBeforeClose callback is executed, if it exists.

2. The onClose callback is executed, if it exists.

3. Unbind all custom view events.

4. Unbind all DOM events.

5. Remove the view's el from the DOM.

6. Unbind all listenTo events.

Table 10-1 lists these callbacks and describes how they can be used.

Table 10-1. Callbacks That Can Be Used Across All Marionette View Types

Callback	Description
onBeforeClose	This allows additional checks to be performed before a view is actually closed. By returning false, the view will be kept open, and the sequence of closing events will be terminated.
onClose	Once the view is closed and cleaned up, this allows the execution of additional custom cleanup code, without the need to override the close function.
onDomRefresh	When a view has been rendered and shown on the DOM, the onDomRefresh function allows you to manipulate the HTML for the view.

ItemView

As illustrated already in this chapter, ItemView is one of the simpler views in Marionette. During the life cycle of an ItemView, a number of events are fired, in addition to the common events for all views. Table 10-2 lists the callbacks that you can add to your ItemView to handle these events.

Table 10-2. ItemView Life-Cycle Event Callbacks

Callback	Description
onBeforeRender	Triggered before the view is rendered. This allows preparation code to be executed before rendering commences, if necessary.
onRender	Triggered once the rendering of the view is complete. This allows custom code to be added to manipulate the view's el further.

CollectionView

We've already seen how the CollectionView utilizes the combination of Backbone.Collection and Marionette ItemViews to provide a clean way of representing the model objects in the collection on the screen.

Just as with ItemView, CollectionView has a number of callback events that can be added to deal with the various events that get triggered during the view's life cycle. Table 10-3 lists these callbacks.

Table 10-3. CollectionView Life-Cycle Event Callbacks

Callback	Description
onBeforeRender	Triggered before the CollectionView is rendered, allowing additional preparation of the root element before rendering the view.
onRender	Triggered once the rendering of the CollectionView is complete. This allows custom code to be added to manipulate the view's el further.
onBeforeItemAdded	Triggered before an ItemView is added to the CollectionView. The ItemView that is about to be added is passed to this callback as a parameter. This can be used to decide whether to add the ItemView, for example, when a filter is in effect for the CollectionView.
onAfterItemAdded	Triggered when the ItemView has been added to the CollectionView. The instance of the ItemView that has been added is included as a parameter in this callback.
onItemRemoved	Triggered when an a model object has been removed from the original collection and, as such, removed from the CollectionView.

Note that the CollectionView will render automatically when its collection has been altered through add, remove, or reset events. This saves the developer from having to listen for such occurrences and rerender the view manually.

Passing Parameters to ItemView

As well as providing a value for the itemView attribute, which must be an object definition rather than an instance, additional itemViewOptions can be passed for cases where the initialize function in the ItemView requires some parameters.

For example, if TimelineItemView had an initialize function defined as follows:

```
initialize: function(options){
    console.log('Initialized with ' + JSON.stringify(options));
},
```

then simply passing any parameters you need via the CollectionView can be achieved by stating these itemViewOptions in the constructor:

```
var timelineView = new com.apress.view.MarionetteTimelineView({itemViewOptions:
{parameter: 'hello itemview'}});
```

Providing Views for Empty Datasets

There may be cases that the collection is empty and there is nothing to render. Considering that there is no template available at the level of the CollectionView, this needs to be handled somewhere else. Luckily, the creators of Marionette included an emptyView attribute that allows a backup view to be used when there are no items to be rendered.

Typically, the value of the emptyView attribute will be another ItemView definition that uses a dedicated template.

Accessing Child Views

In cases that you need to access a particular ItemView within the CollectionView, you can use the children attribute, which provides a list of pointers to each ItemView. You can also access a specific ItemView by model using children. findByModel(model) in cases that you have a reference to the model that relates to the ItemView.

Nested Regions

Marionette provides a Layout object that allows you to create multiple regions in an application and control the overall app layout. A Layout object consists of a number of Region objects and extends from ItemView. This means you can provide a template for the overall application layout structure and then use the regions attribute to specify the areas within the application that will be filled out with other views, or even other nested layouts.

The definition of a layout has two key attributes: the template that will be used and the regions marked inside that template. An example of a Layout definition follows:

```
MyLayout = Backbone.Marionette.Layout.extend({
  template: '#layout-template',
  regions: {
    main: '#main',
    nav: '#nav'
  }
});
```

Just as with the main Backbone.Marionette.Application object, regions can be added and removed using the appropriate functions (addRegion, removeRegion). Deferring the management of regions to the Layout object rather than the overall Application object leads to a cleaner code base.

As Layout extends ItemView, it also inherits the close functionality. This means you can switch layouts by closing one and replacing it with a new one.

Using Layout in Our Example

We can extend our current example to use the Layout object, creating separate regions for the timeline view and the profile. First, we'll need to change the existing ProfileView to be a Marionette ItemView. As we've done before, a simple copy of ProfileView will suffice, renaming it to MarionetteProfileView. To make this an ItemView, we'll just change the type from Backbone.View to Backbone.Marionette.ItemView.

```
com.apress.view.MarionetteProfileView = Backbone.Marionette.ItemView.extend({
        //existing source
});
```

Next, the template for the overall application needs to be created. This is simply a matter of moving everything that was within the body tag, bar the other templates, into a new template with an ID of app-layout-template.

```
<!-- Template for entire app-->
<script type="text/template" id="app-layout-template">
<div id="app" class="grid">
        <div class="row">
            <div class="span8">
                <div id='timeline' class='timeline-view'>
                <h2>My Tweets</h2>
                <div id="timeline-area">
                    <ul id='timeline-list' class='listview fluid'>
                    </ul>
                </div>
            </div>
        </div>

        <div class="span4" id="side">
            <div id="profile" class="profile-view">
            </div>

                <div id="search" class="search-view">
                   <form>
                        <div class="input-control text">
                            <input type="text" id="searchbox" autofocus=""
placeholder="I'm looking for..">
                        </div>
                            <button class="bg-color-blue" id="searchbutton">Search</button>
                   </form>
                </div>
            </div>
        </div>
    </div>
</script>
```

Previously, the Application object used the div with an ID of app as its main region. We'll change this now to be the body tag.

```
AppRegion = Marionette.Region.extend({
      el: 'body',
});
```

The creation of the layout now is simply a matter of defining the template to use and the regions that are marked for the views to be added. This code can be placed directly in app.js.

```
AppLayout = Backbone.Marionette.Layout.extend({
    //template: Handlebars.compile($("#app-layout-template").html()),
    template: "#app-layout-template",
    regions: {
        timeline: '#timeline-area',
        profile: '#side'
    }
});
```

The Layout must be instantiated and added into the mainRegion of the application.

```
var layout = new AppLayout();
MApp.mainRegion.show(layout);
```

Finally, each of the views can be created and added to the appropriate region.

```
layout.timeline.show(new com.apress.view.MarionetteTimelineView({itemViewOptions:
{parameter: 'hello itemview'}}));
layout.profile.show(new com.apress.view.MarionetteProfileView({user: 'sugrue'}));
```

Layout affords a little extra control over the application user interface, without the need to create a number of levels of complicated subviews throughout the application. While it may seem that Application and Layout are similar, you should consider that a Layout has a visual representation, while the Application should be used as a lightweight object for managing the life cycle of your app.

Thorax

Having looked at Marionette in detail, it's worth investigating another alternative framework that helps manage your Backbone applications. Thorax (http://thoraxjs.org, Figure 10-5) was written by Ryan Eastridge and Kevin Decker for the Walmart mobile application. While similar to Marionette in some aspects, the framework is more opinionated, forcing Handlebars as the template mechanism.

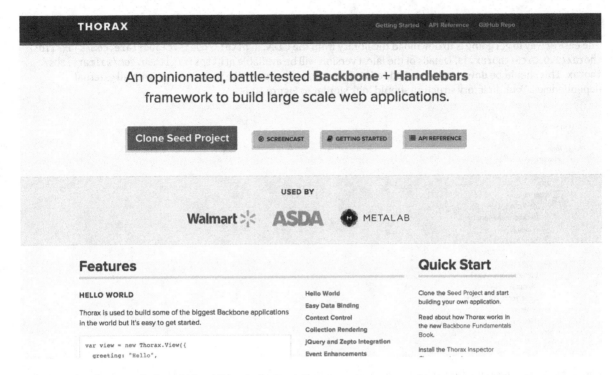

Figure 10-5. *Thorax web site at* http://thoraxjs.com

Thorax Feature Set

Thorax provides a similar feature set to Marionette, covered in the following sections.

Views

Thorax includes extensions to the standard Backbone.View, which utilizes Handlebars templates. Just as with Marionette, there is a CollectionView that helps deal with displaying complete lists of items.

View Management

Views can be easily embedded within other views and are managed properly by Thorax so as to avoid any memory leaks, or *zombie views*.

There is also a LayoutView that acts as a container for another view and allows this contained view to be replaced easily.

Specialized Versions of Model and Collection

When passing through models or collections to your views, Thorax expects these to use the wrappers provided in the framework.

Getting Started with Thorax

The easiest way to get going is to download the library from the CDN, at http://cdnjs.cloudflare.com/ajax/libs/thorax/2.0.0rc6/thorax.js. Details of the latest version will be available at https://github.com/walmartlabs/thorax. This should be downloaded and added to the external directory, like we have done with all external dependencies. Your directory structure should look similar to Figure 10-6.

Figure 10-6. *Directory structure of application including Thorax*

For a really quick start, you can clone the Thorax Seed project from https://github.com/walmartlabs/thorax-seed and follow the instructions to build a basic app, utilizing grunt tasks to generate a stub.

We'll be building a Thorax version of the Twitter, so make a copy of index.html from Chapter 6 and rename it to t.html. For now, the only script you'll need to include apart from the standard combination of dependencies (Backbone, jQuery, and Handlebars) is the new Thorax library.

```
<!-- General Includes -->
<script src="js/external/jquery-1.10.2.js"></script>
<script src="js/external/underscore.js"></script>
<script src="js/external/backbone.js"></script>
<script src="js/external/handlebars.js"></script>
<script src="js/external/moment.js"></script>
<script src="js/external/dialog.js"></script>
<script src="js/external/thorax.js"></script>
```

As in the previous section, when illustrating the features of Marionette, it is useful to create a separate app.js under a thorax directory, which should also be included in the HTML page.

```
<!-- The 'main' for this app -->
<script src="js/thorax/app.js"></script>
```

In the following sections, we'll run through some Thorax basics before moving onto a reimplementation of the Twitter application using Thorax.

An Introduction to Thorax Types

Thorax includes a number of specialized versions of Backbone objects, such as `Thorax.Model`, `Thorax.Collection`, and `Thorax.View`, which all interact seamlessly together. This section will first focus on the data types available. Thorax views will not work with plain `Backbone.Model` or `Backbone.Collection` objects, so it is essential to understand test types. With an understanding of the model and collection types, we'll take a look at some examples of Thorax views.

Thorax.Model

`Thorax.Model` extends Backbone's default model with two functions, one to check whether the model is empty (`isEmpty()`) and another to check whether the model has been populated (`isPopulated()`). When a model is passed to a view, the `isPopulated()` function is used to check whether it is necessary to fetch the model data.

To create a Thorax model, simply use `Thorax.Model.extend` to define the model rather than `Backbone.Model.extend`.

```
MyModel = Thorax.Model.extend({
    //otherwise the model is the same
});
```

Thorax.Collection

Just as with `Thorax.Model`, `Thorax.Collection` adds two functions to the default Backbone implementation. The functions are also the same; `isEmpty()` returns true if the collection has a zero length, and `isPopulated()` is used to determine whether the collection should be fetched when it is passed to a view.

Creating a `Thorax.Collection` is a matter of replacing the usual `Backbone.Collection.extend` with `Thorax.Collection.extend`.

```
MyCollection = Thorax.Collection.extend({
    //otherwise the collection is the same
});
```

Thorax's collection is the same as a standard Backbone collection in every other way.

Thorax.View

The centerpiece of the Thorax library is the `View` object, which adds an element of simplicity and data binding to the default `Backbone.View` object.

Each view needs to have a Handlebars template available for rendering, which is referenced through the `template` attribute. Views will also include either a `model` or `collection` attribute, but note this can be passed at a later stage.

Most views will have at least a `template` and `model` attribute defined as follows:

```
var view = new Thorax.View({
 template: //a compiled template
 model:    //your model
});
```

This template has access to any of the attributes listed in the view, as well as all properties within the model object. The following example illustrates how properties are made available to the view's template:

```
var view = new Thorax.View({
  label: "Title",
  template: Handlebars.compile( "{{label}} : {{bookname}}"),

  model: new Thorax.Model({
    bookname: 'Beginning Backbone'
  }),
});
```

The view must be added to a section of the page before it will be visible. This is done through the appendTo function, which accepts a CSS selector to decide where to attach the HTML that the view has generated.

```
view.appendTo('body');
```

By running the previous code in app.js, you will have a simple view displayed, as in Figure 10-7.

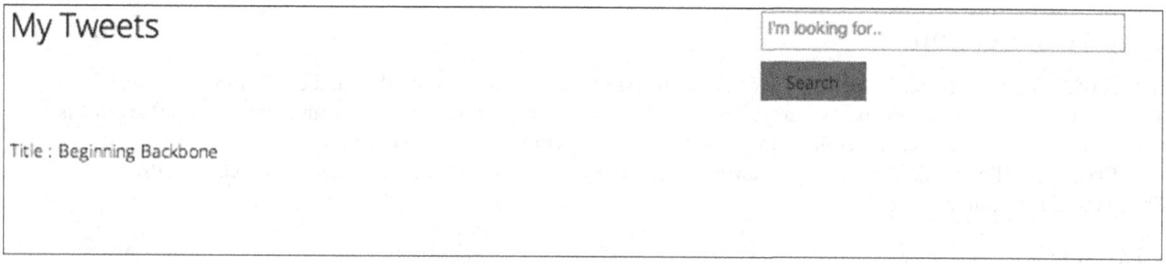

Figure 10-7. *A simple Thorax view*

Using View Context

Thorax.View includes a context property that allows you to expose only parts of the model to the template. This can be useful if you want to control which model attributes the template uses or if you want to alter the attributes in some way before displaying them in the view.

The following code snippet illustrates how the context property can be used to change the bookname value to uppercase. Because the author is not made available in the context, it is not displayed in the resulting HTML output.

```
var view = new Thorax.View({
  model: new Thorax.Model({
    bookname: 'Beginning Backbone',
    author: 'James Sugrue'
  }),
  label: 'Title',
  context: function() {
    return {
      bookname: this.model.get('bookname').toUpperCase()
    };
  },
```

```
template: Handlebars.compile( "{{label}} : {{bookname}} by {{author}}"),
});
```

```
view.appendTo('body');
```

■ **Note**   context applies only to model attributes; any attributes defined in the view will always be visible to the template.

Embedded Views

One of the main reasons to use Thorax is to make the management of subviews simpler and to alleviate any concerns of memory leaks. Using one of the many built-in Handlebars helpers, view, you can easily embed views inside the view template.

First, create a view that you want to use as a child view.

```
var subview = new Thorax.View({
 model: new Thorax.Model({
   description: 'A book to help you get started with Backbone.js',
  }),
 template: Handlebars.compile( "{{description}}"),
});
```

Then, the subview can be passed as another property within the main view. In the following example, this is tagged with the name subview, but it can be any name you want.

The template included here expects a view named subview to be available. By simply using the {{view subview}} statement within your template, the subview is successfully rendered.

```
var view = new Thorax.View({
 model: new Thorax.Model({
   bookname: 'Beginning Backbone',
   author: 'James Sugrue'
 }),
 label: 'Title',
 context: function() {
   return {
     bookname: this.model.get('bookname').toUpperCase()
   };
 },
 subview: subview,
 template: Handlebars.compile( "{{label}} : {{bookname}} by {{author}} <br/> {{view subview}}"),
});
```

```
view.appendTo('body');
```

Layouts

Thorax.LayoutView is a simple way to include a placeholder for other views in your document. It can be useful when you need to replace a view within another.

```
var layout = new Thorax.LayoutView();
layout.appendTo('body');
```

The LayoutView has two functions: setView and getView. When these functions are used, certain life-cycle events will be triggered within the views themselves. Consider the following view:

```
var view = new Thorax.View({
 events: {
   ready: function() { console.log('View is ready');},
   destroyed: function() { console.log('View is destroyed');},
   rendered: function() {console.log('View is rendered');}
 },
 model: new Thorax.Model({
   bookname: 'Beginning Backbone',
   author: 'James Sugrue'
 }),

 template: Handlebars.compile( "{{bookname}} by {{author}}"),
});
```

When this is added to the view, through the setView function, the rendered event will be triggered.

```
layout.setView(view);
```

If the view is replaced with another, the destroyed event will be fired.

```
//replacing with this view. Original view is destroyed
var replacementView = new Thorax.View({
 events: {
   ready: function() { console.log('Replacement View is ready');},
   destroyed: function() { console.log('Replacement View is destroyed');},
   rendered: function() {console.log('Replacement View is rendered');}
 },
 model: new Thorax.Model({
   bookname: 'Beginning Backbone',
   author: 'James Sugrue'
 }),

 template: Handlebars.compile( "{{bookname}}"),
});
```

```
layout.setView(replacementView);
```

The result of the previous code is the destruction of the original view and the rendering of the new view.

■ **Note** There is a useful Chrome extension available, named Thorax `Inspector`, that allows you to inspect Thorax views within your application and see the associated models and collections.

Using Thorax for the Twitter Example

To illustrate how to migrate an existing application to Thorax, we'll migrate both the timeline view, which uses a collection, and the profile view, which uses a model.

Migrating the Profile View

Before we deal with the view, the Profile model will need to be changed to a Thorax.Model object. To do this, simply make a copy of the original Profile.js model and change the extends declaration. For clarity, you may want to place all Thorax models under a separate namespace, as in this example. As you can see, the amount of change required is quite limited.

```
var com = com || {};
com.apress = com.apress || {};
com.apress.model = com.apress.model || {};
com.apress.model.thorax = com.apress.model.thorax || {};

com.apress.model.thorax.Profile = Thorax.Model.extend({

  urlRoot: 'http://localhost:8080/profile',

  parse: function(model) {
    return model;
  }

});
```

With the model in place, we can make a copy of the original ProfileView.js and create a ThoraxProfileView.js file. Thorax will deal with rendering, so the resulting code is much simpler. Additionally, because the model will be created before the view is used, there is no requirement for an initialize function.

```
var com = com || {};
com.apress = com.apress || {};
com.apress.view = com.apress.view || {};

com.apress.view.ThoraxProfileView = Thorax.View.extend({

  el: '#profile',

  template: Handlebars.compile($("#profile-template").html()),

});
```

Ensure that the model and view are available in the HTML page.

```
<!-- Model -->
<script src="js/app/model/thorax/Profile.js"></script>
<!-- View -->
<script src="js/app/view/ThoraxProfileView.js"></script>
```

The profile template in the HTML page is also slightly updated because the model is no longer referenced under the username.

```
<!-- Template for profile -->
<script type="text/x-handlebars-template" id="profile-template">
<div class='tiles clearfix'>
   <div class="tile double bg-color-orangeDark">
      <div class="tile-content">
         <img src="{{profile_image_url}}" class="place-left">
         <h3 style="margin-bottom: 5px;">{{name}}</h3>
         <p>{{description}}</p>
         <div class="brand">
             <div class="badge">{{followers_count}} Followers</div>
         </div>
      </div>
   </div>
 </div>
</script>
```

Finally, update app.js to retrieve the profile model and on success display the profile view.

```
var profileModel = new com.apress.model.thorax.Profile({id: 'sugrue'});
//ensure we have the model before rendering
profileModel.fetch({success: function(){

      //get the profile model first
      var profileView = new com.apress.view.ThoraxProfileView({model: profileModel});

      profileView.appendTo('#profile');

   }
});
```

Running the application will result in the profile being displayed on the HTML page.

Migrating the Timeline View

Although the migration of the timeline view is similar to the previous, you will also need to deal with a collection rather than a simple model. This is dealt with using the special collection Handlebars helper that Thorax provides.

Before dealing with the collection, the Tweet model will need to be updated, as in the Profile model example, to extend Thorax.Model. Once again, the Thorax version of Tweet.js is placed under a different namespace.

```
var com = com || {};
com.apress = com.apress || {};
com.apress.model = com.apress.model || {};
com.apress.model.thorax = com.apress.model.thorax || {};

com.apress.model.thorax.Tweet = Thorax.Model.extend({
```

```
parse: function(model) {

    //USE moment here
    //mode.created_at "Wed Aug 28 06:32:07 +0000 2013"
    var created = model.created_at;
    var friendly = moment(model.created_at, "ddd MMM DD HH:mm:ss ZZ YYYY").fromNow();

    model.friendlyDate = friendly;

    return model;
}

});
```

In the same manner, `Timeline.js` will need to extend `Thorax.Collection`. No other changes are necessary, other than on the namespace.

```
var com = com || {};
com.apress = com.apress || {};
com.apress.collection = com.apress.collection || {};
com.apress.collection.thorax = com.apress.collection.thorax || {};

com.apress.collection.thorax.Timeline = Thorax.Collection.extend({

    //the model that this collection uses
    model: com.apress.model.thorax.Tweet,
    //the server side url to connect to for the collection
    url: 'http://localhost:8080/timeline',

    initialize: function(options) {
        //anything to be defined on construction goes here
    },

    organiseCollection: function() {
        console.log('organising');
    }
});
```

The previous `TimelineView.js` is greatly simplified; because Thorax will deal with all rendering, `TimelineView.js` doesn't need a render function. The `initialize` function is also unnecessary because the collection will be made available before the view is created.

```
var com = com || {};
com.apress = com.apress || {};
com.apress.view = com.apress.view || {};

com.apress.view.ThoraxTimelineView = Thorax.View.extend({
  template: Handlebars.compile($("#timeline-template").html()),
});
```

The previous template assumed that a collection would be provided and iterated through using the each that Handlebars provides. However, Thorax provides a collection helper. This helper allows you to define the tag and class to use at either end of the list, while iterating through the collection.

```
<!-- Template for timeline -->
<script type="text/x-handlebars-template" id="timeline-template">
{{#collection tag="ul" class="listview fluid"}}
        <li>
          <div class='icon'>
                  <img src='{{user.profile_image_url}}'></img>
            </div>
            <div class='data'>
                <h4>{{user.name}}</h4>

                <p>{{format text}}</p>
                <p class="timestamp"><i>{{friendlyDate}}</i></p>
            </div>
        </li>
        {{/collection}}
</script>
```

While updating the HTML, ensure that there is a dedicated section to append the view to. In this case, it is the div with the timeline-section identifier.

```
<div id='timeline' class='timeline-view'>
<h2>My Tweets</h2>
 <div id="timeline-section"></div>
 </div>
```

You will also need to ensure that all the necessary scripts are included in the HTML, in addition to the scripts already included for the Profile view.

```
<!-- Model -->
<script src="js/app/model/thorax/Tweet.js"></script>
<!-- Collections -->
<script src="js/app/collection/thorax/Timeline.js"></script>
<!-- View -->
<script src="js/app/view/ThoraxTimelineView.js"></script>
<!-- Util -->
<script src="js/app/util/Helpers.js"></script>
```

Finally, to render the view, retrieve the collection and build the timeline view once it has been fetched successfully.

```
var timeline = new com.apress.collection.thorax.Timeline();
//force the fetch to fire a reset event
timeline.fetch({reset:true, success: function(){
    var timelineView = new com.apress.view.ThoraxTimelineView({collection: timeline});
    timelineView.appendTo('#timeline-section');
}});
```

After running the previous code, the resulting HTML should look like Figure 10-8.

Figure 10-8. Final view of Thorax Twitter application example

Summary

In this chapter, we saw the benefits of the two leading Backbone add-ons, Marionette and Thorax. With Marionette, it's clear that your application is much more scalable, with applications built through modules and an event-driven architecture that removes unnecessary coupling between objects. The code behind the application is much simpler than with standard Backbone and is less error-prone because of the reduction in boilerplate code. The memory management features mean that you won't fall victim to the typical zombie view issues that many Backbone developers hit. Best of all, Marionette allows you to pick and choose which features of the framework suit your project.

Even though Thorax is opinionated, with the requirement that Handlebars templates are utilized, it provides a really simple way of binding models and collections to views. And as with Marionette, nested views and rendering are dealt with by the framework and allow developers to focus on the core business logic.

This chapter should be enough to get you started with either Marionette or Thorax. If you choose to base your Backbone application on either framework, you'll see that there is a lot to discover. No matter which one you choose, your applications will be more structured and scalable as a result.

CHAPTER 11

■ ■ ■

Best Practices with Backbone

In the previous chapters we've seen how to use Backbone, along with some useful add-ons, to create high-quality web applications. However, as your app scales and begins to gain traction with real customers, you need to be confident in how you use the underlying technology. While frameworks such as Marionette and Thorax reduce the margin of error when it comes to view management, it is still worth understanding the techniques that can ensure you get the most from Backbone. This chapter compiles best practices that developers have employed when using Backbone. You'll see how to manage templates effectively, avoid memory leaks, and ensure that your application has the best performance possible with the tips listed in the following sections.

General Best Practices

Before we go into detailed practices, there are some simple things you should keep in mind when building Backbone applications.

Maintain a Clear Separation of Concerns

Much is made of Backbone's unopinionated nature, where you are free to use the library as you want. Without controls in place, it can be pretty easy to have your code run out of control. It is worth keeping the "separation of concerns" principle in mind. The main example of where this should be upheld is where references are made to views from with a model. While this may appeal in some cases, you should resist this as much as possible.

While a view has a reference to a model or collection in order to populate the data, the model never needs to know about the view that it is being rendered in. Enforcing this separation has a number of benefits:

- Models/collections can be tested without the view needing to be rendered.

- View-related logic will be kept out of the model and left into the view (because the model doesn't know anything about the view).

- If separate views are built for mobile and desktop browsers, there is no additional complication for the model. It remains the same regardless.

All your data classes will be more modular and reusable as a result.

Add Error Handling Patterns to Your Application

For any application that involves the input of data, you will want to have a consistent error handling and notification system in place. When building your application, this should be one of the first things you put in place. It ensures that all other developers in your team follow the same pattern and reduces the amount of duplicated code. It also ensures a better user experience because errors are displayed in a consistent and helpful manner.

Handling Validation Errors

One common pattern is to return an error object from the validate function. When the view is notified of a failure in the validation of the model, through the invalid event, it can then investigate this error object to update the view accordingly.

The following validate method returns an error array containing the individual errors that are encountered during validation. Note that if there are no errors, then nothing is returned from the function, implying a valid model.

```
validate: function(attrs) {
    var errors = [];

    if(attrs.email.indexOf('@') == -1) {
        errors.push({
            'message': 'Invalid email address',
            'attribute': 'email'
        });
    }

    if(attrs.name.length < 1) {
        errors.push({
            'message': 'Name must be specified',
            'attribute': 'name'
        });
    }

    //if there are no errors and no return, then there is no invalid event.
    if(errors.length) {
        return errors;
    }
}
```

The view listens for the invalid event being triggered from the model, inspects the second parameter (the return value from the validate function) for errors, and updates the view accordingly.

```
this.model.on('invalid', function(model, errors) {

        for(var i =0 ; i < errors.length; i++){
            if(errors[i].attribute === 'email'){
                //highlight the email field with errors[i].message
            }
            if(errors[i].attribute === 'name'){
                //highlight the name field with errors[i].message
            }
        }
});
```

A more advanced variation of this pattern suggested by Philip Whisenhunt and Derick Bailey is to trigger individual events for each error that can occur in the validate function, with the advantage that each error can then be handled individually in the view, rather than having a large function as a result of an invalid event being fired. The validate function is much the same, triggering events rather than adding errors.

```
validate: function(attrs) {
   var errors = [];

   if(attrs.email.indexOf('@') == -1) {
      this.trigger('invalid:email', 'Invalid email address', this);
   }

   if(attrs.name.length < 1) {
       this.trigger('invalid:name', 'Name must be specified', this);

   }

}
```

On the view, each of the error events is listened for.

```
this.model.on('invalid:email', function(error) {
      //highlight the email field with the error
});
this.model.on('invalid:name', function(error) {
      //highlight the name field with the error
});
```

As you can see, this provides a more elegant, decoupled approach to error handling.

Add a General Error Alert

For a custom user interface, it is worthwhile to add a single alert dialog that can be used across all of your views. This can be done by extending Backbone.View to create your own superclass or by using the mixin approach detailed in the "Sharing Common Code Between Views" section later in this chapter.

Avoiding Memory Leaks

One of the most common errors across all applications, regardless of programming language or framework, is memory leaks. A memory leak occurs when objects or views that should no longer be in use are still "alive" in the system. This is usually a result of objects not being correctly disposed. In Backbone, this is a common problem, but it's easy to solve once you know how.

Unbind Events When Closing Views

One of the most common reasons for memory leaks in Backbone is when views that are not currently in use, as a result of navigating to a new view, are still bound to events. We've referred to these previously in the book as *zombie views*.

As we've already seen, events are an essential part of the Backbone application infrastructure, allowing real decoupling between views, models, and collections. A symptom for event bindings that are being handled incorrectly would be where a single event is being handled multiple times unexpectedly.

Let's first recap the different ways to handle events in a view. One way that a view can bind itself to change events in a model is through the on function.

```
MyView = Backbone.View.extend({
 initialize: function(){
   this.model.on('change', this.render, this);
 },
});
```

With the previous code, any changes in the model will result in the render function in the view being invoked. Note that in previous versions of Backbone, this function was named bind rather than on; the old name is still supported, but it's best to use on.

Views also use the events hash to bind DOM events to handlers.

```
MyView = Backbone.View.extend({
 events: {
   'click #search': 'runSearch'
 },
 runSearch: function(){
     //search code
 },
});
```

When the application is finished with the view and you render a new view, these events are still bound, and because of this, the view is kept in memory. Developers new to Backbone may assume that the remove function, which removes the view from the DOM, will deal with all events, but this is not true.

You can take a few different approaches in your application code to deal with this.

Use listenTo for Event Handling

One of the advantages of using listenTo for your event handling is that when the remove function is called for a view, the stopListening function is called in turn, thus unbinding any of the events that have been bound using listenTo. The following is an example of how this function can be used to bind to all change events in a model:

```
MyView = Backbone.View.extend({
 initialize: function(){
   this.listenTo(model, 'change', this.render);
 },
});
```

It can be a good rule of thumb to use listenTo in place of either the bind or on function when dealing with events.

Use a Pattern to Close Views Correctly

Another option is to write some additional code for views to ensure that they are disposed of properly. When switching between views in a router, you could ensure that as new views are displayed, any previous view is closed. Derick Bailey proposes a useful pattern for this on his blog, at http://lostechies.com/derickbailey/2011/09/15/zombies-run-managing-page-transitions-in-backbone-apps/, which is used in his Marionette library and is also available in his EventBinder plug-in.

The pattern begins with the addition of a close function for Backbone.View. This can be achieved in a number of ways, but the most effective is to extend the Backbone.Views prototype with a close function. The close function will encapsulate both removing the view from the DOM and unbinding any events.

```
Backbone.View.prototype.close = function(){
        this.remove();
        this.unbind();
        if (this.onClose){
                this.onClose();
        }
}
```

Note that the final few lines of this function refer to onClose(). This is another additional function that can be added to each individual view that should unbind all events that the view has added throughout its life cycle.

```
var MyView = Backbone.View.extend({

  initialize: function() {
    this.model.on('change', this.render, this);
  },
  render: function() {
      // render a template
  },
  onClose: function(){
      //unbind events bound during the views lifecycle
      this.model.off('change');
  }
});
```

As you can see in the previous code sample, the view registers to listen to the change event on the model during initialization and deregisters this listener when the onClose function is invoked.

To make calls to close views, there needs to be an object that keeps track of which view is currently in focus. To do this, Derek Bailey suggested adding a single AppView controller that can be used by the router as views are switched.

```
function AppView(){
  this.showView(view) {
  if (this.currentView){
    this.currentView.close();
  }

  this.currentView = view;
  this.currentView.render();
  $("#mainContent").html(this.currentView.el);
 }
}
```

The AppView object exposes one function, showView. This function closes the currentView, if one exists, before rendering the new view and adding to the page.

Router can now utilize this AppView object when views need to be shown as various routes are triggered. First the view is created, and then the showView function is used to display the view and ensure the previous view is properly disposed.

```
MyRouter = Backbone.Router.extend({
 routes: {
   "": "home",
   "search/:query": "showResults"
 },
 initialize: function(options){
   this.appView = options.appView;
 },
 home: function(){
   var homeView = new HomeView();
   this.appView.showView(homeView);
 },
 showPost: function(query){
   //some code to get search results...
   var searchResultsView = new SearchResultsView({model: results});
   this.appView.showView(searchResultsView);
 }
});
```

Once again, it's worth noting that leveraging frameworks such as Marionette will help you achieve similar results as the previous, but it's always useful to have a better understanding of what is really going on when views are removed.

Rendering Views

You can use a number of practices when dealing with views. These range from improving the granularity of the render functions to improving how you use templates.

Render Only What You Need

All examples so far in this book have dealt with single render functions for each view. While this makes sense, it doesn't take long before you have complex render functions for more involved views. More importantly, there will be cases where you want to ensure that your views remain fresh. Take the Twitter application, for example: there is a single render function that is done when we retrieve new data that renders all the tweets in the timeline. These tweets will appear with timestamps such as "one minute ago." It would be nice to have these times update so they don't become stale, but it is overkill to render the entire collection, or even the single tweet section, each time. It would be more useful if the rendering could be split up so that the timestamp can be updated on its own.

One way of dealing with this is to break up the render function into separate areas. By splitting up templates, it is possible to have the main render function call a number of smaller functions with defined responsibility.

Taking a single tweet, for example, the render function could be split into two parts: one for the main content and one for the timestamp.

```
render: function(){
        this.renderContent().
            renderTimestamp();
        return this;
},
```

The advantage to this approach is that you can later update just part of the view, without needing to rerun the entire render function. The following code snippet shows how such a view could be constructed:

```
var com = com || {};
com.apress = com.apress || {};
com.apress.view = com.apress.view || {};

com.apress.view.TweetView = Backbone.View.extend({

    el: '#tweet',
    $timestamp: null,
    $content : null,
    tweetTemplate: Handlebars.compile($("#tweet-template").html()),
    timestampTemplate: Handlebars.compile($("#timestamp-template").html()),
    tweet : null,

    initialize: function(options){
        this.tweet = options.tweet;
        this.render();
    },

    render: function(){
        this.renderContent().
            renderTimestamp();
        return this;
    },

    renderContent: function(){
        //if the content is already rendered remove
        if(this.$content){
            this.$content.remove();
        }
        //deal with the main content template
        $content = this.tweetTemplate({
                tweet: this.tweet.toJSON()
        });
        this.$el.append($content);
        return this;
    },

    renderTimestamp: function(){
        //if the timestamp is already rendered remove
        if(this.$timestamp){
            this.$timestamp.remove();
        }
        //deal with the timestamp template
        $timestamp = this.timestampTemplate({
                time: this.tweet.getTimestamp()
        });
        this.$('#timestamp').append($timestamp);

        return this;
    }

});
```

Note that there are two separate templates used here and that as each of the lower-level render functions is called, they will first clear the element if it has previously been rendered. Each of the functions also returns a pointer to this, allowing the render methods to be chained in a neater way.

The templates used for the view are as follows. The main content template includes a placeholder for the timestamp.

```
<script type="text/x-handlebars-template" id="tweet-template">
 <p>{{tweet.text}}</p>
 <div id="timestamp"></div>
</script>

<script type="text/x-handlebars-template" id="timestamp-template">
  <p><i>{{time}}</i></p>
</script>
```

For completeness, the code to populate and display this view follows. The Tweet model is a simple Backbone.Model, with just a simple text attribute, as well as a way of representing the timestamp in a readable fashion using moment.js.

```
Tweet = Backbone.Model.extend({

    timestamp: null,
    initialize: function(){
        timestamp = new Date();
    },

    getTimestamp: function(){
        var friendly = moment(timestamp).fromNow();
        return friendly;
    }

});

var tweet = new Tweet({text: 'James'});

var tweetView = new com.apress.view.TweetView({tweet: tweet});
```

Even in cases where you do not need to update parts of the view at specified intervals, splitting up the render function will make your code more readable to others and reduce the risk of the view code becoming unmaintainable.

Reduce Template Bloat with Partials

As an application grows, there will undoubtedly be some repetition in the definition of your templates as parts of some templates are copied into newer ones. This can lead to maintenance problems and breaks the well-respected Don't Repeat Yourself (DRY) principle of software development. This section will look at the solutions available in both Handlebars and Underscore.

Partials in Handlebars

Handlebars provides out-of-the-box support for partials through the `registerPartial` function. When one template includes another partial template in its definition, the `{{> partialname}}` helper is used to place it in the correct location. The following timeline template example shows how this would be possible:

```
<script id='timeline-template' type='text/x-handlebars-template'>
 {{#each tweetlist}}
   {{> tweet}}
 {{/each}}
</script>
```

The template expects another partial to be registered, with the name tweet. As mentioned, this is done using the `Handlebars.registerPartial` function.

```
Handlebars.registerPartial('tweet', $('#tweet-partial').html());
```

The partial itself is defined like any Handlebars template would be. It can be a useful convention to add `-partial` to the end of the template ID for the purpose of fast identification.

```
<script id='tweet-partial' type='text/x-handlebars-template'>
 <div class='tweet'>
   <h2>{{username}}</h2>
   <div class='text'>{{text}}</div>
 </div>
</script>
```

The main template can be compiled as normal within your Backbone view once your partial has been registered in time.

Partials in Underscore

It's also possible to provide partials in Underscore templates. Although there is no helper, like there is in Handlebars, it is still quite simple because of Underscore's JavaScript syntax.

First, the partial template is defined to display a single item, in this case a book.

```
<script type='text/template' id='book-template'>
     <li>
       <b><%=name %></b> by <%=author %>
     </li>
</script>
```

To utilize this partial template, the main template can refer to it as if it were a JavaScript function, taking the item as a parameter.

```
<script type='text/template' id='library-template'>
<ul>
   <% for (var i = 0; i < library.length; i++) { %>
     <% itemTemplate(library[i]); %>
   <% } %>
</ul>
</script>
```

In the Backbone view, both templates need to be available to the render function.

```
LibraryView = BackboneView.extend({({
        template: _.template($('#library-template').html()),

itemTemplate: _.template($('#book-template').html()),

 render: function() {
   var html = this.template({
     library: library /* a collection */,
     itemTemplate: this.bookTemplate
   });

   $(this.el).append(html);
 }
});
```

This approach can be used across all reusable Underscore templates in your application.

Precompile Templates in Handlebars

Template precompilation is the practice of preparing templates at build time to reduce the compilation time required when rendering a view. It can also help you reduce the size of the templating library because the compilation engine is no longer required for the application in production. Handlebars already provides a separation between the full version and the runtime version, as described in Chapter 4.

The savings made when using a precompiled template are not insignificant, especially when dealing with mobile devices.

In Chapter 4, we created a simple Handlebars example that provided a template for the library collection. To precompile this template for using in a Backbone application, you will first need to install the Handlebars node package.

```
npm install handlebars -g
```

Next you will need to take the template out of the HTML page and move it to a separate file. Typically each template is moved to a .handlebars file. In the case of the library template, it makes sense to move it to library.handlebars.

```
<script type="text/x-handlebars-template" id="library-template">
<ul>
    {{#each library}}
      <li>
      {{#log name 4}}{{/log}}
       <em>{{name}}</em> by {{author}}
      </li>
      {{/each}}
 </ul>
</script>
```

To precompile this template, the handlebars command takes the following form:

```
handlebars <input> -f <output>
```

In the case of the `library.handlebars` file, this will be as follows:

```
handlebars library.handlebars -f templates.js
```

This will generate a `templates.js` file that can be used in the HTML. The template will be identified as `library` in this case because the compiler uses the name of the input file as the template name. You can verify this by opening `templates.js` where you will see that the `templates` array includes an entry for `library` at the beginning of the file.

```
(function() {
  var template = Handlebars.template, templates = Handlebars.templates = Handlebars.templates || {};
templates['library'] = template(function (Handlebars,depth0,helpers,partials,data) {
```

■ **Note**   You will be using this array (`Handlebars.templates[]`) to access the precompiled template later.

The `templates.js` file needs to be included in the HTML page, and provided there are no calls in your JavaScript code to compile templates, the Handlebars runtime can be used instead.

```
<script src="js/external/handlebars-runtime.js"></script>
<script src="js/templates/templates.js"></script>
```

Finally, rather than using `Handlebars.compile` for the template in `Backbone.View`, you can access the template through the `Handlebars.templates` array.

```
template: Handlebars.templates['library'],
```

The refactored `LibraryView` remains the same otherwise.

```
LibraryView = Backbone.View.extend({

    initialize: function(){
        console.log('View created');
    },

    events: {
        'click ' : 'alertBook'
    },

    template: Handlebars.templates['library'],
    render: function(){
        var self = this;
        var output = self.template({'library': self.collection.toJSON()});
        self.$el.append(output);
        return self;
    },

    alertBook: function(e){
        alert('Book clicked');
    }

});
```

View Management

There can be a lot of complication around views once your application gets larger. The following section deals with some common issues that Backbone developers find in this area, including how to share common code between views and how to communicate between subviews and their parent view.

Sharing Common Code Between Views

When writing views in an application, it's likely you'll find that there is code that you want to share between them. There are a few approaches to dealing with this; one is to use inheritance. But the most useful technique to sharing code that I have found is by providing mixins, where the common code is provided in a separate JavaScript file that can be incorporated on demand.

As an example, imagine that you wanted common alert functionality across a selected number of views. All functions that could be shared, related to alerts, would be placed in a single file.

```
var Mixins = Mixins || {};

Mixins.Alerts = {

    showSuccessMessage: function(message){
        console.log('Show success message');
    },

    showFailureMessage: function(message){
        console.log('Show failure message');
    }
};
```

Then, when a view is defined, the mixin could be incorporated using the _.extend function.

```
var com = com || {};
com.apress = com.apress || {};
com.apress.view = com.apress.view || {};

com.apress.view.TweetView = Backbone.View.extend(
    _.extend({}, Mixins.Alerts, {
    //standard Backbone view code
})));
```

As a result of this, all the functions defined in the mixin are now available to the TweetView object.

Updating a Parent View from a Subview

At some point in your career as a Backbone developer you will hit a situation where a parent view needs to be updated as a result of a change in a subview. There are two approaches you can take to solve this: one involves passing a reference to the parent view to the subview, and the other relies on the event mechanism.

Passing a reference is the easiest to read and understand but leads to a coupling between the parent and child views. The following code shows how this could be achieved:

```
var MainView = Backbone.View.extend({
 initialize: function() {
   var self = this;
   this._views = [];
   // create a sub view for each model
   this.collection.each(function(model) {
     self._views.push(new SubView({
       model: model,
       parentView: self
     }));
   });
 }
});
```

Now that each SubView has a reference back to the parent view, the call to rerender the parent view could be made from the subview using this:

```
this.parentView.render();
```

The neater event-based solution requires no reference to be passed. Instead, the parent view simply needs to listen for events from the subview.

```
var MainView = Backbone.View.extend({
initialize: function() {
   var self = this;
   this._views = [];
   // create a sub view for each model
   this.collection.each(function(model) {
       var subview = new SubView({
       model: model,
       parentView: self
     });
     self._views.push(subview);
     self.listenTo(subview, 'event', self.render);
   });
}
});
```

The subview just needs to trigger the event in order to get the parent view to enter its render function.

```
this.trigger('event');
```

Network Performance

Once you have proven the functionality of an application, the performance of that application will come under scrutiny. There are a wealth of tools available to help you diagnose where you can make potential improvements, and a number of articles give good advice about this. We've already covered some of these tips previously in the book.

For example, the convention is that all CSS styles should be at the head of an HTML page, and the scripts should all be loaded at the bottom. This ensures that the page will render correctly at the beginning because waiting for CSS scripts to load will block rendering. Meanwhile, downloading JavaScript resources will block other downloads on the page, so these should happen at the end.

However, there are other tips that you should keep in mind when building your Backbone applications.

Minimize Requests on Page Load

One of the top tips with regard to network performance is to make fewer requests. Every single asset that you need in your page is an extra HTTP request. Rather than eagerly populating each of the Backbone.Model and Backbone.Collection objects in your application, take the time to consider which of these are needed immediately when the application is presented to the user.

One option is to use lazy loading, where the call to populate the objects from the server is made just at the time the user requires the data. While this can help minimize the page load time, it can lead to delays when the user does actually request the information.

If your application is built with server-side technologies, such as Grails, JSP, or .NET, it is possible that you could populate some of the initial models and collections with JSON data. This technique has become more popular, especially with Airbnb making its Rendr library available to all as an open source project on GitHub (https://github.com/airbnb/rendr). This project allows Backbone code to be rendered both on the client and on the server. More importantly, it makes it easy to pass the Backbone model content to your page when it is being rendered on the browser, allowing the server to perform the bulk of the network operations.

Finally, you may decide to refactor the API calls that are made from the client to server side as a result of some performance analysis of your application. Building end points that reduce data duplication across the API can be a useful exercise. It is always worth revisiting the API and refactoring as you go along.

Perceived Performance

You can utilize some tricks in your application to make the responsiveness seem to be much faster. In general, you should always be critical of the responsiveness of your app. Developers who are working with the same code from day to day tend to get used to the reaction times of an application, where a user may not be so forgiving.

Optimistic Network Calls

There are certain situations where it is safe to assume that a call to the back end will complete successfully, especially if all validation is carried out on the client side of the application. If you have a view where you save some model attributes to the server, it is typically that you wait for the success handler to be invoked before these changes are displayed or before a success message displays to the user.

```
var MyView = Backbone.View.extend({
 events: {
   'click .save': 'save'
 },

 save: function(e) {
   // save the model
   this.model.save(model.attributes, {
     success: function(model, response, options) {
       // render changes
     },
```

```
      error: function(model, xhr, options) {
        // render error
      }
    });
  }

});
```

If you are confident that the call will be successful and that all necessary validation has been carried out on the client side, then you don't need to wait to display the result of the successful transaction. If something does go wrong, the error handler can pick up the change and run some code to undo the change and inform the user that the operation failed.

There may be cases that this type of optimization is too risky, so it is worth weighing the risk versus the benefit of such changes.

Use Document Fragment for Rendering Collections

When a single view corresponds with an entire collection, updating the view following a change in the collection can appear to happen pretty smoothly because one single render function is invoked, with one call to append to the view's el. However, when you have a separate view for each model object in your collection, every time the collection changes, the rerendering of each of subview can affect performance and make the UI appear to be jumpy.

Consider the following code that takes this approach for a collection:

```
var MainView = Backbone.View.extend({
    initialize: function() {
  var self = this;
  this._views = [];
  // create a sub view for each model
  this.collection.each(function(model) {
    self._views.push(new SubView({
      model: model
    }));
  });
 },
 render: function() {
   var self = this;
   this.$el.empty();
   // render each subview, and append
     for(var i=0; i < this.views.length; i++){
     self.$el.append(views[i].render().el);
   });
 }
});
```

Each time that an append occurs, the DOM needs to recalculate the position and size of everything in the DOM tree, which is an expensive operation when there are a large number of models in a collection. It would be much cleaner to build up the element contents first and have a single append to the DOM. That is exactly what the createDocumentFragment function of the DOM helps you achieve. Supported on all the major browsers, the function creates a Node object in the background, allowing you to prepare the contents before appending to the real document.

This results in the render function in the previous code sample changing to the following:

```
render: function() {
  var self = this;
  self.$el.empty();
  var fragment = document.createDocumentFragment();
  // render each subview, and append
    for(var i=0; i < this.views.length; i++)
      fragment.$el.append(views[i].render().el);
  });
  this.$el.append(fragment);
}
```

Note how a fragment is first created and each of the subviews is added to this. Once the loop has completed and the fragment has all views added, the entire fragment can be appended to the root el for the view.

Use Models to Store Extra Data

The default implementation of most Backbone models is to represent the data that gets persisted to the server only. While this sounds good in principle, there are cases where it causes more trouble. Consider an example where we want to track when an item in a view is selected. In the view class, it's simply a matter of adding a listener for the click event to track which item is selected.

```
com.apress.view.TweetView = Backbone.View.extend({
    //other code
    tweet : null,
    events: {
        'click': 'markSelected'
    },

    markSelected: function(options){
        console.log('marking..');
        var self = this,
            $target = $(options.currentTarget);
        $target.addClass('selected');

    },
    //other code
});
```

If you want to check what the currently selected model object is, you need to traverse the DOM and find which element has the selected class.

In cases like this, it makes sense to track the state in the model object. In this way, you can iterate through the collection to find the model object where the selected attribute is equal to true. This would change the markSelected function to the following:

```
markSelected: function(options){
      console.log('marking..');
      var self = this,
          $target = $(options.currentTarget);
      self.tweet.set('selected', true);
      $target.addClass('selected');
},
```

Note that this does add some overhead of managing variables and deciding which variables should be persisted to the server. However, discovering item state within the application is not as expensive as discovering which classes are applied to the corresponding DOM element. It also helps with the testability of the model objects because the selected state is effectively decoupled from the view.

Cache Objects Where Possible

Rather than retrieving new instances of views or models that are used across the application, it is good practice to cache such objects. A user object is a good example of this, where the object is shared across many views in the application. If you created a new instance of the user object each time you moved to a new page, it would be wasteful, particularly if the object doesn't frequently change.

The router is the best example of a place where such a pattern can be useful. When initialized, the user model is set to undefined.

```
initialize: function() {
    this.cached = {
        userModel: undefined
    }
},
```

If a route is triggered within the router, the model can be retrieved if undefined, or otherwise the cached version can be returned.

```
mainView: function(parameter) {
    this.cached.model = this.cached.model || new UserModel({});
    new View({
        userModel: this.cached.userModel
    });
},
```

If another view uses this, such as a profile view, it doesn't need to retrieve the model from the server.

```
profileView: function(parameter) {
    this.cached.model = this.cached.model || new UserModel({});
    new ProfileView({
        userModel: this.cached.userModel
    });
},
```

There may be cases where you need to force the model to be retrieved. In these cases, you can add a change listener in the model itself to prompt a fetch to take place. The following example forces a fetch to occur if the password is changed:

```
initialize: function() {
    this.on("change:password", this.fetch, this);
}
```

Caching objects can be useful and will increase the performance of the application, at the cost of a slight memory overhead as the objects are kept alive. You should also be aware of cases where the model object isn't updating as you'd expect because of caching. The best advice is to use this pattern with caution.

Summary

This chapter listed a number of the most important practices to keep in mind when building professional Backbone applications. Memory management will be key among the concerns of most app developers, while performance, responsiveness, and general code management are also high on the list. Because of Backbone's unopinionated nature, developers are afforded a lot of freedom on how to construct applications. With the practices in this chapter in mind, you will be able to steer your team away from some of the common traps that exist for Backbone developers.

With all of this in mind, it can make a lot of sense to utilize the plug-ins listed in Chapter 7 or to leverage the Marionette or Thorax libraries discussed in Chapter 10, particularly because most errors in Backbone applications are a result of badly managed views.

Thanks to Phillip Whisenhunt, Addy Osmani, Derick Bailey, Ian Storm Taylor, Rico Sta Cruz, and Oz Katz for their insightful articles that highlighted a number of the best practices, tips, and patterns used in this chapter.

■ ■ ■

CHAPTER 12

Creating a Manageable JavaScript Code Base

Now you know how to build Backbone applications, introduce a build system, and ensure quality code with test frameworks. The last piece of the puzzle is keeping the code in a maintainable state. JavaScript applications are often criticized for becoming a mess of spaghetti code over time, and left unchecked, it could happen to your Backbone app, too. This chapter brings you some tips to help ensure your code remains understandable, modular, and testable over its lifetime. In this chapter, we'll introduce RequireJS as a way to ensure your application is truly modular, and we'll discuss some useful design patterns that enforce structure and clarity in your Backbone applications.

Using RequireJS to Create Modular Applications

Throughout this book, namespaces have been utilized to ensure that no conflicts occur when both views and models have the same name. However, this solves only one aspect of modularity. You still need to ensure that your scripts are loaded in the correct order, based on dependencies. Once the application grows, the interactions between different objects become more difficult to manage. RequireJS is one of the best ways to deal with this issue.

Another important consideration for an application is that of reusability. There may be parts of code that make sense to embed in other views. A classic example of this would be Google Talk: you can communicate with someone in a stand-alone view, as well as having a view embedded at the side of the Gmail web page or as part of a conversation at Google Docs. Rather than writing the same code a number of times or, even worse, copying that code, taking a modular approach means that parts of the code can be used in more than one place.

Traditional languages, such as Java, C++, and C#, all have their own way of declaring dependencies on other classes using an `import/include` syntax. In JavaScript, this isn't possible. Instead, developers must ensure that the load order is correct so that any files that a particular piece of JavaScript depends on have been loaded correctly first. While this is possible with smaller applications, it soon grows out of scale and becomes a maintenance nightmare.

When it comes to creating modules in JavaScript, RequireJS is considered the leading option and provides a great solution for all the problems listed earlier.

What Is RequireJS?

RequireJS (`www.requirejs.org`, Figure 12-1) is an implementation of the Asynchronous Module Definition (AMD) API. This API specifies a way of defining modules such that the module, along with any of its dependencies, can be loaded asynchronously. While this resolves issues around dependencies, it also helps with the performance of the web application because scripts are no longer loaded in a synchronous manner.

```
/* ---

RequireJS is a JavaScript file and module
loader. It is optimized for in-browser use, but
it can be used in other JavaScript environments,
like Rhino and Node. Using a modular script
loader like RequireJS will improve the speed and
quality of your code.

IE 6+ .......... compatible ✔
Firefox 2+ ..... compatible ✔
Safari 3.2+ .... compatible ✔
Chrome 3+ ...... compatible ✔
Opera 10+ ...... compatible ✔

Get started then check out the API.

--- */
```

Latest Release: 2.1.9
Open source: new BSD or MIT licensed
web design by Andy Chung © 2011

Figure 12-1. Requirejs.org

Incorporating RequireJS into a JavaScript application requires some changes across the board, both in the module definition and in the initial set of script tags that are used in your main HTML page. The next section discusses the use of RequireJS in detail.

Using RequireJS

Before looking at how to integrate RequireJS into a Backbone application, it is easier to understand how RequireJS works by viewing its use in isolation, independent of any other JavaScript libraries.

You will need to download RequireJS from the web site at www.requirejs.org/docs/download.html. As in previous examples, this can be saved in a js/external directory. However, RequireJS should have additional attributes that are used in its script tag when loaded from the HTML page. The data-main attribute is used to instruct RequireJS to load the script that it points to after RequireJS loads itself. This is a single entry point for the entire application, and as such no other scripts need be included in your HTML page.

The following HTML code illustrates this:

```
<!DOCTYPE html>
<html>
    <head>
        <title>RequireJS Example</title>
        <!-- data-main attribute tells require.js to load
```

```
        scripts/main.js after require.js loads. -->
    <script data-main="js/main" src="js/external/require.js"></script>
    </head>
    <body>
        <h1>My App</h1>
    </body>
</html>
```

In this case, data-main points to js/main, meaning that main.js, which resides in the js directory, will be the first script to be loaded. RequireJS will always assume that any script dependencies are JavaScript, so there is no need to specify the trailing .js for the file name. Figure 12-2 shows the folder structure necessary for this simple application.

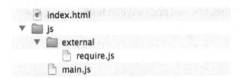

Figure 12-2. *Simple application structure for a RequireJS application*

All code that RequireJS loads from now will be from the js directory because the folder in which the main script loads from is considered to be the value for the baseUrl configuration in RequireJS. However, it is possible to set this value manually. Any additional configuration for RequireJS, such as this, will usually take place in the main script.

Table 12-1 describes some of the most useful configuration options that can be used when setting up RequireJS.

Table 12-1. *Useful RequireJS Configuration Options*

Option	Description
baseUrl	This is the root directory to use for loading all modules in RequireJS. If this has not been set in the configuration and there is no data-main for it to be calculated from, then the default value will be the location of the HTML page that loads require.js.
	It is possible to set the baseUrl to be on a different domain because RequireJS will support cross-domain script loading.
	The following example illustrates how the baseUrl is set to point to the app directory:

	`require.config({`
	`    baseUrl: "/js/app",`
	`});`

paths	The paths hash can be used to set up mappings for modules that are not found directly under the specified baseUrl. This can be useful to set up such mappings to shorten the paths required when detailing module dependencies.
	The following example shows how the lib path is set to map to js/external/lib.

	`require.config({`
	
	`    paths: {`
	`        'lib': 'js/external/lib'`
	`    }`
	`});`

(continued)

Table 12-1. (*continued*)

Option	Description
shim	This allows the configuration of dependencies, exports, and custom initialization for old scripts that do not use define(). This configuration will be required when adding dependencies for jQuery, Underscore, and Backbone in your application. Each item in the list of shims is given a module ID export and can optionally include a list of dependencies. An example of this configuration is provided in the "Including RequireJS in a Backbone Application" section.

map	This allows a module ID to be mapped to another for a given module prefix. This can be useful in cases where you have two different versions of a module but other modules are dependent on different versions.
	
	The following example shows how two different modules (modone and modtwo) can both refer to the api module as api but use different versions.
	
	`requirejs.config({`
	`    map: {`
	`        'modone': {`
	`            'api': 'api1.0'`
	`        },`
	`        'modtwo': {`
	`            'api': 'api1.1'`
	`        }`
	`    }`
	`});`

config	The config option allows a general configuration object to be passed to RequireJS. This can contain any options that you want to be available to a module. This is available by using require.config() in your modules.
waitSeconds	This sets the number of seconds to wait before aborting the attempt to load a script. The default value is 7, and setting this value to 0 will disable this timeout so that RequireJS will never give up on loading a script.
deps	This specifies an array of dependencies to load immediately after the configuration of RequireJS has been processed.

■ **Note**   RequireJS will use module IDs to load all modules. However, if you need to include nonmodule files, you can ensure that the dependency string ends with a .js or begins with a protocol such as http:// or https://.

For this simple example, there is no additional configuration necessary, so main.js remains empty. However, it will be responsible for starting the application once some modules have been defined.

Defining and Using Modules

Creating a module will allow you to create an object that has a defined scope and has a list of dependencies on other modules that exist in your application. The define function is used to create these modules, and depending on the type of module you are defining and how it is being set up, the parameters to this function will vary.

Modules with Name-Value Pairs

If the module you are creating has no functions and is just a set of name-value pairs, it can be defined by passing through the name-value pairs in an object to the define function. For example, the following code, contained in Book.js, would create a module named Book that contains a particular set of data.

```
define({
    title: "Beginning Backbone.js",
    author: "James Sugrue"
});
```

To include this module in main.js, the require function is used. There are two parameters in the require function: an array of module names that are needed and a callback function that takes each of those modules as parameters.

In this example, you can simply require Book and use that as a parameter in the callback function. Note that you can name this parameter whatever you want. The mapping of parameter to module depends on the order the module is listed in the array and its position in the list of parameters.

```
require(['Book'], function(book){
    console.log('Title: ' + book.title);
});
```

The result of the previous code execution should be to print "Title: Beginning Backbone.js" to the console.

Modules with Setup Logic

More complex modules may need to execute some logic before returning the module definition. In such cases, the define function can accept a function as its parameter. This function should run through the appropriate steps before returning the module.

The following example will change the book title to uppercase as an initial setup step:

```
define(function(){

    var title = 'Beginning Backbone.js';
    var author = 'James Sugrue';
    title = title.toUpperCase();

    return {
            title: title,
            author: author
    };
});
```

Assuming that the previous module is saved in SetupBook.js, when it is used in main.js, it will print the title of the book in uppercase.

```
//Setup function example
require(['SetupBook'], function(book){
    console.log('Title: ' + book.title);
});
```

Modules with Dependencies

When a module has dependencies, they can be loaded in its `define` function, in a similar approach to how the `require` function is used. In this case, the `define` function accepts two parameters. The first is an array of module IDs that the module itself is dependent on. The second parameter is a callback function that accepts each of the dependent modules as parameters. This function returns an object that defines the `Library` module.

In the following example, `Library.js` is dependent on `Book.js` in order to define some content for the library. The module returns an object with functions in addition to the simple name-value pairs used up until this point.

```
define(["./Book"], function(book) {

    return {
        name: "My Library",
        getContents: function() {
            var books = [];
            books.push(book);
            return books;
        }
    }
}
);
```

The function is not executed until the dependent module, Book, has first been loaded. `Main.js` will no longer require the Book module and instead will load the `Library` module.

```
require(['Library'], function(library){

    console.log('Library Name: ' + library.name);
    for(var i = 0; i < library.getContents().length; i++){
        console.log('Book: ' + library.getContents()[i].title);
    }
});
```

Running this code will result in the name of the library, as well as a list of the contents of the library, being printed to the console (the list of contents is currently just the simple Book module defined earlier).

Note the module does not need to return objects but can instead add a function that provides a return value.

Including RequireJS in a Backbone Application

If you are refactoring a Backbone application to take advantage of the modular structure encouraged by RequireJS, you will need to do a little work to get code ready. If you are building a new Backbone application, you may want to skip ahead to the section on Yeoman, which describes a simple quick-start method of creating a RequireJS-based Backbone app.

To illustrate how to incorporate RequireJS into existing applications, let's take another look at the example Twitter application from Chapter 6.

Initial RequireJS Inclusion

First create a complete copy of the code from Chapter 6, and add `require.js` in the `js/external` directory. To follow the standard RequireJS convention, create a `main.js` file that will deal with the initial configuration. This should be placed in the `js` directory. All the script includes in the original `index.html` file can be stripped down to the standard RequireJS include.

```
<script data-main="js/main" src="js/external/require.js"></script>
```

This initial step provides no functionality, but it covers the three main steps to get started on moving to RequireJS:

1. Download RequireJS.

2. Remove existing script tags in the main HTML page.

3. Include RequireJS with a `main.js` file to deal with the initial setup.

Configuring Backbone for RequireJS

With `main.js` in place, you can now perform some of the initial RequireJS configuration that is needed in order to have libraries such as Backbone, which are not written as modules, to be usable by the RequireJS system. This was referred to briefly in the "Using RequireJS" section under the shim configuration option.

First we need to create an initial configuration object for RequireJS in `main.js`.

```
require.config({
  });
```

Each of the paths to our various libraries should be added in the `paths` section of the configuration. This tells RequireJS where it can discover libraries such as Backbone, jQuery, and Underscore. Each of these is given an ID.

```
require.config({
paths: {
      jquery: './external/jquery-1.10.2',
      backbone: './external/backbone',
      underscore: './external/underscore',
   }
});
```

Note that there is no need to append `.js` to the end of the paths for the libraries; RequireJS does this automatically.

One of the benefits of this configuration is that even though we are referring to jQuery as `jquery`, it can point to a specific version. This is the only place in the entire code that the version needs to be considered. As new versions of jQuery are made available and used in your application, the update to the path just needs to be made in this location. Not that jQuery must always be referred to as `jquery` within RequireJS. It is already AMD compliant, but it is a named module, and that name must not deviate from `jquery`.

The next part of the configuration that needs to be dealt with is the shim, where each of the libraries that are not already created using the RequireJS `define()` syntax need to be made available. Because jQuery already defines itself as a module, you will not need to include it in the `shim` section.

Each library is identified using the same name because it has been given in the `paths` section. Each library may have a number of dependencies, which are listed as an array of strings under the `deps` attribute. In the following example, Backbone has dependencies on both Underscore and jQuery. Because Underscore itself has no dependencies, it does not need to have any `deps` defined.

Each of the libraries listed in the shim needs to have an exports attribute defined, which provides access to the global variable used to access the library. For Underscore, this is _, just as if you were using the library without RequireJS, and Backbone obviously uses Backbone as its export.

```
shim: {
    underscore: {
        exports: '_'
    },
    backbone: {
        deps: [
            'underscore',
            'jquery'
        ],
        exports: 'Backbone'
    },
},
```

To ensure that this is all OK, add the following line after the RequireJS configuration in main.js. It simple uses RequireJS to load Backbone and makes a call to start the history. If anything goes wrong here, you will see an error in the browser console.

```
require([
    'backbone'
], function (Backbone) {
    Backbone.history.start();
    console.log('All ok');
});
```

Our sample application also has dependencies on a few other libraries, including Handlebars and Moment. js. These also need to be included in the path and shim sections of the configuration. The following code shows the complete RequireJS configuration for the Twitter example application:

```
require.config({
    shim: {
        underscore: {
            exports: '_'
        },
        backbone: {
            deps: [
                'underscore',
                'jquery'
            ],
            exports: 'Backbone'
        },
        handlebars: {
            exports: 'Handlebars'
        },
        moment: {
            exports: 'moment'
        },
```

```
        dialog: {
            exports: 'Dialog'
        },

    },

    paths: {
        jquery: './external/jquery-1.10.2',
        backbone: './external/backbone',
        underscore: './external/underscore',
        handlebars: './external/handlebars',
        moment: './external/moment'

    }
});
```

Refactor Your Application with RequireJS

With the RequireJS configuration in place for all external libraries, the next task is to refactor all of the JavaScript code that you have already created for the application to work with this modular approach.

In general, you should be able to apply the following pattern to all of your code in order to make things compliant. Start by appending the following to the beginning of your file. This is where you define the dependencies that your file has, with each of these dependencies passed to the callback as parameters.

```
define([ ], function() {
```

The code that already existed in the file can remain intact, and the file can be closed with this:

```
// export what you have created:
    return object;
});
```

Now, anytime that another JavaScript file calls require on the defined module, it will receive the correct object. To get a better understanding of how to migrate the code of the application, let's first consider the Timeline view, which is the core of the app. The TimelineView object itself has a number of dependencies:

- The collection: Timeline.js

- The model: Tweet.js

- The Handlebars helpers: Helpers.js

To make the view a module, all of the downstream dependencies will also need to be converted to modules. The best place to start is at the bottom of the pile, the Tweet model object. This has a simple list of dependencies, Backbone and Moment.js, both of which are already defined in the RequireJS configuration. First these defines need to be put at the beginning of the file.

```
define(['backbone', 'moment'], function(Backbone, moment) {

    var com = com || {};
    com.apress = com.apress || {};
    com.apress.model = com.apress.model || {};
```

```
com.apress.model.Tweet = Backbone.Model.extend({

    parse: function(model){

        var created = model.created_at;
        var friendly = moment(model.created_at, "ddd MMM DD HH:mm:ss ZZ YYYY").fromNow();

        model.friendlyDate = friendly;
        return model;
    }

});

return com.apress.model.Tweet
});
```

The end of this file is appended with a return statement, which refers to the `com.apress.model.Tweet` variable and then closes the `define` function. This is the simplest refactor because it has no dependency on any other self-created object.

Next the collection `Timeline.js` needs to be refactored. This will be slightly different because it is the first of the objects that has a dependency on other custom objects. The collection object has dependencies on Backbone and on the Tweet model that has just been converted to a module.

```
define([ 'backbone', 'app/model/Tweet'], function(Backbone, Tweet) {

var com = com || {};
com.apress = com.apress || {};
com.apress.collection = com.apress.collection || {};

com.apress.collection.Timeline = Backbone.Collection.extend({

    //the model that this collection uses
    model: Tweet,
    //the server side url to connect to for the collection
    url: 'http://localhost:8080/timeline',

    initialize: function(options){
        //anything to be defined on construction goes here
    },
});
    return com.apress.collection.Timeline;
});
```

Although the conversion pattern is the same as previously stated, any references made to the Tweet model have changed from `com.apress.model.Tweet` to `Tweet`. This is because the module has been exposed under that name, rather than the namespace version. In fact, you may consider dropping the namespace concept from your code when using RequireJS.

The `TimelineView` follows the same approach, although it has a longer list of dependencies, including Handlebars and jQuery, as well as the `Timeline` object.

```javascript
define(['jquery', 'handlebars', 'backbone', 'app/collection/Timeline'], function($, Handlebars,
Backbone, Timeline) {

var com = com || {};
com.apress = com.apress || {};
com.apress.view = com.apress.view || {};

com.apress.view.TimelineView = Backbone.View.extend({

    el: '#timeline',

    template: Handlebars.compile($("#timeline-template").html()),

    timeline: null,

    events: {
        'click .profile': 'showDialog'
    },

    initialize: function(options){
        var self = this;

        //create a collection for this view to render
        self.timeline = new Timeline();
        //initial render
        self.render();

        //force the fetch to fire a reset event
        self.timeline.fetch({reset:true
            });

        self.listenTo(self.timeline, 'reset', self.render);

    },

    render: function(){
        var self = this;
        if(self.timeline.models.length > 0){
            var output = self.template({tweet: self.timeline.toJSON()});

            self.$el.append(output);
        }
        return self;
    },

    showDialog: function(options){

        var self =this,
            $target = $(options.currentTarget),
            username = $target.data('user');
```

```
    /**
     * Reuse the profile view
     **/
    var profileView = new com.apress.view.ProfilePopupView({user: username});

  }

});


  // export stuff:
  return com.apress.view.TimelineView;
});
```

Note that the reference to the Timeline collection is changed here too. Rather than this:

```
    self.timeline =new com.apress.collection.Timeline();
```

it uses the RequireJS module reference.

```
    self.timeline = new Timeline();
```

Finally, the Handlebars helper needs to be made accessible from RequireJS. The module does not need to export anything; it just needs to execute code to add the helper to the Handlebars module.

```
define(['handlebars'], function (Handlebars) {

    Handlebars.registerHelper('format', function (str) {
        if(str){

            //highlight the @part
            //http://www.simonwhatley.co.uk/parsing-twitter-usernames-hashtags-and-urls-with-javascript
            str = str.replace(/[@]+[A-Za-z0-9-_]+/g, function(u) {
                    var username = u.replace('@','')
                    return '<a href="#" data-user="' + username +'" class="profile">@'+username+'</a>';
            });

            return new Handlebars.SafeString(str);
        }else{
            return str;
        }

    });

});
```

To execute these modules and see the `TimelineView` in action, some additional code needs to be added to `main.js`. Both Backbone and the `TimelineView` are required for the application now, each of which will load its own dependent modules. The `Helpers` module is also included as a requirement here so that it will add its helpers to Handlebars.

```
require([
    'backbone', 'app/view/TimelineView', 'app/util/Helpers'],  function (Backbone, TimelineView) {

    var timelineView = new TimelineView();
});
```

The view is created by referring to the `TimelineView` module that was passed as a dependency. This section at the end of `main.js` will complete the entire application setup, as previously covered in `app.js`, provided each of the objects is converted to modules. It's important to keep an eye on the dependencies each file has. Views will typically have a need for jQuery ($) and Handlebars to be imported, as well as Backbone and your own custom modules. If you have been following the namespace convention, you can easily identify them because they all begin with `com.apress`.

Once all of the code has been successfully migrated, the following code should execute the app in the same condition as it was in Chapter 6:

```
require([
    'backbone', 'app/view/TimelineView', 'app/view/ProfileView', 'app/model/Search',
    'app/view/SearchView', 'app/router/AppRouter', 'app/util/Helpers'
], function (Backbone, TimelineView, ProfileView, Search, SearchView, AppRouter) {

    var timelineView = new TimelineView(),
    profileView = new ProfileView({user: 'sugrue'}),
    searchModel = new Search(),
    searchView = new SearchView({model: searchModel}),
    appRouter = new AppRouter({searchModel: searchModel});
Backbone.history.start();
});
```

Using Yeoman to Get Started Quickly

In Chapter 10 we discussed how Grunt provides generators to help you get started with a complete application structure quickly. Yeoman (`http://yeoman.io`, Figure 12-3) makes this process even easier, with generators available for Backbone applications that utilize RequireJS.

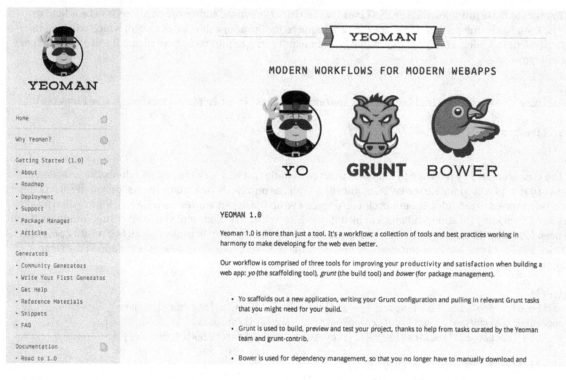

Figure 12-3. Yeoman web site at http://yeoman.io

Yeoman, created by the Google Chrome Developer Relations team, is a tool stack that brings together three tools to improve your productivity when creating web applications. It includes Grunt, which we discussed in depth in Chapter 9, as well as two other tools: Bower and Yo.

Bower is a package manager for libraries and frameworks that are used within web applications. In a similar fashion to NPM, Bower allows you to download the libraries you need through the command line and brings all the dependent libraries along with it. This is a huge improvement in the process of downloading a library and finding its dependencies.

Yo is at the core of Yeoman, providing a scaffolding tool to build web applications from scratch from the command line. A number of generators are already available, including a Backbone generator, which we will focus on in the subsequent section.

Installing Yeoman

As with many JavaScript tools, Yeoman is installed using the npm command from Node.js. All you need to do is use the following command:

```
npm install -g yo
```

If you are using version 1.2.10 or newer of Node, you will have `grunt-cli` and `bower` also installed for you at this point. If not, you can install these dependencies manually using the following command:

```
npm install -g grunt-cli bower
```

Test your installation by typing yo on the command line. You should see output similar to that in Figure 12-4.

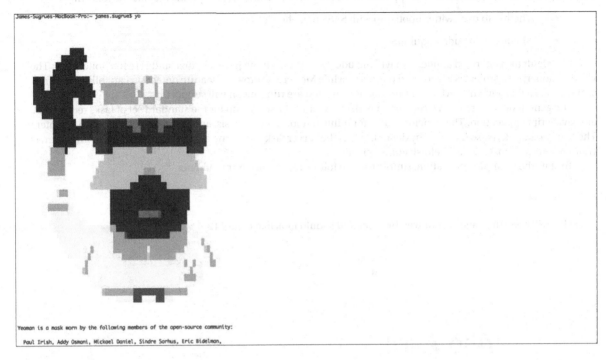

Figure 12-4. Output from running the yo command

The default installation will include two generators: a mocha generator and a web app generator. The next section will cover how to install and use the Backbone generator.

Using the Backbone Generator

The installation of generators takes place from within the yo command line. After typing yo, you will see the option "Install a generator." Once selected, you can search for a generator and select the one that you require. In this case, select generator-bb, as in Figure 12-5.

```
[?] What would you like to do? Install a generator
[?] Search NPM for generators: backbone
[?] Here's what I found. Install one?
   generator-backbone-amd
   generator-backbone-module
 > generator-bb
   generator-maryo
   generator-phonegap-backbone
   Search again
   Return home
```

Figure 12-5. Output from Yeoman when installing the Backbone generator

To run the Backbone generator, simply type yo backbone on the command line. You will be presented with a number of options for your Backbone application. At the time of writing, these options include the following:

- Whether to use Twitter Bootstrap with SASS or CoffeeScript

- Whether to include RequireJS

By default the generated application will include jQuery, Backbone.js, Modernizr, and HTML5 Boilerplate. The HTML5 Boilerplate project is a front-end template, while Modernizr provides feature detection capabilities for your application so that you know what features the browser you are running on will support.

The generator also creates a Grunt script with everything already set up for the standard set of tasks required in any JavaScript application. These include tasks for minification, static analysis, and testing, as discussed in Chapter 9. The live reload task is also included by default. When the server task is running and a change is made to any source file, your web browser instance will refresh automatically.

To start the example application, simply run the following on the command line:

```
grunt server
```

This will open the page in your web browser and should look like Figure 12-6.

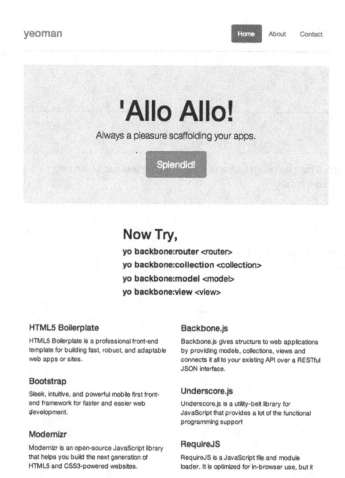

Figure 12-6. *A Backbone application generated by the Yeoman Backbone generator*

Rather than manually adding models, collections, views, and routers, the generator provides useful shortcuts to create additional views. For example, to create a simple view, just use a command such as the following:

```
yo backbone:view Timeline
```

This will generate two files. First is an ejs template, which can be swapped out if you want to use one of the template systems discussed in this book instead. It also creates a view that matches the name passed, in this case Timeline.js. If you have chosen to use RequireJS with your application, the generated code will look as follows:

```
/*global define*/

define([
    'jquery',
    'underscore',
    'backbone',
    'templates'
], function ($, _, Backbone, JST) {
    'use strict';

    var TimelineView = Backbone.View.extend({
        template: JST['app/scripts/templates/Timeline.ejs']
    });

    return TimelineView;
});
```

I consider this to be the easiest way to get going with a new application and use RequireJS without needing to deal with all the boilerplate.

Design Patterns for Backbone Applications

When designing applications, it is worth applying some of the design patterns, such as those discussed in the famous Gang of Four book, *Design Patterns: Elements of Reusable Object-Oriented Software*. These patterns encompass some well-understood approaches that have been used to solve common issues around the design of software applications. Although there are many that you could apply to your application, this section focuses on two of the most useful for Backbone applications: the Facade pattern and the Mediator pattern.

Leveraging the Facade Pattern

The idea behind the Facade pattern is to hide complex implementation-level details so that the module exposes only the bare minimum to any calling code. This pattern is known as a *structural pattern* because it identifies a simple way to realize relationships between entities. The classic definition from the Gang of Four book says that the Facade pattern should do the following: "Provide a unified interface to a set of interfaces in a subsystem. Facade defines a higher-level interface that makes the subsystem easier to use."

While the facades you create in a Backbone application may involve encapsulating the work of many modules into one single module that the caller uses, it is more common that you simply produce modules that export only the essential functionality. The main thing you want to do with facades is to ensure that other developers who use your module never need to worry about lower-level details.

One place where the facade can be useful is with Model objects. With the default Backbone model object, you can get any attribute by name. While this is nice and simple, the code that uses the model may be at risk if the data structure changes. Adding getter and setter functions can insulate you from these changes so that the only code that needs to deal with data structure changes is in the model.

Consider the following example, from Chapter 6, where we get our data from a third-party API, such as Twitter, and represent it using a Backbone model:

```javascript
var com = com || {};
com.apress = com.apress || {};
com.apress.model = com.apress.model || {};
com.apress.model.Tweet = Backbone.Model.extend({
    parse: function(model){
        var created = model.created_at;
            var friendly = moment(model.created_at, "ddd MMM DD HH:mm:ss ZZ YYYY").fromNow();
            model.friendlyDate = friendly;
        return model;
    }
});
```

If the data structure for a tweet was to change and the Tweet object was used in more than one place, the changes would be disruptive to our code. It would be better to provide getter functions to gain access to the attributes we need.

```javascript
var com = com || {};
com.apress = com.apress || {};
com.apress.model = com.apress.model || {};
com.apress.model.Tweet = Backbone.Model.extend({
    parse: function(model){
        var created = model.created_at;
var friendly = moment(model.created_at, "ddd MMM DD HH:mm:ss ZZ YYYY").fromNow();
model.friendlyDate = friendly;
        return model;
    }
    getText: function(){
        return this.get('text');
    },
    getProfileImage: function(){
        return this.get('user').profile_image_url;
    },
    getUserName: function(){
        return this.get('user').name;
    }
});
```

Facades can be utilized in any module created in your application. For example, instead of returning the base model object, you could instead just export a function that users of the module require. In the following code example, two functions that represent complex operations are kept private to the module, and a simple convert function is made available to the caller.

```
/*global define*/
define([
    'underscore',
    'backbone'
], function (_, Backbone) {
    'use strict';
    var ConversionModel = Backbone.Model.extend({
        defaults: {
        },
        complexOperation: function(value){
    //complex work in here
        },
         secondOperation: function(value){
    //a second operation
}
});
    return {
convert: function(value){
        return ConversionModel.complexOperation(value) + ConversionModel.secondOperation(value);
    }
}
});
```

Using the Facade pattern, the underlying implementation details may change without worrying about any other pieces of code that use your module.

Leveraging the Mediator Pattern

Another popular pattern in JavaScript applications is the Mediator pattern, which helps enforce better levels of decoupling between modules. The Mediator pattern is known as a behavioral pattern because it deals with the relationships and responsibilities between objects. The definition in the Gang of Four book states that the pattern does the following: "allows loose coupling by encapsulating the way disparate sets of objects interact and communicate with each other. Allows for the actions of each object set to vary independently of one another."

The best analogy for this pattern is an airport control tower: the tower (mediator) looks after who can take off and land, and all communication to and from planes goes through the control tower, rather than having each plane communicate with one another.

Large-scale applications can benefit by introducing a single mediator to provide a single point where events are passed, and this central module decides which modules should be notified.

The following code snippet shows an example mediator implementation. Two functions are exposed by this module. First is a subscribe function that modules can use to register their interest for a particular event type. There is also a notify function, which allows any module to inform the mediator of new events.

```
define( function(){

        //a list of channels, which itself has a list of subscribers
        var channels = [];

        var publish  = function(eventType, params){
            //find subscribers
            if(channels[eventType]){
```

```
            for(var i= 0; i < channels[eventType].length; i++){
                var channel = channels[eventType][i];
                channel.callback.call(channel.context, params);


            }
        }
    };

    return {
        subscribe: function(eventType, callback){
            if(!channels[eventType]){
                channels[eventType] = [];
            }
            channels[eventType].push({context: this, callback: callback});
        },
        notify: function(eventType, params){
            publish(eventType, params);
        }
    }
  }
);
```

As each module registers, it is added to a list of channels. Note that this is a simple implementation that doesn't provide an unregister function.

The use of this module is quite simple. Any module can register interest with a callback to handle a particular event.

```
require(['Mediator'], function(mediator){

    var callback = function(args){
        console.log('Handling name change. Value is ' + args.name);
    };

    mediator.subscribe('name.change', callback);

});
```

In the case of the previous code, there is a callback subscribed to handle any name.change notification. To trigger this notification, the notify function is invoked.

```
mediator.notify('name.change', {name: 'Beginning Backbone.js'});
```

This results in the callback related to this event being notified. This is a small-scale example that illustrates how the pattern can be used. You'll find lots of implementations of this type of publisher-subscriber type of pattern across the usual code repositories such as GitHub.

Providing a central control module for all the events in your application makes your application more manageable. As well as being able to distribute notifications across all modules, the mediator can be extended to suppress notifications when the application is in certain states.

Summary

This chapter has dealt with some of the best ways to ensure your application remains modular and testable. We've seen how RequireJS can be used to break up your code into simple modules with real dependency management included. As well as making the code maintainable and testable, RequireJS also creates a structure that will make understanding and navigating through the code easier for new developers joining your team. In addition to seeing how RequireJS can be added to an existing Backbone application, Yeoman was introduced in this chapter as a mechanism for creating new Backbone projects from scratch without the need to write so much boilerplate code and still have the benefits of RequireJS.

Finally we looked at how two classic design patterns, the Facade pattern and the Mediator pattern, can be utilized to make your code even more manageable. The key thing to remember is that even though JavaScript is a dynamic language and allows you to do almost anything you want, there is always the opportunity to apply real structure to your code to make it future-proof and ready for any application requirements that get added late in the project life cycle.

Index

Get the eBook for only $10!

Now you can take the weightless companion with you anywhere, anytime. Your purchase of this book entitles you to 3 electronic versions for only $10.

This Apress title will prove so indispensible that you'll want to carry it with you everywhere, which is why we are offering the eBook in 3 formats for only $10 if you have already purchased the print book.

Convenient and fully searchable, the PDF version enables you to easily find and copy code—or perform examples by quickly toggling between instructions and applications. The MOBI format is ideal for your Kindle, while the ePUB can be utilized on a variety of mobile devices.

Go to www.apress.com/promo/tendollars to purchase your companion eBook.

Apress®
THE EXPERT'S VOICE™